Studies in Economic Transition

General Editors: **Jens Hölscher**, Reader in Economics, University of Brighton; and **Horst Tomann**, Professor of Economics, Free University, Berlin

This series has been established in response to a growing demand for a greater understanding of the transformation of economic systems. It brings together theoretical and empirical studies on economic transition and economic development. The post-communist transition from planned to market economies is one of the main areas of applied theory because in this field the most dramatic examples of change and economic dynamics can be found. The series aims to contribute to the understanding of specific major economic changes as well as to advance the theory of economic development. The implications of economic policy is a major point of focus.

Titles include:

Irwin Collier, Herwig Roggemann, Oliver Scholz and Horst Tomann (*editors*)
WELFARE STATES IN TRANSITION
East and West

Hella Engerer
PRIVATIZATION AND ITS LIMITS IN CENTRAL AND EASTERN EUROPE
Property Rights in Transition

Hubert Gabrisch and Rüdiger Pohl (*editors*)
EU ENLARGEMENT AND ITS MACROECONOMIC EFFECTS IN EASTERN EUROPE
Currencies, Prices, Investment and Competitiveness

Oleh Havrylyshyn
DIVERGENT PATHS IN POST-COMMUNIST TRANSFORMATION
Capitalism for All or Capitalism for the Few?

Jens Hölscher (*editor*)
FINANCIAL TURBULENCE AND CAPITAL MARKETS IN TRANSITION COUNTRIES

Jens Hölscher and Anja Hochberg (*editors*)
EAST GERMANY'S ECONOMIC DEVELOPMENT SINCE UNIFICATION
Domestic and Global Aspects

Mihaela Kelemen and Monika Kostera (*editors*)
CRITICAL MANAGEMENT RESEARCH IN EASTERN EUROPE
Managing the Transition

Emil J. Kirchner (*editor*)
DECENTRALIZATION AND TRANSITION IN THE VISEGRAD
Poland, Hungary, the Czech Republic and Slovakia

Tomasz Mickiewicz
ECONOMIC TRANSITION IN CENTRAL EUROPE AND THE COMMONWEALTH OF INDEPENDENT STATES

Julie Pellegrin
THE POLITICAL ECONOMY OF COMPETITIVENESS IN AN ENLARGED EUROPE

Stanislav Poloucek (*editor*)
REFORMING THE FINANCIAL SECTOR IN CENTRAL EUROPEAN COUNTRIES

Gregg S. Robins
BANKING IN TRANSITION
East Germany after Unification

Johannes Stephan
ECONOMIC TRANSITION IN HUNGARY AND EAST GERMANY
Gradualism and Shock Therapy in Catch-up Development

Johannes Stephan (*editor*)
TECHNOLOGY TRANSFER VIA FOREIGN DIRECT INVESTMENT IN CENTRAL AND
EASTERN EUROPE THEORY

Hans van Zon
THE POLITICAL ECONOMY OF INDEPENDENT UKRAINE

Adalbert Winkler (*editor*)
FINANCIAL DEVELOPMENT IN EASTERN EUROPE
The First Ten Years

Studies in Economic Transition
Series Standing Order ISBN 0–333–73353–3
(*outside North America only*)

You can receive future titles in this series as they are published by placing a standing order. Please contact your bookseller or, in case of difficulty, write to us at the address below with your name and address, the title of the series and the ISBN quoted above.

Customer Services Department, Macmillan Distribution Ltd, Houndmills, Basingstoke, Hampshire RG21 6XS, England

Economic Transition in Central Europe and the Commonwealth of Independent States

Tomasz Mickiewicz

First published 2005 by
PALGRAVE MACMILLAN
Houndmills, Basingstoke, Hampshire RG21 6XS and
175 Fifth Avenue, New York, N.Y. 10010
Companies and representatives throughout the world

PALGRAVE MACMILLAN is the global academic imprint of the Palgrave Macmillan division of St. Martin's Press, LLC and of Palgrave Macmillan Ltd. Macmillan® is a registered trademark in the United States, United Kingdom and other countries. Palgrave is a registered trademark in the European Union and other countries.

ISBN-13: 978–1–4039–4162–6
ISBN-10: 1–4039–4162–9

This book is printed on paper suitable for recycling and made from fully managed and sustained forest sources.

A catalogue record for this book is available from the British Library.

Library of Congress Cataloging-in-Publication Data
Mickiewicz, Tomasz.
    Economic transition in Central Europe and the Commonwealth of Independent States / Tomasz Mickiewicz.
        p.   cm. — (Studies in economic transition)
    Includes bibliographical references and index.
    ISBN 1–4039–4162–9 (cloth)
    1. Europe, Central—Economic policy.   2. Former Soviet republics—Economic policy.   3. Post communism—Economic aspects—Europe, Central.   4. Post communism—Economic aspects—Former Soviet Republics.   I. Title.   II. Series.
    HC244.M477 2005
    330.94′009171′7—dc22   2005049292

10   9   8   7   6   5   4   3   2   1
14   13   12   11   10   09   08   07   06   05

Printed and bound in Great Britain by
Antony Rowe Ltd, Chippenham and Eastbourne

For Ania and Stanisław

'There is no doubt that the history of our revolution should provide a lesson of modesty for our philosophers and politicians; indeed, never before were there more far-reaching events better and longer prepared yet less expected.'

—Alexis de Tocqueville, *L'Ancien Régime et la Révolution*

Contents

List of Figures

List of Tables

Acknowledgements

I wish to express my gratitude to my colleagues from SSEES UCL, who found time to read various sections of the manuscript and offered valuable comments: Ruta Aidis, Chris Gerry, Piotr Jaworski and Mariusz Jarmużek. I would also like to thank Jens Hölscher and the participants of the MET conference in April 2005 and, last but not least, the editorial staff of Palgrave Macmillan, Keith Povey, Amanda Hamilton and Katie Button in particular.

TOMASZ MICKIEWICZ

List of Abbreviations

ALMP	Active labour market policies
BIS	Bank for International Settlements
CASE	Centrum Analiz Społeczno Ekonomicznych (Centre for Social and Economic Research)
CE	Central European
CEE	Central and Eastern European
CIS	Commonwealth of Independent States
CMEA	Council of Mutual Economic Assistance
CPE	Centrally planned economy(ies)
CPI	Consumer price index
CSSR	Czechoslovak Soviet Socialist Republic
EBRD	European Bank for Reconstruction and Development
EEC	European Economic Community
EU	European Union
FDI	Foreign direct investment
FSU	Former Soviet Union
FYR	Former Yugoslav Republic
GDP	Gross domestic product
GMM	Generalized method of moments
GNP	Gross national product
GUS	Central Statistical Office (Poland)
IMF	International Monetary Fund
IOSCO	International Organization of Securities Commissions
IPO	Initial public offering
IT	Information technology
LOLR	Lender of last resort
NBFI	Non-bank financial institution
NEP	New Economic Policy (USSR)
NMP	Net material product
NPV	Net present value
OECD	Organization for Economic Cooperation and Development
OLS	Ordinary least squares
PCA	Principal component analysis
PPF	Production possibility frontier
PPP	Purchasing power parity
QR	Quantitative restriction
SEE	South East European
SME	Small and medium-sized enterprise

SOE	State-owned enterprise
SSA	sub-Saharan Africa
SUR	Seemingly Unrelated Regression (model)
TE	Transition economy(ies)
TFP	Total factor productivity
USSR	Union of Soviet Socialist Republics
VAT	Value added tax
WTO	World Trade Organization

Introduction

This book is about the economic transition in Central Europe and the CIS countries. The process replaced the command economy based on administrative orders, seen as a main coordination mechanism, with one relying on private property, free prices, state regulation and policy incentives. Fifteen years ago, twenty-seven countries in Europe and Central Asia embarked on their economic transition path. For some, the outcome was a considerable success. Several other are still struggling to shed the inheritance of the past and to correct more recent policy mistakes. Why were post-Communist recessions so long in some countries and growth so disappointing? Why was fiscal performance so different? Was democracy a factor that facilitated reforms or, rather, slowed them down? The book discusses these questions in the context of new empirical evidence, including a critical examination of the main themes in the economics of transition literature. The arguments are presented in an accessible format, with a stress on narrative discussion, without compromising the main theoretical insights.

In Chapter 1, we discuss the old regime and the reasons for the slowdown and ultimate demize of the command economy system. Chapter 2 introduces the main components of the reform programme and discusses the interdependence between stabilization, liberalization and the 'hardening' of the budget constraint. A discussion of stabilization and exchange rate policies continues in Chapter 3. We ask if, and under what circumstances, the stabilization had a recessionary impact. In Chapter 4, we turn to the process of privatization, the key aspect of institutional change. Part I of the book concludes in Chapter 5 with a discussion of unemployment, when we ask why labour market outcomes were so different in the various transition economies.

In Part II of the book, we use empirical evidence to test several theoretical hypotheses related to the transition process. In Chapter 6, we ask possibly the most fundamental question: why some countries went through a ten-year long recession, while others emerged from the post-Communist recessions after a mere two years. What was the relative impact of stabilization policies, liberalization policies and initial conditions? Next, we go into more detail. Chapters 7 and 8 focus on public and private finance, respectively. In Chapter 7, we test hypotheses related to the impact of the reforms on government expenditure, revenue and fiscal balance. Chapter 8 focuses on private finance and explores the factors responsible for both the development and the efficiency of the financial sector in the transition countries.

In Chapters 9 and 10, we return to the linkages between the political system, reform and economic growth. In Chapter 9, we explore whether democracy was good for reform, and for which reform in particular. In Chapter 10, building on an already vast empirical literature, we add new results, exploring the links between political freedom, reform, macroeconomic stabilization and liberalization, applying a model which takes into account the multidirectional nature of the interactions between these three dimensions. Some brief final remarks conclude the study.

The book maintains a broad, comparative perspective. With one or two exceptions, there are no sections that present single country-based studies of economic policies and our motivation was to avoid duplicating the existing literature. In particular, Gros and Steinherr (1995, 2004) offer good insights into the economic policies and institutional reforms applied in Russia, in Central Europe (in particular, the Czech Republic, Hungary, Poland), in the former Yugoslavia and last but not least in East Germany. In addition, while we refer to the economic theory of transition, we avoid replicating the existing mathematical models. In this respect, the book by Roland (2000) remains the best compendium available. An earlier, shorter book by Blanchard (1997), focusing on models of reallocation and disorganization, provides an equally stimulating read. We comment on some of these themes in the light of empirical evidence in Chapter 6.

Following the same logic, we do not cover topics on which we feel unable to add anything new to the existing literature. Gros and Steinherr (2004) present results on the significance of EU markets for all the transition countries, including those furthest away from Western Europe, and discuss the argument for trade integration with the EU, and the benefits of joining. Rozelle and Swinnen (2004) offer an authoritative summary of the results of (either complete or incomplete) liberalization and the introduction of private property rights in the agricultural sector of the transition countries. While we touch on corporate governance in Chapter 4, the topic deserves a book to itself. The literature on corporate governance is large, but let me just refer to a recent good summary by the colleague from whom I have learned possibly the most in this respect: Filatotchev (2003). While the book touches on the issues of income distribution and poverty in Chapters 4, 5 and 9, no systematic treatment is given. Again, our main excuse is that we saw no realistic chance of adding anything new to the existing research. The book by Milanovic (1998) on inequality and poverty has stood the test of time and still offers very good insights on the subject. Alongside unemployment, poverty should remain a key focus of economic policy, but with our own focus on recession and income growth, we are partly excused by Milanovic's own observation: 'changes in income are the most decisive factor influencing poverty' (1998: 23). Poverty and misguided policies leading to economic decline have been closely related.

Part I
What Happened?

1
The Old Regime and the Opening Balance of Transition

Introduction

At the beginning of 1989, Europe was a different place. The continent was dominated by the largest country on earth, which no longer exists: the Union of Soviet Socialist Republics (USSR). It embraced an economic system labelled by different names, 'command economy' being one of the more accurate. Yet seventy years earlier, the USSR had replaced another huge empire, Tsarist Russia, which had collapsed in 1917 near the end of the First World War. Later, towards the end of the Second World War, in 1944–5, a command-type economic system was imposed on several European countries – Bulgaria, Czechoslovakia, the Eastern part of Germany, Estonia, Hungary, Latvia, Lithuania, Poland and Romania.[1] Lithuania, Latvia and Estonia were annexed by the USSR and declared Soviet Republics. The remaining countries preserved varying degrees of autonomy, yet with the monopoly of political power guaranteed to local Communist parties.

This international economic and political system collapsed in 1989, a year that began with the official re-emergence of the independent 'Solidarity' trade union in Poland (led by an electrician from the Lenin Shipyards in Gdansk, Lech Walesa), and ended with the fall of the Berlin Wall. The dictatorships in Central Europe were collapsing, either peacefully or violently and, unlike his predecessors, the Soviet leader Mikhail Gorbachev decided not to send tanks to help the native Communist parties stay in power. In fact, in some cases he actively supported local liberals against hardliners. Gorbachev's aim was to reform the Soviet system, not to replace it, yet once the change gathered momentum the social and political dynamics of anti-Communist revolution turned out to be impossible to stop.

Economic transformation followed. On 12 September 1989, Poland gained the first non-Communist government for fifty years, with the office of Minister of Finance taken by one of the economic advisors of 'Solidarity', an academic from the Warsaw School of Economics, Leszek Balcerowicz. Only three months later, on 17 December 1989, a package of economic reforms orientated towards stabilization and liberalization was introduced in the Polish parliament, and implemented on 1 January 1990 (Balcerowicz 1992). The programme became a benchmark for other post-Communist countries, which could learn from both the successes and the mistakes of one of the more fascinating experiments in economic history.

The command economy

To assess the scale of economic change that followed from the fall of Communism, one has to appreciate how different the command economy was from the market economy setting in most middle- and high-income countries around the world. While the command economy now seems to be in the remote past, its heritage was a decisive factor in the economic developments which followed the liberalization programmes during the 1990s and are still having an impact in the first decade of the twenty-first century. As in any other economic system, the command economy can be described by four basic dimensions: (1) decision-making rules, (2) the mechanism of information flows, (3) property rights, and (4) the nature of incentives and the system of goods distribution.[2]

In terms of decision-making, the command economy system of production was organized in a centralized, hierarchical way. Enterprises were at the lowest level, industrial conglomerates at an intermediate level and branch ministries and the central planning commission at the highest level, with final authority resting with the Political Bureau and (Politburo) the First Secretary of the Communist Party. From a formal point of view, little discretion was left to enterprises in their decisions on output mix, output level, prices, choice of trade partners, investment and finance.

This mode of economic organization could be easily contrasted with the market economy, where the choices of enterprises were based on decentralized information conveyed by market prices. In the command economy, the information on which decisions were to be based was passed on by the planning directives, which determined what the enterprise should produce, and how.

However, there were parts of the economy which remained outside the centralized control – i.e. where price information still affected the decisions of economic actors. This kind of systemic inconsistency led to tensions in the overall coordination mechanism. In particular, the margin of freedom related to households which, unlike firms, retained choice in consumption and labour supply decisions. 'Unofficial' economic activity was widespread. Kornai (1986) provides an interesting analysis for Hungary. Around 1980, for instance, 42 per cent of new houses were built by individual households themselves (with the help of self-employed construction workers, on many occasions working part-time, i.e. 'moonlighters'). In general, the 'unofficial' economy covered a large section of services. The inconsistency between household decisions and output decisions by the planning administration was a continual problem. One solution, obviously not very popular, was to impose restrictions on consumer decisions. In some countries, at some periods, consumption was rationed, typically by the use of coupons. Similarly, freedom of labour was restricted – for instance, where higher-education graduates were told to accept specific jobs. The most infamous example of incorporating labour into the command and planning mechanism related to the vast system of forced labour camps which played a decisive role in the economic development of the USSR, especially in huge infrastructure projects, at least until the mid-1950s. Only after death of Stalin in 1953 was the Gulag system scaled down.[3]

Restrictions imposed on enterprises in their decision-making were mirrored by the nature of property rights. Private ownership of capital was restricted to a limited number of licensed small-scale enterprises operating at the fringes of the economic system. Interestingly, while the overwhelming majority of enterprises were not private, their formal ownership status was unclear. It is common to refer to them as 'state-owned enterprises' (SOEs), reflecting the fact that key control rights remained with the state economic administration; the individual companies were effectively part of the state. Nevertheless, their formal ownership status was ill defined; the enterprises were officially declared as 'socialist' – i.e. owned by the people, not by the state treasury, unlike nationalized companies in other parts of the world outside the Soviet Bloc. Moreover, in the late Communist period, significant control rights were transferred to workers' councils inside enterprises. This change was stipulated in Poland during the first period of the independent 'Solidarity' union (1980–1) and remained in place throughout the 1980s in spite of martial law and political repression. Self-governance was also extended to enterprises in Hungary, and in the USSR in the late 1980s, under Gorbachev. Those solutions drew from the experience of Yugoslavia, a country that remained outside the Soviet Bloc and introduced the self-governance model first. In economic theory, the old name of a Roman province (Illyria) was used to label the self-governance model of enterprize as 'Illyrian': it was first described by Ward (1958) in his seminal paper in the *American Economic Review*. Agriculture was another sector with a significant margin of private producers. In Poland, that private margin was restored when a short period of collectivization was followed by the concessions made during the wave of post-Stalinist liberalization after 1956.

Decision-making rules, information channels and property rights alone cannot make an economic system work without being supplemented by a coherent set of *incentives* for economic actors. While the founding father of Communism, Karl Marx, envisaged a world without money, in practice the system had to rely on monetary income as a main channel determining the access to goods and therefore their final distribution. Wage income and social transfers remained key categories of income, with property income and (official) income from self-employment playing a much smaller role, when compared with the high- and middle-income market economies (Milanovic 1998).

Yet, while the role of monetary incentives was dominant, it was still restricted and was complemented by other distribution mechanisms. First, a combination of administrative prices and free-demand decisions by consumers resulted in market disequilibria and shortages. The latter implied that money income was a necessity but not a sufficient condition for acquiring goods. For that reason, other distribution mechanisms operated, starting with queuing and – possibly more important – networking and corruption. Payments in kind for workers were also widespread. Enterprises functioned not only as production units but also as providers of services for workers, including housing, child care, holidays and recreational facilities and health care (Rein, Friedman and Wörgötter 1997). To provide access to these mainly via work was functional from the system point of view, as it gave incentives for higher work participation; indeed, activity rates in all these countries were high.

While discussing the incentive system, one has also to take into account the duality which was the command economy's defining feature. The administrative hierarchy (all the way up from enterprises to the central planning commission) was always shadowed by the Communist party structure, where party officials were expected to act as (supposedly highly motivated) controllers. This vast monitoring system was meant to overcome motivational problems. The party controllers were granted important privileges and offered special access to housing, cars and luxury goods via exclusive distribution channels (vouchers, special shops). According to the official blueprint, all this gratification was only supplementary – the system was supposed to rely heavily on the ideological motivation of the party controllers acting in the 'social interest', i.e. overcoming the 'petty egoism' and 'indifference' of economic actors at various levels of the production process. Until the mid-1950s (the death of Stalin), ideology was always comple-mented not only by material incentives but also by a reign of terror, and in the case of party apparatchiks it is difficult to disentangle genuine enthusiasm from the disciplining effect of fear: psychologically the latter has as strong a positive effect as the former, as self-delusion is part of human nature. Regardless of the weight we may attach to those two components, it appears that, with time, the appeal of ideology faded away, the era of overwhelming terror ceased, and material incentives to match aspirations proved difficult to deliver. The necessary minimum social support base began to shrink.

What went wrong?

Shortages and disequilibria resulted in deadweight cost and inefficiency. Nevertheless, the command economy survived for seventy years in Europe.[4] The system did offer basic economic stability for the population: while on the one hand freedom of labour was restricted, on the other there was no unemployment. Standards of living were not improving fast, yet extreme poverty was eradicated. The premium for education (as, say, measured by the difference between non-manual and manual wages) was minimal, but more education was offered than in countries at a comparable level of income *per capita* (Jackman and Rutkowski 1994; Milanovic 1998; Mickiewicz and Bell 2000). From the political perspective, while episodes of mass repression reoccurred (the Soviet invasion of Hungary in 1956 and of Czechoslovakia in 1968, martial law in Poland in 1982), in most places and for most of the time after the mid-1950s the level of political repression in Communist countries was relatively low, especially when compared with many dictatorships in Latin America, Asia and Africa at that time. The interesting question for both economic and political historians is thus what went wrong, and why the system collapsed so dramatically.

It was easier to see the early signs of a crisis from within than for outside observers. More than one generation of Western scholars took the official Soviet growth statistics seriously, and many were impressed with USSR achievements. After all, it was both a military superpower and the only country able to compete successfully with the US in the space programme. But not everybody was misled. A group of UK based scholars published a book in 1982 with the novel title, 'Crisis in the East European Economy' (Drewnowski 1982): 'There is a spectre haunting Eastern Europe: the spectre of zero growth' the opening sentence by Peter Wiles reads, and he provides a catalogue of likely and unlikely factors that were contributing to economic slowdown and decline (Wiles 1982). Much of that discussion has stood the test of time. Following and expanding it (with the benefit of hindsight), one can distinguish between two interrelated clusters of explanations:

(1) *Systemic* features of the command economy, which were present from the very beginning but whole effects became negative only when they interacted with changing external circumstances;
(2) *Non-economic* factors.

The first cluster of factors – i.e. the systemic features of the command economy that contributed to economic slowdown – related to inadequate incentives, semi-autarky, structural inertia and the priority that was given to military expenditures. We shall discuss these in turn.

Incentives

The issue of incentives has been at the centre of the debate on economic efficiency under a command economy. On one hand, Oskar Lange (1936) argued that the efficient prices equivalent to the perfect competition solution might be calculated by the planners. It would mean that along the informational dimension the command economy system could match or even surpass the market economy system.[5] Von Mises' reply (1966 [1949]) was that information alone could not be a sufficient condition for efficiency; it would have to be matched by the two parallel dimensions of private property rights and incentives conditioned by them:

> They want to abolish private control of the means of production, market exchange, market prices, and competition. But at the same time they want to organize the socialist utopia in such a way that people could act as *if* these things were still present. They want people to play market as children play war, railroad, or school. They do not comprehend how such childish play differs from the real thing it tries to imitate. (Von Mises 1966 [1949]: 706–7, emphasis in the original; see also Temkin 1989 for an overview of this discussion.)

Nevertheless, the problem of incentives was recognized more by central planners than by Marxist economists, and alternative bundles of ideology, intimidation and material incentives were applied to overcome it. In the long run, only the latter proved to have some lasting effect. Even so, the fundamental problem remained: how to shape the objective function on the level of individual economic actors in an efficient way. Rewards for the fulfilment of the plan were relatively simple to implement, but these left many issues outstanding. The plan could not cover all contingent states of the world: it had to remain an incomplete contract. In particular, incentives play a critical role in the process of innovation, which is least easy to organize within the framework of a centralized economic administration. By definition, innovation cannot be incorporated into an economic plan. Inadequacy of the innovation process became a serious constraint in the later phase of the socialist development – with both the changing nature of the economic environment (the growth of information technologies, etc.) and the higher level of GDP and therefore more sophisticated developmental needs. The paradoxical nature of the science and technology system under the command economy relates to the fact that on the one hand it was orientated towards the needs of enterprises, yet on the other innovation activities had to be incorporated into the economic administration and planning system and therefore remained organized within branch research institutes attached to the corresponding branch ministries, with few cross-section links and inadequate diffusion of technology into products:

> As technology is primarily a firm-specific asset, the consequence of this systemic defect was that the links between R&D and production were generally weak. (Radosevic 1999: 283–4)

Semi-autarky

Internationalization may be a viable development strategy, alternative to domestically originated innovation. Foreign trade and investment are the key channels for the transfer of knowledge and technology. After the Second World War, internationalization became one of the key factors of global development, yet the logic of planning administration prevented the centrally planned economies (CPEs) from participating fully in the benefits. The openness of these countries remained low, while it grew rapidly elsewhere. Figure 1.1 illustrates this, using the exports/GDP ratio for 1990,[6] i.e. for the initial point of the transition programmes. As larger economies tend to trade less, the openness (vertical axis) is plotted against the size of GDP (horizontal axis), showing a typical negative correlation. In the lower left corner of the graph we see a group of post-Communist economies with very little trade (Albania, Macedonia, Mongolia). The contrast with the outside world would be even more dramatic if it were not for the fact that some former Soviet republics were very much dependent on intra-USSR trade (Kazakhstan, Moldova), which became external trade on the breakdown of the Soviet Union. For Russia, in 1990, 64.4 per cent of its foreign trade was within the former Soviet Union (FSU), and only 35.6 per cent with other countries

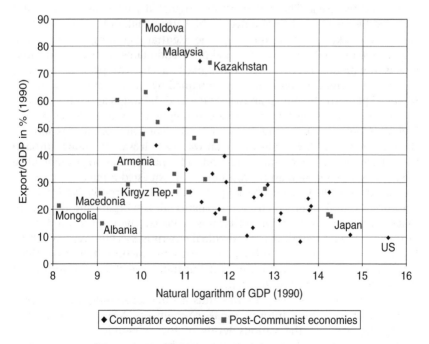

Figure 1.1 Size of the economy and openness
Source: Computed on the basis of World Bank data.

(Smith 1996). Generally, if CPEs traded, they traded mostly with themselves – i.e. within the Soviet Bloc. Later on, the capacity to re-orient the trade towards the EU and other developed market economies became an important factor determining economic success.

Semi-autarky was partly a policy choice and partly a systemic feature of the planning system, for which the outside world was an alien, uncontrollable cause of disruption. It was a source for the residual resources that had to be imported to close the material balances of the plan. Exports were generated to pay for them. A related problem was that suitable exports were difficult to find. In 1983, 70 per cent of Soviet exports to the hard currency area were in the form of energy exports, with four-fifths being oil (Schroeder 1986).

Structural inertia

The third related systemic feature, with negative effects increasing over time (i.e. in the later stages of development), was structural inertia. To understand the roots of the problem, one has to look at how the planning mechanism worked in practice. Economic plans were constructed for long periods (five years, sometimes also for three years or seven years), yet in practice the basic tool used in economic administration was the *detailed annual plan*. The planning process involved three stages: plan development, plan implementation and feedback. The first of those originated with general guidelines provided by the Central Committee of the Party (Politburo). Those directives were then taken into account by the Central Planning Commission, responsible for establishing provisional production targets. Those production targets (the production plan) had to be linked directly with plans for supplies, employment and transport, and accompanied by the investment plan, the financial plan, the income plan (which decided the wages and other income of the population), the corresponding consumption plan and the trade plan, including both domestic and foreign exchange of commodities. As soon as the draft version of the production plan was ready it was sent down through the corresponding branch ministries and industrial associations to individual enterprises for comment and confirmation of requested inputs.

Next, the details were sent back up the same administrative ladder to the Planning Commission, which had to balance all key inputs and outputs to make the plan consistent. Once that was achieved, the implied production targets were again sent down to individual enterprises as binding law, which became the basis for the subsequent year's production (Kurowski 1991; Gregory and Stuart 1995). Figure 1.2 illustrates the flow of information during the construction of the plan.

The formulation of the plan was thus a time-consuming and complex process with very high informational requirements. Moreover, it implied bargaining between the various levels of the economic administration, where the position of enterprises *vis-à-vis* the higher levels of economic administration was strengthened by informational asymmetry (only enterprize managers had full knowledge of the real technological requirements).

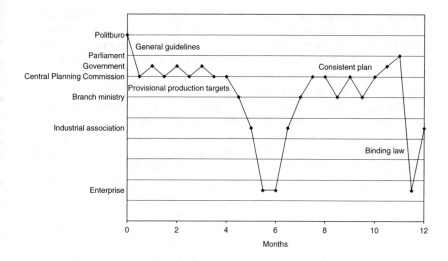

Figure 1.2   Construction of the annual plan: flow of information
Source: Adapted with some modifications from Kurowski (1991).

From the point of view of the enterprize it was beneficial to have lower production targets, for two reasons. First, some slack in production targets was always beneficial, as supplies of raw materials and intermediate products beyond technological requirements might help to save on effort and minimize a risk of production disruption. Secondly, declaring ambitious production was a strategy which entailed the risk for enterprize managers that this year's achievements could be transformed into higher expectations from the planners next year.[7] In response to the expected slack, rewards were typically linked to over-ambitious production targets. Yet, in response, there was more pressure from enterprises to increase the target amount of supplies and resources, including labour and capital. A repetitive bargaining game resulted between enterprises and the higher levels of the planning administration. The pressure on supplies, matched with the aim of the planning authorities to maximize production and price controls, led to chronic shortages. The complexity of the planning mechanism implied that frequently the plan arrived late and enterprises had to rely on provisional figures, with a risk of subsequent disruption. And even if the plan was ready, the logic of the planning mechanism required that much of it was in fact based on an assessment which had a one-year lag built in to it, as this is how long it took transform the initial data into a coherent plan (see Figure 1.2). In practice:

> The plan for year *t* was, in effect, little more than a revision and update of the plan for year *t*-1 . . . Although it simplified the planning process, it built in considerable inflexibility. (Gregory and Stuart 1995: 275)

Structural change and innovation were the disrupting factors which complicated the task of planning even more. The interests of all involved, including the enterprises, were to expand their own production, with no place left for new entrants (and no exit mechanism). New large firms emerged as a result of centralized investment projects, but even those were primarily oriented towards filling the existing gaps in the material balances of the plan.

In the initial phase of development, growth in the Soviet Bloc was fuelled by extensive methods. The increment of working-age population was high and the under-employed labour force in agriculture was transferred to industry. Similarly, production of raw materials and fuels had been expanding. All that changed in the later phase, as it did outside the Soviet Bloc. However, the structural inertia of the system prevented it from adjusting efficiently:

> The extreme sensitivity of the Soviet economy to changes... is due to its extreme rigidity, including the inability to adjust the system of investment to variations in the rate of growth of the supply of labour and capital... In other words, the Soviet economy has been able to grow without great difficulty while it was sufficient to produce no matter what and no matter how: labour was plentiful and even waste of capital looked like growth. (Sirc 1981: 74–6)

Thus, the system worked satisfactorily as long as the structures evolved in a predictable way, especially during the early industrialization phase. Problems arose when there was a sudden shift in the relative availability of resources, resulting in a need to switch to new technologies, which could cause an upheaval in the whole complex network of planning balances. An example of such an external shock came at the beginning of the 1970s, and again after 1979, with a dramatic increase in international oil and energy prices. While for the most of the developed economies this implied a long period of structural adjustment, the Communist leaders declared the oil crises another sign of the decline of the capitalist system, with no implications for the socialist world. The command economies of Central and Eastern Europe carried on along the old path of energy-intensive development, expanding old technologies, and importing production lines which were just becoming obsolete in the West because of the shift in cost structures. Over time, the gap widened, leaving the command economies with the highest level of energy intensity of production. In 1960, average *per capita* energy consumption in high-income market economies was on average around 3,000 kg of oil-equivalent per year, around 2,000 in CPEs and around 200 kg in market economies at a similar level of income *per capita* (middle-income countries). The latter group is more relevant for comparison, as generally the production/energy ratio displays a hump-shaped relationship with income *per capita* – for the highest level of income, the energy intensity of consumption increases, counterbalancing the effect of the higher efficiency of use, as exemplified by the US.

Between 1960 and 1980, the rate of growth of energy consumption in the CPE group was visibly faster than in market economics. Moreover, during the 1980s, while the energy consumption in the high-income economies oscillated around the same level, it continued to grow in the CPE group. By the end of the 1980s, it was similar in both groups, approaching 5,000 kg. Yet, in the relevant comparator group of the middle-income market economy, it was only around 1,000 kg – i.e. five times lower (Tolba and El-Kholy 1992: 376).

Figure 1.3 illustrates the closing balance of the command economy period.[8] It is clear from Figure 1.3 that at the beginning of the 1990s the energy efficiency of production was uniformly low in the (post)-Communist economies. The most dramatic cases relate to the former Soviet republics, including the Russian Federation. Similar figures can be obtained for the steel intensity of GDP (see Winiecki 1987, 2002; Winiecki and Winiecki 1992).

The negative economic impact of the growing absorption of energy by the domestic sector was amplified by opportunity costs. A low level of exports to developed market economies combined with the necessity of imports from that area for modernization made the marginal impact of the decrease in exports particularly harmful. Expanding domestic consumption of energy

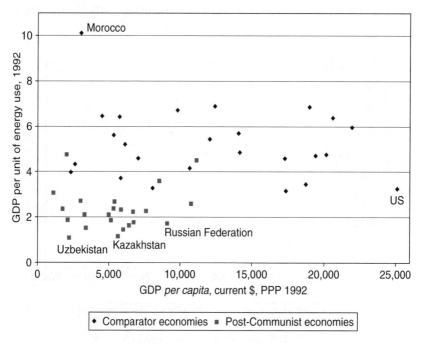

Figure 1.3 Income *per capita* and energy efficiency of production
Source: World Bank, *World Development*.

combined with dependence on energy, and more generally on commodity exports to the West, presented a difficult trade-off for the central planners. In the late 1980s, the negative effects were amplified by two additional factors. First, reckless extraction policies led to depletion of some of the most easily available oil pools and ore deposits (Gros and Steinherr 2004). In particular, production of crude oil in Russia levelled out, oscillating around 10,000 barrels a day (Gregory and Stuart 1995). Second, the international price of a barrel of oil was slashed by 60 per cent, going down from $29.3 in 1985 to $12.1 in 1986 (constant 1980 $US) and remaining at a low level until the end of the decade, which turned out to be the last in the history of the CPEs (Tolba and El-Kholy 1992).

The high energy intensity of GDP resulted both from cost inefficiencies and from distorted production structures. The CPEs were characterized by a high share of steel and heavy industry in the industry sector, and by a high share of the latter in the whole economy. This may be typical for some export-driven economies, but the CPEs were not of this kind, as already discussed. They were rather faced with structural distortion (Mickiewicz 2003). Figure 1.4 illustrates the point.

In Figure 1.4, one may note the three post-Communist countries with a particularly high share of industry in employment: Romania, Russia and Ukraine. All three subsequently faced a particularly difficult transition.

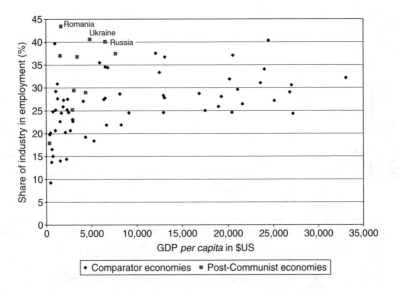

Figure 1.4   GDP *per capita* and share of industry in employment, 1990
Source: *UN Statistical Yearbook* (1995) and WIIW database, Vienna Institute for International Economic Studies.

Normally we see the hump-shaped relationship between the level of GDP *per capita* and the industry share. Development in poor countries is accompanied by the build-up of employment in industry transferred from agriculture. The share of industry is highest in the middle-income economies and with further development it stabilizes and shrinks, making room for an expanding service sector. In this respect, the initial drive for industrialization in the CPEs was consistent with the standard pattern of development.

Priority was given to both heavy industry and to the primary sector. In Marxist doctrine, this is referred to as 'the law of the priority development of production of producer goods'. It assumed (wrongly) that:

> the production of consumer goods does not grow parallel to that of the whole economy but that initially producer goods are used to produce other producer goods and that only eventually, if ever, there is a switch to consumer good production. (Sirc 1981: 75)

It was the latter which never fully materialized, and the resulting structural distortions increased with time. The problem was that due to structural inertia and maintaining the wrong priorities, the CPEs remained on a track which led them further and further away from an efficient development path based on both consumer goods and modern services. Pulled by the overgrown energy-inefficient industry – the steam engine of the planned economies – the socialist train ultimately came to the end of the line and was derailed.

Military spending

One is tempted to link the high share of steel and heavy industry to the fourth systemic feature identified at the beginning of this section – i.e. to the policy priority given to military spending. The input–output data demonstrate that civilian spending, as with civilian construction and civilian durable goods, may have been even more steel-intensive (Leontief and Duchin 1983). Nevertheless, military expenditure always played an important role. The peak of the 'Cold War' was during the first ten years after 1945, with intensive military effort by both the USRR and the US. Yet, since the mid-1950s, the relative level of spending by the US was reduced and that of the USSR was increased. In 1957, the US share in world military expenditures was 45 per cent and that of the USSR was 20 per cent. By 1978, the former had decreased to 26 per cent, and the latter had increased to 26 per cent (Leontief and Duchin 1983: 6). Yet a similar volume of spending meant a higher share in GDP, given the USSR's much lower GDP level. Moreover, at the beginning of the 1980s the USSR faced an additional military burden triggered by the decision to invade Afganistan and the technological challenge from the US 'Space Wars' programme. Arguably, by that time, the marginal opportunity cost of shifting additional resources to the military–industrial complex was already very high and led to disruptions in other parts of the economic system. On the other hand, civilian production did not benefit greatly from technology diffusion.

The argument so far has led from the deteriorating economic performance of the command economy system to the pressure for change, with the latter resulting ultimately in economic transformation. Indeed, there is overwhelming evidence that disillusion with the economic results of the socialist system was a decisive factor behind the pressure for political change, as demands for more political freedom were always mixed with purely economic demands, as illustrated by the Polish 'Solidarity' trade union movement which emerged in the summer of 1980 and remained active despite repression over the next decade.

The Communist leaders fell victim to their own ideological beliefs. The economic superiority of the command economy was a cornerstone of the ideology, and high growth rates were supposed to be its prime manifestation. An ultimate logical implication was to aim at some specific date for overcoming the leading market economies – the US in particular – as for instance declared by Soviet leader Nikita Khrushchev in the mid-1950s. Yet none of those predictions materialized. Moreover, the liberalization that followed the death of Stalin made the countries of Central Europe more open. In turn, freedom of movement and experience of a higher quality of life in the neighbouring European Economic Community (EEC, the predecessor of the EU) was a dangerous factor undermining the official claims of the superiority of the Communist system. By the late 1980s, the Soviet leaders, and Mikhail Gorbachev in particular, were well aware of the necessity for economic reform. Nevertheless, their effort to improve the economic system while limiting the scope of political liberalization turned out to be an impossible task.

Arguably, the most acute policy dilemma linking economic policy with politics related to price liberalization. This issue was also linked to the wider question of price policies and 'socialist macroeconomic cycles'. As identified by Kolodko (1979), the command economy was subject to the economic cycle just as much as the market economy. In the phase of expansion, the investment programme was overstretched and the number of projects mushroomed beyond the capacity of the system to deal with them. Too many investment projects resulted from the coinciding interests of the planning administration and individual enterprises to expand production and remove the bottlenecks in the economic system, with no strong individual interests supporting efforts to match the resulting claims on resources with scarcity constraints. This free-rider problem resulted in the dispersion of investment, long completion times for projects and production gains that came too late and did not match expectations. In the next phase of the cycle, to stabilize the situation, savings had to be made and raiding the private consumption pool was the easiest remedy. A slowdown in the supply of consumer goods matched with administrative prices led to price increases having a socially visible and painful, one-off, discrete character.

With time, and with political repression mechanisms being scaled down, these increases become more and more difficult to implement politically, triggering social unrest and protests.

Generally the inefficiency built into the investment processes meant that high growth rates could be generated only by disproportionately high investment rates, at the cost of consumption. This is illustrated by a snapshot of the investment shares in GDP and GDP growth rates in the final period of Communism. For the market economies, there is a positive and significant correlation between investment and growth. For CPEs, there is none. Vietnam, with some market reforms already implemented during the 1980s (see Riedel and Comer 1997), enjoyed a period of fast economic growth without an over-stretched investment programme. On the other hand, many CPEs were already in recession or near-stagnation, in spite of maintaining huge investment spending programmes. Mongolia, with a record-breaking 46 per cent of its GDP spent on investment, generated only 4.2 per cent GDP growth, and one may ask how much of that was simply increasing the production of investment goods for future investment in production of investment goods, and so on. At the same time, Chile experienced 10.6 per cent growth, with an investment share in GDP of 25.1 per cent, and Ireland was growing at the rate of 5.8 per cent, spending 18 per cent of its income on investment (see Figure 1.5).

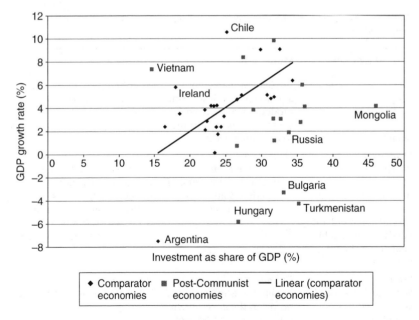

Figure 1.5 Investment and GDP growth, 1989
Source: World Bank, *World Development Indicators*.

The final stalemate? A political economy perspective

By the mid-1980s, with deteriorating performance, it became more and more difficult to find a balance between the desired level of military spending and the high level of investment required to fuel the chosen pattern of growth on the one hand, and the consumption level that maintained some minimum social acceptance necessary for the system to function without major political unrest on the other. While some CPEs (Czechoslovakia, East Germany, Romania) remained centralized and unchanged until the very end, partial reforms were attempted in several CPEs including Hungary, Poland and Russia. It is often argued that the reforms did not produce the expected efficiency gains due to their partial character and inconsistency: a mixed system of economic coordination may be suboptimal not only for a market economy, but also for the classic centralized model of socialism. But the failure of the Communist leaders to reform successfully may be also explained from a political economy point of view – one can argue that while reforms were necessary, the Communist governments were neither credible enough nor strong enough to face the social cost. The situation resulted in a prisoners' dilemma, which may be illustrated by Table 1.1. For each of the four possible outcomes, the first figure in the brackets represents a ranking of outcomes from the social point of view, and the second figure that from the central planners' point of view (Mickiewicz 1988).

Table 1.1   The prisoners' dilemma: economic policy stalemate in the last stage of the command economy

Central planner:	**Strategy 1:**	**Strategy 2:**
Society:	Implement market reform and accept that it will shift production away from central planners' priorities to consumer goods	Do not implement reform; economic inefficiency continues, while traditional economic priorities are retained
Strategy 1: Accept the initial costs of reforms (prices rise in relation to nominal incomes; some implicit subsidization of basic goods eliminated by changes in the price structure)	*Outcome A*: Successful reform: restructuring of prices and production, some initial social cost (+1, +1)	*Outcome D*: Society is paying for the reform, which is not implemented; savings resulting from decrease in real incomes used to support traditional priorities (–2, +2)
Strategy 2: Social unrest – social costs of reforms not accepted	*Outcome B*: Production is restructured; however, the government is supporting the level of real incomes (borrowing from abroad?) (+2, –2)	*Outcome C*: Status quo; no reform (–1, –1)

Successful market reform (*Outcome A*) is superior to the status quo. However, it is not achieved: reforms are not implemented (*Outcome C*).

The paradox can be explained by problems resulting from the *time inconsistency* of the reform process and the impossibility of a credible commitment by an undemocratic government. Reform can thus be seen as a two-stage task, where the initial phase of price liberalization has a negative impact on real incomes. After it is implemented, the authorities may carry on with institutional market reforms, measures for freedom of entry, privatization and external openness which should lead to a growth in income (*Outcome A*). However, alternatively, they can use the resulting stabilization to support traditional systemic priorities (*Outcome D*). In the latter case, society is paying the costs of the promised reform, which is not implemented; this outcome is the best from the point of view of the authorities and worst from the point of view of society. The government is unable to commit itself credibly to follow Strategy 1; that could be possible only with restoration of democratic control. Given this, the best strategy for society is to refuse to pay the costs of reform, rejecting the economic policy of the government which has no social legitimization and expecting that either the government will find a solution to the problems it has created, even if reforms are implemented (*Outcome B*) or will maintain the status quo (outcome C).

Thus, in this world of a non-cooperative game, the rational strategies of all involved lead to a stalemate and aborted reforms, even if a movement from C to A would be Pareto-efficient. In most Communist countries the game was implicit, not explicit. There was not enough social representation to negotiate with the government, nevertheless the threat of social unrest was real. In Poland, the pattern can be identified in the negotiations between 'Solidarity' and the government in 1980–1, and again in 1987–9. During the latter episode, the authorities decided to hold a referendum, proposing to introduce economic reforms, with initial social costs implied by price increases. The proposal was accepted by a small section of population only, as the dominant strategy was a simple boycott leading to invalidation of the referendum due to low attendance. Both in 1981 and in 1987, 'Solidarity' was criticized by outside observers for 'irrational' behaviour. The interpretation given above (Mickiewicz 1988) shows that it was perfectly rational to reject 'price reforms' introduced by a government lacking political legitimization. This interpretation was confirmed two years later, when the new non-Communist, 'Solidarity' government was able to introduce far-reaching reforms, with an even more significant social cost, without provoking social unrest.

If the above interpretation is correct, it could point to the impossibility of reform or change of a command economy system without political change. Yet change was becoming a necessity, given deteriorating economic results. This led the authorities to negotiate political reforms, and 'round table' discussions between the government and independent social representation

Table 1.2 The opening balance: post-Communist economies, 1990[a]

Country name	GNI, PPP (current international $ million)	Population, total	GNI per capita, PPP (current internat. $)	Industry, value-added (% GDP)	Exports, goods and services (% GDP)	External debt/GDP (%)	External debt/Exports (%)	GDP/energy use[c]
Albania	9,025.64	3,282,000	2,750	48.2	14.9	16.6	111.6	4.719837
Armenia	12,211.40	3,545,000	3,440	52.0	35.0			1.853619
Azerbaijan	36,882.73	7,159,000	5,150					1.501622
Belarus	73,132.41	10,200,530	7,170	47.2	46.3	52.4		1.74408
Bulgaria	46,718.37	8,718,000	5,360	51.3	33.1	15.6	158.3	2.075735
China	1,594,130.69	1,135,185,024	1,400	41.6	17.5	18.3	88.9	2.334284
Czech Rep.	119,093.91	10,363,000	11,490	48.8	45.2		40.5	2.569731
Estonia[b]	12,713.20	1,571,000	8,090	49.7	60.3	0.9		1.613445
Hungary	93,979.91	10,365,000	9,070	39.1	31.1	64.1	205.9	3.562825
Kazakhstan[b]	103,755.80	16,266,250	6,380	44.6	74.0	0.1		1.141505
Kirghiz Rep.	16,205.51	4,395,000	3,690	35.8	29.2			2.686325
Latvia	22,737.57	2,670,700	8,510	46.2	47.7	0.5	1.1	2.348068
Lithuania	31,891.45	3,722,000	8,570	30.9	52.1	0.4	0.8	2.208035
Macedonia, FYR	8,732.91	1,903,000	4,590	46.7	25.9			

Moldova[b]	22,843.50	4,362,000	5,240	33.3	89.4	0.4		2.094474
Mongolia	3,387.48	2,106,000	1,610	40.6	21.4			2.300305
Poland	205,162.68	38,118,800	5,380	48.3	27.6	80.7	292.2	2.65555
Romania	145,538.53	23,207,000	6,270	50.0	16.7	3.0	17.8	1.698988
Russia	1,497,556.06	148,292,000	10,100	48.4	18.2	10.2	56.4	2.245187
Slovak Rep.	47,649.59	5,283,000	9,020	59.1	26.5	13.0	48.9	4.5096
Slovenia[b]	24,232.73	1,998,100	12,130	45.6	63.1			1.838056
Turkmenistan	21,713.72	3,668,000	5,920	29.6				
Ukraine	358,724.37	51,892,000	6,910	44.6	27.6	0.6	2.2	1.433306
Uzbekistan	51,356.68	20,420,000	2,520	33.0	28.8			1.074833
Vietnam	64,536.84	66,200,000	970	22.7	26.4	359.6	1361.0	3.049592

Source: World Bank Development Indicators.
Notes:
[a] For the former republics of the USSR, data on external debt relate to 1992.
[b] For Estonia, Kazakhstan, Moldova and Slovenia export data relate to 1992.
[c] Energy/GDP: PPP $ per kg of oil equivalent, 1992.
GDP = Gross domestic product.
GNI = Gross national income.
PPP = Purchasing power parity.

Table 1.3 The opening balance: comparator countries, 1990

Country name	GNI, PPP (current international $ million)	Population, total	GNI per capita, PPP (current internat. $)	Industry, value-added (% GDP)	Exports, goods and services (% GDP)	External debt/GDP (%)	External debt/Exports (%)	GDP/ energy use[b]
Argentina	241,277.70	32,527,000	7,420	36.0	10.4	44.0	425.0	6.729418
Austria	145,056.28	7,725,700	18,780	30.9	39.6			6.378514
Brazil	801,898.23	147,940,000	5,420	38.7	8.2	25.8	314.4	6.416394
Chile	61,495.80	13,099,000	4,690	41.5	34.6	63.4	183.1	5.187386
Egypt	128,738.17	52,442,000	2,450	28.7	20.0	76.4	381.1	4.321693
Finland	86,674.75	4,986,000	17,380	29.2	22.8			3.176463
France	1,019,410.12	56,735,000	17,970	26.5	21.2			4.709553
Germany[a]	1,536,286.26	79,433,000	19,200	33.1	26.3			4.761975
Greece	118,081.96	10,161,000	11,620	25.5	18.5			5.447119
Indonesia	333,337.33	178,232,000	1,870	39.1	25.3	61.1	241.1	3.993804
Ireland	41,099.46	3,505,800	11,720	31.8	57.0			4.839881
Italy	977,699.80	56,719,000	17,240	30.8	19.7			6.870801
Japan	2,476,708.20	123,537,000	20,050	41.2	10.7			5.968128
Korean Rep.	382,138.74	42,869,000	8,910	43.1	29.1	13.8	47.6	4.144351

Malaysia	83,004.57	18,201,900	4,560	42.2	74.5	34.8	46.7	3.719639
Mexico	515,859.68	83,226,000	6,200	28.4	18.6	39.8	213.7	4.58916
Morocco	67,062.85	24,043,000	2,790	32.4	26.5	94.7	358.1	10.12036
Portugal	110,437.83	9,896,000	11,160	28.7	33.2			6.876195
South Africa	281,336.45	35,200,000	7,990	40.1	24.4			3.274795
Spain	500,099.87	38,836,000	12,880		16.1			5.683627
Sweden	150,715.63	8,559,000	17,610	28.1	30.1			3.453745
Tunisia	30,871.57	8,156,000	3,790	29.8	43.6	62.6	143.6	6.444978
Turkey	274,817.09	56,126,000	4,900	29.8	13.3	32.8	246.8	5.606571
UK	955,583.50	57,561,000	16,600	31.4	24.0			4.589401
US	5,876,806.58	249,440,000	23,560		9.7			3.244226

Source: World Bank Development Indicators.

Notes:

[a] For Germany, data relates to 1991 (i.e. post-unification).

[b] Energy/GDP: PPP $ per kg of oil equivalent, 1992.

FYR = Former Republic of Yugoslavia.

GDP = Gross domestic product.

GNI = Gross national income.

PPP = Purchasing power parity.

became the trademark of the peaceful political transition implemented in Central and Eastern Europe during 1989. The aim was no longer to reform, but to *transform* the system.

An alternative interpretation of the link between political reform and the economy can be derived from Barro (1997). According to this, the implosion of the Communist system can be seen as a spectacular historical event, yet one which is still consistent with global trends. Political freedom can be seen as a 'luxury good' – i.e. one for which demand appears only at some specific level of income. There is not much need for political freedom in poor countries, where basic material necessities take precedence over civic liberties. This reasoning is based on the empirical link between income *per capita* and political freedom. Indeed, at the beginning of the twenty-first century, the two command economies which remain most rigid in terms of political repression are also those which have failed in terms of economic development: Cuba and, even more so, North Korea. From this perspective, the political change in Central Europe and the Soviet Union could be triggered by the relative success of the command economy system there, not by its failure. Even if the system were not able to converge with the advanced market economies, it was still producing satisfactory rates of economic growth (Tables 1.2, 1.3). In the longer run, the standard of living improved, and that triggered demand for political change.

Notes

1. The command economy was also adopted by Yugoslavia and Albania, yet politically those two countries remained outside the 'Soviet Bloc' – i.e. outside 'the sphere of influence' of the USSR, as defined by the lack of a Red Army military presence.
2. The distinction between those four dimensions draws on Gregory and Stuart (1995). Decision rules and property rights are related dimensions (some control or decision rights are embedded in property rights), but we follow the traditional distinction here. See also Kornai (1992), Milgrom and Roberts (1992), Gros and Steinherr (1995, 2004), Temkin (1996) and others.
3. See Applebaum (2003) for an extensive account based on a wide range of sources, many of which became available only after the fall of Communism. Between 1929 and 1953, 18 million people passed through 476 camps scattered across the Soviet Union; at least 3 million perished.
4. Or for sixty years, if we exclude the initial phases of 'war communism' and the 'New Economic Policy' (NEP) in the USSR (see Gros and Steinherr 2004). At the beginning of the twenty-first century, the system is still operational in North Korea and Cuba. In addition, China and Vietnam offer two important examples of economic systems which can be functionally described as a unique evolving mixture of a command economy and a market economy.
5. 'Why is there an objective price structure in a competitive market? Because, as a result of the parametric function of prices, there is generally only *one* set of prices which satisfies the objective equilibrium conditions – i.e. equalises demand and supply of each commodity. The same objective price structure can be obtained in

a socialist economy if the *parametric function of prices* is retained. On a competitive market the parametric function of prices results from the number of competing individuals being too large to enable any one to influence prices [on] his own. In a socialist economy, [since the] production and ownership of...productive resources [apart from] labour [are] centralised, the managers certainly can and do influence prices by their decisions. Therefore, the parametric function of prices must be imposed on them by the Central Planning Board as an *accounting rule'* (Lange 1936:63, emphasis in the original). Note that the argument used by Lange implies that a market socialist system with free prices *and* state ownership of capital assets is also feasible, provided that the enterprises are not large – i.e. are unable to inflict monopolistic distortions. Thus, why centralized administrative control over enterprises (including prices controls) is important for the socialist system is not really explained. The answer is that centralized control is crucial, not just because of the monopolistic position of enterprises but because of the incentive problem, which Lange was unwilling to admit. Decentralized enterprises with no transferable property rights to capital assets would still not guarantee that the assets were matched with those who could use them in the most efficient way.

6. All the data correspond to Tables 1.2–1.3, pp. 20–3.
7. This is the so-called 'ratchet effect'. See Milgrom and Roberts (1992); Roland (2000).
8. Energy use is affected by the production structure. Economies based on tourism, for example, may be very energy efficient in this respect (see Morocco in Figure 1.3).

2

The Transition Programme: Interdependence between the Key Components

The main components of reform

Economic transition consists of changing the system of control rights, incentives and information in an economy. The change should result in a better 'match' between control rights and residual claims, making the motivation of economic agents consistent with the aim of value maximization. As discussed in Chapter 1, one important element of efficiency relates to *flexibility*: the producers should adequately respond and adjust to changes (1) in the real structure of costs (scarcity), and (2) in the set of preferences of buyers. However, it is not only the behaviour of producers, but also of other economic agents, that matters: households should be motivated to save instead of hoarding goods, and investors to chose the long-term best value-adding projects.

Following Balcerowicz (1995: 239) we may distinguish between the three main components of transition:

(1) *Liberalization*

- Microeconomic liberalization of prices (elimination of price controls)
- Currency convertibility and removal of all major quantitative restrictions (QRs) on foreign trade; removal of external barriers to entry
- Removal of internal barriers to entry (i.e. to developing and setting up new private enterprises)

(2) *Macroeconomic stabilization* policies
(3) *Institutional reform* (changes in existing institutions; privatization of state enterprises, reorganizing the state administration, reform of the tax system, financial system reform).

Both liberalization and stabilization can be introduced immediately. On the other hand, it takes time to prepare a new legal and organizational framework (institutional reform).[1] This observation leads us immediately to one of the main issues of the transition programme: given the complementarities between the institutional reforms and the two other building blocks, is inconsistency in timing unavoidable, and does it have any serious negative effects on the results, at least temporarily? The question is therefore whether some elements of the liberalization component (and/or stabilization) should wait until the institutional reforms are complete. Roland (2000) offers an extensive theoretical analysis of this issue. We will provide new empirical results on the effects of the speed of reform in Chapter 6, but in this chapter and Chapter 3 we shall focus on the interdependence between the stabilization and liberalization components, arguing that it is inefficient to stabilize without liberalization and that stabilization has to be introduced quickly, as it is beneficial, regardless of the characteristics of the economic system.

Before we turn to this question, it may be useful to present a more detailed mapping of the key components of transition. The standard list of indicators is produced for all transition economies by the European Bank for Reconstruction (EBRD) and Development and published in the annual *Transition Reports* (EBRD 1995–2005). The list was been expanded in 2003 to add legal and infrastructure indicators, which we do not discuss here. The core set of eight indicators is presented below; for each indicator, the tasks are presented in order from the less to the more complicated (EBRD 2001, 2003):

(1) *Internal price liberalization* The definition of this measure was modified in 2003 (with corresponding scores adjusted for previous years). At present, it focuses entirely on the removal of administrative prices and price controls and the phasing out of state procurement at non-market prices, and excludes utility tariffs. In the original version, it also included utility pricing – i.e. the relation of prices to economic cost – and generally adequate regulation of utility prices. At present, the latter issue is treated separately under a new heading of the 'infrastructure index'.

(2) *External liberalization* (2a) *Foreign trade*: removal of most quantitative and administrative restrictions on import and export (agriculture being a typical exception); removal of high export tariffs; abolition of direct involvement in exports and imports by the state administration and state-owned foreign trade companies – foreign trade monopolies no longer granted to the latter, no barriers in access to foreign exchange, uniformity of custom duties for non-agricultural goods and services, membership in the World Trade Organization (WTO), which implies meeting the standard criteria of the international trade system; (2b) *Foreign exchange*: no multiple exchange rates, full current account convertibility.

(3) *Competition policy* Unrestricted entry to most markets; competition and anti-trust institutions and legislation; enforcement actions to counteract any abuse of a dominant market position and to strengthen competition, break-up of monopolies.

(4) *Large-scale privatization*   Here, progress is measured by the percentage of large-scale enterprise assets being transferred to private owners, with 25 per cent, 50 per cent and 75 per cent being used as threshold levels for assessment; the subsequent criterion is the quality of governance of these enterprises.

(5) *Small-scale privatization and freedom of entry*   Complete privatization of small companies resulting in ownership rights that can be transferred with no restriction; effective tradability of ownership rights for land, freedom of entry for new enterprises.

(6) *Governance and enterprise restructuring*   'Hard' budgets. tight credit and subsidies policies; enforcement of bankruptcy legislation; effective corporate governance provided by capital markets and banks; active owners and investors; well-functioning markets for corporate control; evidence of efficient restructuring and investment.

(7) *Bank reform and interest rate liberalization*   Full interest rate liberalization; no preferential access to cheap refinancing; banking laws and regulations consistent with Bank for International Settlements (BIS) standards related to capital requirements, supervision and market discipline (Basel Committee on Banking Supervision 2004); availability of a full set of banking services; financial deepening; significant provision of lending to private enterprises, privatization of banks.

(8) *Securities markets and non-bank financial institutions (NBFls)*   Fully developed NBFls (collective investment schemes, private insurance and pension funds, leasing companies); substantial market liquidity and capitalization of the stock exchange; substantial issue of securities by private enterprises; convergence of securities laws, regulations and practice with international standards set by the International Organization of Securities Commissions (IOSCO) (IOSCO 2003); protection of minority shareholders and, generally, all other customers of financial services; fair, efficient and transparent organization of financial markets, minimizing systemic risk, secure clearance and settlement procedures.

Possibly, the only important omission among this set of indicators relates to *fiscal reform*. One related issue – 'soft' budgets and subsidies – appears under dimension (6) (Governance and enterprise restructuring), yet the reform of both government revenue and expenditures is a wider issue, central to the success of the transition programme, and deserving of more attention. The omission is partly explained by the fact that macroeconomic assessment is treated separately by the EBRD, with the focus on the budget deficit. Yet, the structural aspects of the fiscal sphere deserve more attention on their own and cannot be reduced to an issue of government balance. Both reform of the distortionary tax structure and introduction of an efficient and effective pattern of social spending is crucial. On the revenue side, Schaffer and Turley's (2001) work offers a useful supplement to EBRD indicators; they calculate ratios of effective to statutory taxation, low values of which can be taken as measures of problems with tax compliance and collection, many of which are related directly to 'soft' budgeting by firms. It is also interesting to compare the EBRD groupings with the categories proposed by Balcerowicz (1995) discussed at the beginning of this chapter. Internal and external liberalization and small-scale privatization are all components of liberalization. They can be introduced relatively quickly. The remaining five dimensions (privatization of large enterprises, competition policy, corporate and financial governance) rely on institutional, legal and administrative reform, which is time-consuming and more difficult to implement. This is confirmed by the quantitative analysis presented in the Appendix to this chapter (pp. 40–4): there are marked differences in the speed with which the particular elements of reforms were introduced, and the empirical clustering of reforms is consistent with insights based on the distinction between liberalization and institutional reforms already discussed.

It is easier to justify the omission of stabilization components from the transition indicators. Stabilization may be assessed using the macroeconomic indicators covered in the EBRD reports, and there is no need for special transition indicators here, as standard measures of inflation, the budget deficit, the current balance, unemployment and GDP growth apply. Nevertheless, there is a direct link between macro stabilization and micro liberalization, as we shall argue in the next section. Subsequently, we shall discuss 'hard' budget constraints, an issue that is central to the success of transition programmes, and which cuts across several dimensions.

Why stabilization should be accompanied by price liberalization

Both liberalization and stabilization aim at eliminating disequilibria: price controls assume disequilibria, otherwise they would be meaningless, and inflation is a sign of a disequilibrium position on a macro level, otherwise prices would not have to adjust. The situation generally deteriorated over time in the command economies. One explanation may combine the focus on labour markets and on final goods markets. In the initial phase of development, the command economies could rely on a pool of under-employed labour that could be attracted from the countryside to the new socialist industry. In addition, the pace of population increase was high. However, later, labour became scarce. Despite administrative controls aimed at preventing competition, enterprises attempted to compete for labour by offering larger salaries to motivate higher participation and greater effort. This was possible due to 'soft' financial constraints on enterprise spending. The resulting increase in disposable income was not matched by supply and, to make matters worse, the administration maintained a priority of producer goods over consumer goods in production plans. While wages were rising, prices were not allowed to rise fast enough to absorb the full increase in demand, as that would have made the erosion of real wages more visible (see also pp. 17–18). As a result, an 'inflation gap' was allowed to develop. People were left with excess cash, because there were not enough goods available at official prices. Saving was not an attractive option, as the real interest rate on deposits was negative. State banks under government control maintained uniformly low deposit interest rates. The government attempted to absorb some of the cash by offering various pre-payment schemes for durable goods such as cars and housing (Kolodko 1987). Nevertheless, the propensity to save was low, and the 'inflation gap' led to 'forced savings'. The latter term is incorrect if taken in its precise meaning: nobody was 'forced' to save. It was always possible to maintain higher cash balances; in fact, market disequilibrium created some additional incentives, as easy access to cash was a necessary condition to buy goods, which appeared in shops in a haphazard manner. In addition, foreign currency and hoarding of goods could be used as substitute savings. In most of these countries, foreign currency was relatively easily accessible, and even where it was illegal to keep foreign cash, the risk involved was too small to prevent a shift of savings towards foreign currency. Hoarding of goods also resulted in disequilibrium spreading between the markets for different goods. Anything durable could be stored, starting with food products such as sugar, flour, or oil. Thus, maintained cash balances of the domestic currency were 'forced' only in the sense that the prices of the alternative options (unofficial exchange rates, 'black market' prices of goods) were driven high by demand.

The mechanism of disequilibrium was described above as originating from macro imbalances between incomes and the value of consumer goods production, which may be an appropriate subject for stabilization policy. However, disequilibrium on the consumer goods market may also result from an inadequate price structure. Thus, both a macro and a micro dimension has to be addressed if efficient equilibrium is to be restored. To illustrate the point, it is useful to recall the basic rational choice framework. The analysis below draws from Podkaminer (1987a, 1987b). We illustrate the concept of the 'inflation gap' first (Figure 2.1).

In Figure 2.1, the nominal income is equivalent to y, illustrated by the budget line, between points $(y/\bar{p}_1)$ and $(y/\bar{p}_2)$, where $\bar{p}_1$ and $\bar{p}_2$ denote administratively set prices for two representative products. However, the nominal budget line is not a binding constraint for real consumption opportunities; instead, those are delimited by the quantities of goods produced (the shaded area in Figure 2.1). Here, disequilibrium resulting from macroeconomic imbalances prevails and the microeconomic impact of distorted price structure has no direct effect on consumption possibilities.

Figure 2.2 illustrates a more interesting case, where consumer choice is affected as much by price distortions as by macro imbalances. A surprising result is that under disequilibrium, consumption of some products (such as q_1 on Figure 2.2) may be higher than the optimum. This follows from the fact that disequilibrium tends to spill over from one market to another.

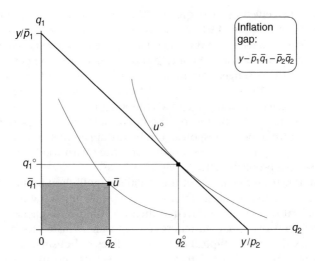

Figure 2.1 Podkaminer's model of the 'inflation gap'

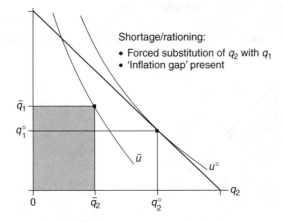

Figure 2.2 Podkaminer's model of forced substitution

When consumers cannot buy enough of q_2, they choose to buy q_1 as a second best. Consumption of the latter good is higher than under market equilibrium with liberalized prices.

Podkaminer (1987a, 1987b) argue that q_1 may refer to food and q_2 to durable goods. While the prices of durable goods were too low (and supply inadequate), the excess demand spilled over to the food market. A few years later, the outcome of price and supply liberalization confirmed the correctness of this analysis. In Poland, the consumption of meat – the category in which supply was most widely perceived as inadequate – did not change after the liberalization of prices and supply (4.91 kg/person in 1993 as compared with 4.83 kg/person in 1988, GUS data). On the other hand, there was a spectacular increase in the consumption of some durable goods. For instance, the percentage of households with passenger cars increased from 30 per cent to 45 per cent between 1988 and 1993. All this happened in spite of an 18 per cent increase in the relative prices of non-food goods to food goods in the same period.[2]

Understanding of the nature of disequilibrium thus is important, as it affects the choice of policy response. Led by the apparent symptoms of disequilibrium, the authorities were mostly concerned with food supply, while the most serious problems actually lay elsewhere.

We turn now from the nature of the initial disequilibrium to the economic transition. In practice, in all successful reform programmes stabilization and price liberalization were introduced at the same time, and quickly. In areas, where price controls remained (energy), they were adjusted towards world market levels. The major typical exception relates to housing. A theoretical argument may be constructed to show that because the sources of initial disequilibria were both macro imbalances and micro distortions in relative prices, macroeconomic policies alone were not sufficient to establish an efficient equilibrium.[3] This is presented below.

Point D, in Figure 2.3 illustrates consumer choice under initial disequilibrium. Again, real incomes are defined by the budget line between points $(y/\bar{p}_1)$ and

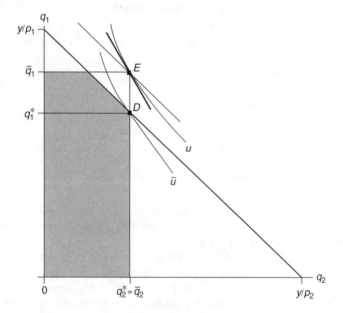

Figure 2.3   The inefficiency of macro stabilization without price liberalization

($y/\bar{p}_2$). The inefficiency of this initial set of prices and incomes relates to the following characteristics:

- At D, the *real prices* are wrong. The real price of q_1 is too high, q_1 is too expensive, and therefore the resulting real income is too low. There is also some waste – i.e. the amount of q_1 consumed (q_1^*) is lower than the amount of q_1 produced ($\bar{q}_1$).
- At D, the *relative prices* are wrong. This corresponds to the fact that the slope of indifference curve at point D is steeper than the slope of the budget line. The first corresponds to the ratio of marginal utilities, the second to the price ratio.

Thus, we have

$$\frac{MU_2}{MU_1} > \frac{P_2}{P_1},$$

or

$$\frac{MU_2}{P_2} > \frac{MU_1}{P_1}$$

Therefore, at D, the consumer would like to buy more q_2 instead of q_1, given the imposed price structure. There is microeconomic disequilibrium, as she is constrained by the supply of q_2, not by prices.

- Moreover, relative prices at D give *wrong incentives* to producers. The high relative price of q_1 in relation to q_2 creates incentives to producers to divert resources from production of q_1 and to increase production of q_2. That may move the system even further into disequilibrium.

Now compare the outcomes of two alternative policies, both moving the system to point E in Figure 2.3. The solid black budget line crossing E is an outcome of the policy, which eliminates the 'inflation gap', with full price liberalization. The thin budget line crossing E is an outcome of stabilization without full price liberalization. The analysis is presented in terms of two goods, which enables us to illustrate it graphically, but it can be generalized easily to the multiple goods case. In any event, there is only one unique price ratio (price structure), which will guarantee equilibrium at E, namely the price ratio for which the budget line is tangent to the relevant indifference curve (say, of a representative consumer). This set of relative prices is illustrated by the solid budget line crossing E and can be achieved by price liberalization.

Assume, instead, that the chosen set of prices (this time, still administratively controlled, either fully or partly) is given by an alternative thin budget line crossing E. Here, q_1 is more expensive and q_2 less expensive as compared with the equilibrium price set. There is still excessive demand for q_2 and apparent disequilibrium, even if all real income is spent at E. What is likely to follow is an attempt to stabilize by depressing real incomes, moving the system back to some point below E – for instance, back to point D. However, the important point to note is that micro disequilibrium cannot be eliminated by depressing real incomes alone. It is very unlikely that by shifting the budget line down in a parallel way one would arrive at the tangency point with the indifference curve. Thus, with a distorted price structure, there will be signs of disequilibrium, even if the macro policy is restrictive.

Price liberalization was the most fundamental element of reforms and the fastest to implement. As estimated by Berg (1994), only a month after full price liberalization in Poland (January 1990), the simple correlation between Polish relative prices and the relative prices in West Germany (as measured by a basket of thirty core consumer products) had increased to 0.81. It was only 0.29 before the transition.

We look next at the empirical evidence on the timing of stabilization and liberalization, which is illustrated by Figure 2.4. Stabilization programme dates are taken directly from EBRD (1999), and they coincide with the timing of the decrease in the inflation rate. Liberalization is measured by an aggregate indicator identical to that used by Falcetti, Raiser and Sanfey

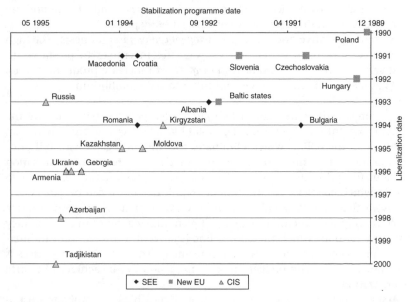

Figure 2.4   Timing of stabilization and liberalization
Sources: EBRD (1999–2005); Falceti Raiser and Sanfey (2002)
Note: SEE = South East Europe.

(2002) – i.e. by a simple average of three EBRD indicators related to (1) price liberalization, (2) trade liberalization and (3) small-scale privatization and freedom of entry. Here, we define 'liberalization' as a specific moment of time when this measure increases above a pre-defined threshold, following the approach adapted earlier by De Melo and Gelb (1997). Liberalization happens when the average of the three indicators takes a value of 3 or higher for the first time. The choice of threshold value results from taking the first liberalization programme introduced in Poland in January 1990 as the benchmark: in the first year of reforms, this composite liberalization index jumped from 1.7 to 3.0.[4] Interestingly, using this measure, three post-Communist countries had not implemented liberalization at the time of writing (2005): Belarus, Turkmenistan and Uzbekistan remain below this threshold, and therefore should not be considered as 'transition economies', but rather as some hybrid form of command economy with limited elements of the market.

There is a strong correlation between the timing of liberalization and stabilization: where differences exist it is liberalization which was introduced more slowly than the stabilization package. It is also interesting to take a closer look at outliers.[5] Three countries liberalized without effective stabilization: Croatia, Macedonia and Russia. In all three, the economic results were not satisfactory. At the other end of the spectrum, Azerbaijan, Bulgaria and Tajikistan attempted to stabilize without liberalization and the results were not good either. In all the successful reforms, the timing of both elements coincides.

The 'hard' budget constraint as a necessary condition for adjustment

In the previous section we discussed the case of disequilibria where the QRs were binding – i.e. they were more harsh than the nominally defined consumer budget. This was associated with inefficiency, which could not be overcome by macro stabilization alone. Price liberalization was necessary to eliminate the problem. Here, we turn to the opposite case, which is also inefficient. We discuss what happens when the budget constraint is not binding, being 'soft', in the sense that the economic agent can reach beyond it. The question is, under what circumstances does the budget constraint cease to be *effective* – when it is not determining economic agent behaviour? While quantitative constraints which are more harsh than the budget line are typical for consumers, the opposite case of a 'soft' budget may relate to enterprises. However, the two problems are strictly related. If the financial constraints are not binding, some others have to be. It is likely that where economic agents are not restricted by finance, they will ultimately face quantitative constraints. The 'financial veil' hides the fundamental scarcity of resources: when it is torn, the latter are faced directly. However the 'soft' budget constraint has yet another effect – it is not just replacing one set of constraints with another; in that case, it would not be 'soft' in any sense. A strong element of *redistribution* is involved. From the general equilibrium perspective, making the budget 'softer' for some economic agents implies that constraints are becoming more severe for others. As stated by Kornai (1986):

> The concept of 'budget'... is of a general nature and serves to denote the plan for revenue and expenditure of any economic unit: household, enterprise, government agency or non-profit institution. (Kornai 1986: 33)

Kornai made the issue of the 'soft' budget the cornerstone of his comparative system analysis (1979, 1980, 1986). The 'soft' budget situation may result from one of the following circumstances (Kornai 1986):

(1) Firms are *price-makers*, not price-takers; in a pure competitive model, a company is not able to transfer any idiosyncratic increase in costs onto its customers via increasing prices, as its sales will fall to zero; thus control over prices always introduces some slack, even if the demand curve is not vertical.

(2) The *tax system* is 'soft': 'formulation of tax rules has been influenced by the firm, the firm may be granted exemption or postponement as an individual favour; taxes are not collected strictly' (1986: 41).

(3) *Subsidies* exist, that may come in the form of contributions to investment funding with a financial cost below opportunity cost, or weak repayment obligations, some continuous production subsidies, or ad hoc subsidies to cover a one-off loss.

(4) The *credit system* is 'soft': availability of credit is not linked to the net present value (NPV) of a project, the terms of the financial contract are not always enforced and there is a built-in expectation that they may not be followed at the time the credit is granted.

(5) *External financial investment* is on 'soft' conditions, similar to point (4); this channel is relevant where equity markets exist. In the case of the command economy there was uniform ownership of enterprises, which had no separate equity.

If the budget is 'soft', firms with negative NPV may survive, and growth opportunities are no longer correlated with the value of the firm. From the general equilibrium perspective, this situation implies the transfer of resources from value enhancing producers to those which may generate little value-added or may even be value-destroying. The firm shares the risk with the government; the additional profits may be skimmed off, but losses may also be shifted onto somebody else. The structure of incentives is affected. Instead of a 'real economy', it becomes more profitable for managers to focus on the 'control sphere' (Kornai 1986) – i.e. on lobbying for decisions and administrative, fiscal and financial actions of corresponding decision makers (supporting organizations) to 'soften' the budget constraints. The corollary is that the budget constraint is not uniformly 'soft' for every firm, as it depends on their lobbying potential.

Here, we may focus on the role of social networks. Alternatively, we may think about bargaining, and list the possible threats available to budget-constrained organizations, including disruptive strike action.[6] The parallel perspective is that the extent of the 'soft' budget will also depend on how attractive it is for the supporting organization (typically the government administration) to intervene to relax the constraints. For this reason, the budget may be relatively 'softer' for the largest companies, for which the political cost and external economic effects of bankruptcy may be the strongest. Shleifer and Vishny (1994) and Boycko, Shleifer and Vishny (1996) take labour spending as an example of a situation where the preferences of the sponsor (the supporting organization) may differ from those of the managers of the budget-constrained organization. The politicians may prefer higher spending than that resulting from profit maximizing choice, to maintain either higher employment or higher wages, which may be linked to either 'patronage jobs' which lead to individual exchange of favours, or to electoral and political support. To motivate the managers, they have to be compensated. This is easier in state-owned companies than in private companies, because the private owners are full residual claimants, and more costly to compensate. It follows from this line of analysis that the extent of a 'soft' budget should be positively correlated with the extent of state ownership of the productive assets (see also Kornai, Maskin and Roland 2003).

Under a 'soft' budget, the responsiveness and adjustment to changes in the economic environment is lower. In particular, the firm is not compelled to adjust fully to external prices (either because the financial constraints are not binding or because it is a price-maker) (Kornai 1986). In the previous section, we saw an example of the complementarity of two elements of the transition programme (liberalization and macro stabilization, both being necessary conditions for restoring equilibrium). Our discussion on the 'soft' budget extends this list. The objective of transition is to achieve a situation where the decisions of economic actors result in efficient adjustment to the structure of real costs (scarcity) and consumer preferences, as revealed by liberalized prices. Restoring equilibrium, as discussed in the previous section establishes a basic set of price information, which may guide enterprises in an efficient direction. Transformation of the corporate control sphere (including ownership reform, as discussed in Chapter 4) may align the motivation of economic agents with the incentives offered by the economic environment. However, our discussion of 'soft' budget implies that *changes in corporate control and re-introduction of the profit incentive are not a sufficient condition for successful liberalization*: even if the economic agents who control the firm are driven by the profit motive, this does not in itself determine their behaviour completely; the characteristics of the *economic environment* also matter. Only when profit incentives are combined with a 'hard' budget constraint are efforts directed towards 'real actions' (adjusting quantities, technological decisions, etc.). Combining profit incentives with a 'soft' budget constraint gives at least an equal or greater role to the manipulation of the control sphere: financial variables, price increases, lobbying for government subsidies, etc. In fact, *in this respect, more not less disruption may result: as with the profit motive, the incentives for lobbying are now much stronger.*

Direct EBRD operationalization of a 'hard' budget is more narrow than that used by Kornai (1986). It is included under the heading of 'Governance and enterprise restructuring (6)' and relates to government subsidies and 'soft' credit. However, other aspects of the 'hard' budget are dealt with; they are spread over several indicators. The indicator of banking sector reforms (7) is a good measure of the quality of credit systems and the elimination of that channel of the 'soft' budget. Price-setting is dealt with under 'competition policy (3)'. Good regulation may be a substitute for competition, where the latter is difficult to stimulate via free entry. And prices may become an element of the 'soft' budget in another way, namely where there is state procurement (1) of the firm's products at non-market prices. This is included under the EBRD indicator 'Internal price liberalization'. Thus, at least four our of eight EBRD indicators cover various aspects of the 'soft' budget issue.

While the extent of the 'soft' budget may be dramatically reduced, it cannot be entirely eliminated where any forms of external finance are present. This complication results from the ambiguity built into any form of finance. A time lag is always present between any provision of finance and repayment, and so is imperfect information and an element of risk. For that reason, any finance has a potentially 'soft' element: it may be subject to renegotiation or default without the full consequences being borne by the receiver of the finance. This deficiency is unavoidable due to the fundamental issue of *time inconsistency* (Kornai, Maskin and Roland 2003): in many situations it is not possible for the sponsoring (supporting) organization – i.e. the provider of finance – to commit credibly at the time the financial contract is signed. The reason is that in subsequent periods it may be beneficial to both parties to renegotiate, when the initial financial investment becomes sunk cost. Anticipating this, the budgeted organization, which has an informational advantage, may propose that negative value-added projects be financed. A corollary is that eliminating any possibility of a 'soft' budget will come at a cost, as it not always possible to separate good and bad projects – the budget also be too 'hard' in some cases.

The latter case follows from what Kornai (1986) defined as a pure case of a 'hard' budget constraint, where all external finance is eliminated. In that case, the firm's survival depends exclusively on the proceeds from sales and on the costs of inputs, which bear an element of risk which is not related to the internal efficiency of the firm. As a result, in the short term the firm may have to build excessive cash reserves to smooth cash flow over time. Moreover, growth and technical progress depend on the same factors: the financial resources necessary for expansion of the firm are created exclusively by internal accumulation. That becomes a serious problem for the economy where scope for structure change is high, and some bottlenecks cannot be sorted out quickly based on internal finance alone. Calvo and Corricelli (1992) promoted the point of view that the *credit constraint* was an important factor which contributed to initial recession. Indeed, there is no reason why the initial distribution of relative price shocks across enterprises and the resulting distribution of shocks to revenue should be closely correlated with the forward-looking (after-adjustment) NPV of companies. From this perspective, the availability of finance for restructuring becomes the key issue. If the latter were missing, some valuable capital could be destroyed in the process of initial change, leading to an overall output loss. However, as always, there is a trade-off. At the onset of transition, the state banks were not prepared for the task of efficient credit allocation and commercial lending (see Chapter 8). As argued by McKinnon (1992, 1993) forcing enterprises to rely on internal cash flow as a predominant source of finance may be a second-best solution, given the initial inadequacy of the financial system. The risk of a financial crisis following the opening of an easy channel of 'soft' financing and accumulation of bad loans may be too serious relative to the cost of restricting finance opportunities to enterprises.

Kornai (1995) illustrates the transition from the 'soft to 'hard' budget using survey data, where Hungarian firms were asked to state what were the main barriers they faced to an increase in production. Figure 2.5 plots Kornai's data on the graph showing the category of firms pointing to the given obstacle (the answers may sum to more than 100 per cent, due to multiple choices).

The survey identified six categories of barriers. Four are characteristic of quantitative constraints on the supply side (shortage of materials and labour) and two are constraints that are more typical for the market economy: consumer demand and finance. There is a striking time pattern, where all the quantitative, supply-side constraints become marginal while demand and finance become most important. In general, quantitative constraints and 'soft' finance are two sides of the same coin. Where the latter barrier does not hold, the economy falls back on the more fundamental quantitative constraints, where shortages replace the price coordination mechanism. The latter is restored by the liberalization process: companies compete for revenues from consumers and finance from external investors.

Another interesting indicator comes from Berg (1994), who compares profits (1) before and (2) after taxes and subsidies for the 500 largest enterprises in Poland. The simple correlation between the profits before and after taxes and subsidies in 1987 was zero. It had increased to 0.38 in 1989, after

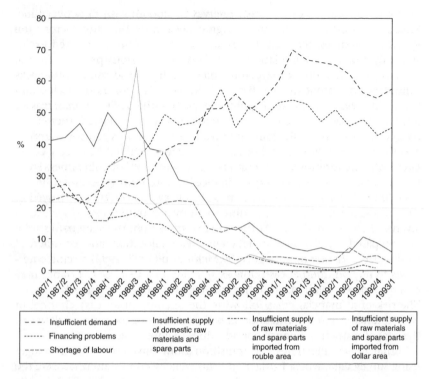

Figure 2.5   Impediments to production, Hungarian survey, 1987–93
Source: Kornai (1995, Table 4).

the first elements of reform had been introduced. In 1991, one year into the full
transition programme, it had increased further, to 0.71. The link between the
cash flow generated from sales and the final financial position of companies –
broken under old regime – was restored by the transition programme.

Appendix   Liberalization and institutional reforms: factor analysis applied to EBRD indicators

As already discussed, while not without problems the set of indicators
constructed annually by the EBRD is the most widely accepted aggregate
measure of the quality of reforms. EBRD indicators relate to eight dimensions:
(1) Internal price liberalization; (2) External liberalization; (3) Competition
policy; (4) Large-scale privatization; (5) Small-scale privatization and freedom
of entry; (6) Governance and enterprise restructuring; (7) Bank reform and
interest rate liberalization; (8) Securities markets and non-bank financial

institutions (EBRD 1995–2005; Falcetti, Raiser and Sanfey 2002). The scores are: 1, 1+, 2–, 2, 2+, 3–, 3, 3+, 4–, 4, 4+. Following standard practice, we transform minuses into – 0.333 and pluses into + 0.333. In 2003, the definition of the price liberalization index was changed, but the scores used here are based on the old definition.

The EBRD groups the eight indicators into three components: 'enterprise reform', 'markets and trade' and 'financial institutions', denoted respectively as *'Enterprises'*, *'Markets'* and *'Finance'*. Indeed, the individual indicators are correlated, which calls for imposing some organizing structure. Here, we were interested in checking if the EBRD grouping was confirmed by the empirical pattern as revealed by formal data-reduction techniques. What components of reform are typically implemented jointly? For that purpose, we used a sample which included 340 available scores from the set of thirteen annual data points over 1990–2002 for twenty-seven countries.[7] For selected indicators, information was available for 1989–94 as well, but only on the components related to liberalization.

Successful application of data-reduction techniques relies on the correlation between dimensions being neither too low nor too high. The links between dimensions (EBRD indicators) is confirmed by Bartlett's test of sphericity, which is significant at the 0.000 level. On the other hand, the degree to which individual indicators correlate is not too high; it is confirmed by the fact that the determinant of an R-matrix is 0.00007, which is sufficiently high (the conventional threshold is set at 0.00001). The correlation matrix reveals that the pair of indicators with the highest correlation is 'Bank reform' and 'Governance' (0.916). The strong link between corporate governance and the quality of the financial system is not a surprise, as corporate governance is nothing else but a system that protects the providers of finance (Shleifer and Vishny 1997), and any deepening of the financial system is difficult to achieve without it.

An overall measure of sample adequacy is that of Kaiser–Meyer–Olkin (KMO), which is 0.924, well above the critical level of 0.5. Further analysis of sample adequacy for individual variables is based on reproduced correlations (i.e. based on the model). It reveals that all diagonal elements are well above 0.5, confirming the result for the aggregate KMO test. For off-diagonal elements, we wish relatively few to be high. Five (17 per cent) of the non-redundant residuals have absolute values above 0.05.

Descriptive statistics are given in Table 2A.1.

It is interesting to note that both price liberalization and competition policy indicators have the lowest standard deviation, albeit for very different reasons. Elementary price liberalization was introduced early in practically all the transition countries (and the average of this indicator is the highest). That confirms the intuition discussed in more detail in the main body of this chapter: price liberalization is a first and indispensable element of the transition programme. In addition, the mean values of

Table 2A.1   Descriptive statistics: EBRD indicators, twenty-seven countries, 1990–2002

Indicator	Mean	Standard deviation
Freedom of entry and small-scale privatization	3.01	1.17
External liberalization (trade and exchange rate)	2.97	1.29
Internal price liberalization	2.63	0.70
Large-scale privatization	2.30	1.01
Bank reform	2.04	0.88
Governance and enterprise restructuring	1.88	0.74
Competition policy	1.79	0.69
Securities markets and non-banking financial institutions	1.75	0.73

indicators are also high for both external liberalization and freedom of entry and small-scale privatization. All three were traditionally merged in research into a composite measure of liberalization. At the other end of the spectrum, we find competition policy and non-banking financial institutions – here, the mean indicator (and standard deviation) are the lowest, indicating that those two components of reforms were the most difficult to implement.

Generally, in terms of standard deviations, external (trade) liberalization stands apart as the element of reform where policy differences are most clearly visible. These differences are likely to be linked to the political dimension. As will be shown in Chapter 9, this is the dimension of reform that is most affected by the quality of the *mediating institutions of democracy* , as trade liberalization effects considerably change the balance of costs and benefits for the various groups of economic actors.

Principal component analysis (PCA) was applied as a factor-extracting technique. The application of Jolliffe's criterion (retaining factors with eigenvalues over 0.7) results in the extraction of two factors which jointly explain 87 per cent of the variance. As there is no reason to suppress correlations between factors, we used oblique rotation (Oblimin with Kaiser normalization). The use of oblique rotation was supported by correlations between factors revealed by the component correlation matrix.

The results of rotated solution are summarized in Table 2A.2. To make the analysis clearer, we retained only values above 0.4.

The three components chosen by Falcetti, Raiser and Sanfey (2002) to represent liberalization – (1) Price liberalization (2) External liberalization and (3) Small-scale privatization and freedom of entry – are indeed all included in one component (2), EBRD where they play the dominant role. However, we find that progress in banking reform and privatization has also run typically parallel to basic liberalization. On the other hand, the first principal component relates to those institutional reforms that are more difficult to implement. The most important elements here are capital market reform and competition policy. Overall, the results suggest that the groupings

Table 2A.2   The pattern matrix: liberalization and institutional reforms

Indicator	Component 1: Institutional reforms	Component 2: Liberalization
Internal price liberalization		1.007
External liberalization		0.778
Free entry and small-scale privatization		0.654
Banking reform	0.606	0.424
Large-scale privatization	0.626	
Governance and enterprise restructuring	0.709	
Competition policy	0.976	
Securities markets and non-banking financial sector institutions	0.985	

obtained cut across the groups of indicators identified by the EBRD (1995–2005) and split naturally into two groups with an easy intuitive interpretation: component 1 may be labelled 'institutional reforms' and component 2 'Liberalization'. In the long time span encompassing most of the transition perspective, there is more variation in institutional reforms than in liberalization policies – the first component explains more variance in reform indicators that the second.

Figure 2A.1 presents the same information graphically. Price liberalization dominates the second principal component, and is practically absent in the

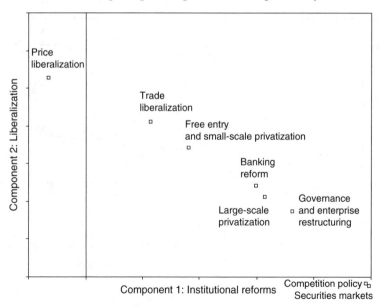

Figure 2A.1   Component plot in rotated space: liberlalization and institutional reforms

first. At the end of the spectrum we find competition policy and NBFI reforms ('securities'), which play a dominant role in the first component, being practically absent in the second.

We may also use the result, to illustrate the pattern of reforms for different countries. Figures 2A.2 and 2A.3 illustrate the progress of reforms for the six largest transition economies.

It is interesting to notice the different dynamics of the liberalization and institutional reform processes. Figure 2A.3 shows that liberalization was typically introduced quickly over a period of one or two years. Hungary and Poland were already liberalized in 1990, so the moment of liberalization is not illustrated on the graph; for all other countries, the moment when the liberalization programme was introduced is easily identifiable. This illustrates the approach adopted earlier in this chapter and more importantly in Chapter 6, where the threshold level of reforms is identified and based on the basic liberalization indicators. Comparing the six major transition economies, one may see that while the liberalization process started late in some countries, the end result is not very different. In particular, the convergence of Romania towards the level of liberalization observed in the three Central European (CE) economies is noticeable (in 2001 in particular, following the earlier reversal of liberalization in 1996). Reversal of economic liberalization in Russia (after the 1998 rouble crisis) may be seen as temporary, as liberalization measures were reintroduced after 2000.

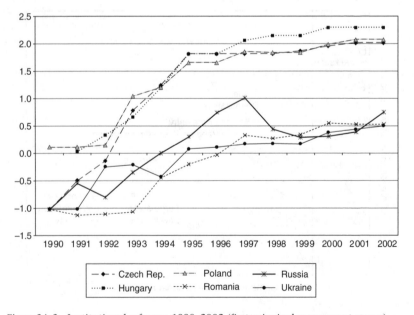

Figure 2A.2   Institutional reforms, 1990–2002 (first principal component scores)

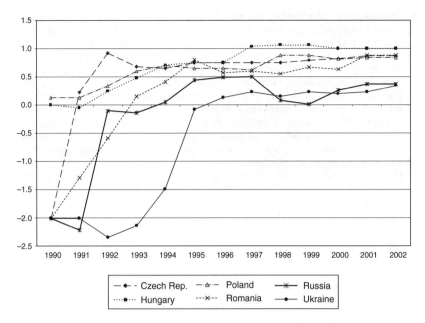

Figure 2A.3 Liberalization, 1990–2002 (second principal components scores)

In contrast with liberalization, the time path of the institutional reform indicator is slower, and the differences between the three CE economies (EU member states since 2004) and the two major CIS economies and Romania are more substantial. No clear pattern of convergence can be detected until 2002, and reversal of institutional reforms in Russia in 1998 has a more lasting effect than the reversal of basic liberalization, albeit there are now signs of reform being reintroduced.

Notes

1. Taken together, microeconomic liberalization and institutional reform can be labelled 'systemic transformation' (Balcerowicz 1995).
2. However, as noticed by Bell and Rostowski (1995), this price effect was overshadowed by the increase of the relative price of services (by 119 per cent as compared with food). They also note a possible impact of changes in real income on demand. Generally, if there was a fall in real income between 1988 and 1993, the share of food consumption should have increased, which did not happen, strengthening the conclusion about the nature of the initial disequlibrium.
3. Roland (2000) demonstrates why partial price liberalization may lead to inefficient outcomes, using political economy as an argument.
4. To make it consistent with indicators for the early period drawn from Falcetti, Raiser and Sanfey (2002), the scores correspond to the old index of price liberalization (i.e. before the 2003 modification) (see EBRD 2003 and the explanation on p. 27).

5. Outliers can be identified by taking either a difference in time between the stabilization and privatization dates, or by running an ordinary least squares (OLS) regression and picking up the countries with the highest absolute values of residuals. Both methods produce the same results in terms of ranking.

6. The budgeted organization is represented by managers bargaining with the supportive organization. However, the strike action may have the tacit support of managers, where it is targeting the supporting organization (say, a branch ministry in the case of state-owned firms). Generally, any kind of disruption with external effects creates a credible threat – think about large infrastructure companies, such as public transport. As always, the informational asymmetry between the budgeted organization and the sponsor (supporting organization) will also strengthen the position of the former.

7. Eleven scores were missing; these relate to the former republics of Yugoslavia in earlier years.

3
Stabilization

Introduction

There is a divergence between the short-term and long-term effects of transition, and it is likely that confusion between the two has had implications for policy-making.

In January 1990, Poland introduced a joint rapid liberalization and fixed exchange rate-based stabilization programme. Czechoslovakia followed a year later and both countries immediately went into sharp recession. On the other hand, the third early reformer, Hungary, followed more gradual liberalization programme. Using the EBRD benchmark, full liberalization in Hungary can be dated from 1992, two years later than in Poland.

With the benefit of hindsight, the policy differences between these three CE countries look insignificant now, and so does output cost. In fact, the recession in Hungary was marginally deeper than in the two other countries (see data in Table 6A.1, p. 113). All three were fast reformers, their transition programmes were relatively consistent and implemented without any major setbacks and the overall output loss was relatively small, as compared with many other transition countries, in the CIS and the Balkans in particular.[1]

However, all this was not known at the beginning of 1992. The Polish and Czechoslovakian programmes were quickly branded with the negatively charged name of 'shock therapy', which – as it appeared – was producing nothing but recession. At about that time, in 1992, in spite of the apparently negative experience of the early reformers, Slovenia and the three Baltic republics introduced comprehensive liberalization and stabilization programmes; however, most other transition countries chose their own slow reform paths. As we know now, with detrimental effect.

In parallel, the apparent negative experience of the first two years of transition programmes led to the emergence of a 'gradualist' critique. Where it went into detail, much of it focused on some element of stabilization design, such as 'excessively tight monetary policy' and 'excessive devaluation'

(Portes 1994; see also Nuti and Portes 1993) and stressed the importance of the interdependence between financial issues and macroeconomic policy (McKinnon 1993). However, similar points were also frequently accepted by the proponents of fast stabilization and liberalization: they stressed that the policy mistakes were difficult to avoid, and that they were corrected as soon as they were spotted (Gomulka 1995). Arguably, mistakes in the calibration of policy variables were unavoidable given the fact that no basic macroeconomic parameters were easy to forecast at the beginning of transition. In general, from today's perspective, there is far less controversy than initially appeared.

In this chapter, we intend to offer a brief overview of the stabilization experience, addressing the causes of its potential contribution to temporary output decline. As already discussed, while the Polish and Czechoslovakian recessions were short-lived, ironically both had more negative implications for some other transition economies: many decisions about stabilization and liberalization design were made around 1991 and 1992, when the two forerunners were in the midst of the J-curve-type recession and as a result mistaken policy conclusions were drawn. But the issue is more than of just historical interest. High-inflation episodes are now reoccurring and the stabilization experience of the transition countries may offer lessons for the future. The emphasis in this chapter will be on short-run stabilization policy design: stabilization is not sustainable without fiscal stability, which in turn depends on institutional reforms related to both taxes and expenditures.

We will make Poland our point of reference for the stabilization programmes introduced in the transition economies in the early 1990s. As already discussed, Poland implemented the first one-off transition – a liberalization–stabilization programme – and became a benchmark for other countries which could learn from both Poland's successes and its mistakes.[2]

'Heterodox' stabilization: the exchange rate and credibility

The methods applied in the Balcerowicz Programme (implemented in Poland on 1 January 1990) were based to some extent on experiences of earlier stabilization programmes in other countries (especially several Latin American countries and Israel in the mid-1980s). As already discussed, Czechoslovakia started its own programme a year later. The Russian government initiated its transition programme in January 1992, but liberalization was gradual and the stabilization programme was postponed until April 1995. Strong opposition to the 1992 early stabilization efforts of Yegor Gaidar's government came from industrialists lobbying for the preservation of the 'soft' budget constraint and led to inconsistencies in macro policies and blocked early progress in stabilization (Gros and Steinherr 1995; Mau 1996).

Following Bofinger, Flassbeck and Hoffman (1997), two basic criteria can be applied to classification of stabilization programmes: their cross-section produces four categories. The first distinction relates to the *'orthodox'* versus the *'heterodox'* programme. The 'orthodox' programme relies on monetary policy (cutting down the rate of nominal money growth, increasing the nominal interest rate) and adjustment in fiscal policy (reduction of the government budget deficit). In turn, in the 'heterodox' programme, these elements are also present but they are complemented by some direct controls on nominal prices, wages in particular. The second distinction is between *money-based* and *exchange rate-based* programmes. In the first version, the exchange rate remains flexible, while in the second it is fixed, at least for some limited period of time, announced at the beginning of the programme. The main motivation for fixing the nominal exchange rate is that it provides a transparent and efficient way of signalling, which affects the inflationary expectations of economic agents. In contrast, reliance on pre-announced monetary targets alone may result in a protracted recession if expectations are slow to recognize the policy shift. This effect may be explained in more than one way; an example of a simple theoretical framework is to think about wages as resulting from some implicit or explicit bargaining aimed at expected *real* wages. The latter depend in turn on price expectations. For this reason, a decrease in inflation which is not accompanied by a downward adjustment in expectations may lead to high real bargained wages. In turn, these negatively affect both employment and production decisions of companies. Recession follows. The credibility of the government is therefore essential to limit the costs of disinflation. Here, we come back to the issue already discussed in Chapter 1: the reform stalemate in the late Communist period and the lack of stabilization resulting from the low credibility of the government: any apparent stabilization could be followed by another inflationary hike, so there was no rationale for adjusting expectations. Credibility was gained only after the replacement of a weak authoritarian government by a democratic setting.

In general, there is a complementarity between exchange rate design and the 'heterodox' approach. Similar to a fixed exchange rate, 'heterodox' elements aim at direct control of some nominal variables, in particular wages. Sticking to these targets is a signal of government determination, so the underlying motivation is similar. One has to stress, however, that in the Polish programme (and in subsequent similar programmes in the other economies emerging from the command system), wage controls were implemented in a less rigid form than in Latin America – not as direct controls, but only in the form of penalty taxes on excess wages, leaving enterprises some marginal flexibility in wage decisions (Bofinger, Flassbeck and Hoffman 1997). In addition, credibility was increased in the Polish programme via a $1 bn stabilization standby loan offered by the International Monetary Fund (IMF) to discourage speculative attacks on the exchange rate.

'Heterodox', exchange rate-based programmes were implemented in Poland (1990), Czechoslovakia (1991) and the three Baltic states (1992–3). In the programmes attempted in Bulgaria and Romania in 1991, the exchange rate element was missing. Both failed.[3] However, a similar programme based on a floating exchange rate, introduced in Slovenia in 1991, succeeded. In contrast to all the above, the IMF-sponsored stabilization programmes introduced in Kazakhstan, Russia and Ukraine in 1994–5, were all 'orthodox', with no exchange rate element present. And while not without disturbances, they ultimately brought disinflation (Bofinger, Flassbeck and Hoffman 1997). Thus, from the point of view of the longer-term objectives of disinflation, the policy lessons are not clear-cut.

The initial position: internal and external disequilibria

Internal disquilibrium in the form of repressed inflation has already been discussed in Chapter 2. Some of that spilled over into open inflation. The initial budget deficit is difficult to assess, as there was no strict separation between the public finances and the (state-owned) banking system, with a large number of additional para-budgetary organizations channelling away vast sums of money, the social security fund being the largest of these. Yet, the public expenditure and revenues were certainly not balanced. If internal disequlibrium was a serious problem, external disequilibrium was even more so. Not only Poland, but also a number of other former command economies, faced a foreign debt crisis coupled with a difficulty in generating sufficient trade surplus to service debt payments. The origin of the debt crisis can be traced back to the period of détente in the 1970s, following the Helsinki agreement and some expansion in economic contacts between East and West. After the first oil crisis (1973), the international financial system was flush with money coming from the Middle East to Western banks and real interest rates were low. At that time, the countries of Central and Eastern Europe started to borrow to support modernization programmes, which was important as their economies were facing the first signs of fading economic growth (see Chapter 1). Yet, at the same time the Communist decision-makers missed the contemporaneous technological shift, as the world economy started to adjust to high energy prices (and a new structure of costs in general), introducing energy-saving techniques. There were neither incentives nor price information built into the old system to guide the necessary restructuring. Wrong technologies, coupled with general inefficiency of investment processes, did not produce the expected increase in exports to repay the debt a few years later (see Chapter 1; for more, see Poznanski 1996). While the situation was serious in Bulgaria, Hungary, and Yugoslavia, Poland was simply unable to generate sufficient amount of exports to service its foreign debt. For that reason, during the initial stage of the transition programme the external equilibrium was a clear priority (Table 3.1).

Table 3.1 Hard currency debt, 1989

	Ratio of gross interest to net exports %)	Gross debt *per capita* (US dollar)	Absolute level of gross debt (billion US dollars)
Poland	42	1,058	40.4
Hungary	19	1,858	19.7
Yugoslavia	18	743	17.6
Bulgaria	17	1,149	10.0
East Germany	13	1,312	21.7
Czechoslovakia	6	480	7.2
USSR	4	170	49.5
Romania	2	9	0.2

Source: Estrin (1994: 6). For a complementary set of indicators, see also Table 1.2, pp. 20–1.

The stabilization package

While from the analytical viewpoint stabilization policy can be separated from institutional reforms, some of the latter are prerequisites for the former in the post-command economy context. Before any particular set of monetary and fiscal policies can be implemented those spheres have to be disentangled from state planning administration and made an autonomous task of both the newly designed Central Bank and the Ministry of Finance, which has to assert its priority over the traditional interests of branch ministries.

Similarly, it is difficult to separate the macro policy stabilization package from both internal and external liberalization, as without the latter two the prices, exchange rate and foreign trade will be directly *administered* instead of being subject to *policy* decisions.

With these caveats in mind, the set of nine objectives for a programme of macro stabilization accompanied by liberalization and the necessary institutional reforms may be summarised as follows:[4]

(1) *Fiscal policy*: the aim was to reduce the state budget deficit from the estimated staggering 8 per cent in 1989 to 0.8 per cent in 1990, using both expenditure and revenue measures (given the surplus on the extra-budgetary government funds, in practice, the consolidated government budget was to be balanced). The primary target for expenditure reduction was the vast system of enterprise subsidies (including both product subsidies and investment) granted under the old regime. On the revenue side, a complicated system of tax credits was eliminated, making taxes more uniform (Bauc, Dabrowski and Senator 1994).

(2) *Monetary policy*: net domestic assets were to grow more slowly than inflation, leading to a decrease in the stock of real money. This effect was to be

concentrated in the first quarter of 1990. Later on, real money was to grow in line with the expected increase in the demand for money, after progress with stabilization had been achieved. Parallel to this, the discount rates offered by the National Bank were to become the main policy instrument, expected to be positive. In general, the independence of the National Bank from the government increased (Bauc, Dabrowski and Senator 1994).

(3) *Financial system*: the objective was to eliminate the system of preferential credit rationing (and corresponding negative interest rates). All past credit agreements were to be corrected, making the real interest rate positive, while 'a part of increased interest payments on old debt was allowed to be capitalised' (OECD 1992: 14; Bauc, Dabrowski and Senator 1994).

(4) *Exchange rate*: the adjustment process had started already in 1989, with the decisive devaluation by 32 per cent introduced on 1 January 1990, jointly with internal convertibility. The free/'black market' exchange rate was taken as a point of reference and the exchange rate was set at the level of zł9,500/$1, stable for at least three months. 'Enterprises were henceforth not permitted to keep their export receipts in foreign exchange accounts', however 'currency was available on demand for current transactions' (OECD 1992: 14).

(5) The programme was supported by a $1 bn *stabilization loan* from the IMF (not used, as it turned out).

(6) *Automatic indexation of wages* was removed and a 'heterodox' income policy was introduced instead.[5] A punitive tax on wage increases above the specified level was imposed on state firms (almost all large and medium-sized firms were state-owned at the beginning of the reform programme). Initially, the taxable increase in wages was calculated in reference to the overall wage bill; later (for 1991), the average wage was made the reference point. The change was intended to prevent large employment reductions, due to rising concerns about unemployment.

(7) All *quantitative trade restrictions* on imports and most of those on exports were eliminated. Instead, a uniform set of import tariffs between 10 per cent and 20 per cent was established (Bauc, Dabrowski and Senator 1994).

(8) *Price liberalization* was implemented, except for energy, utilities, housing and transport. Food prices had already been liberalized, just before the introduction of the main programme, by the last Communist government in August 1989. The energy price, even if it remained officially under government control, was increased by a dramatic 400 per cent, bringing it up to the equilibrium level. Some remaining price controls were gradually removed, including liberalization of the price of coal in July 1990 (Bauc, Dabrowski and Senator 1994).

(9) *Freedom of entry* was granted and a small privatization programme started almost immediately; privatization of large enterprises was delayed and implementation of the bankruptcy law was initially slow.

Inconsistency between the elements of reform?

When price controls prevail at the initial point of reform and, as a result, a monetary overhang is present (see Chapter 2), price liberalization leads to a one-off jump in the price level. The resulting contradiction between liberalization and stabilization is apparent, and may have serious implications if the initial price adjustment is not distinguished from some persistent inflationary impulses. The adjustment towards equilibrium is almost instantaneous and does not have any lasting effect. This is mostly a non-issue, as this effect was well understood by policy-makers, even if the scale of initial price adjustment came as a surprise (Sachs 1993).

A more serious inconsistency results when stabilization is accompanied by some nominal restrictions. Here, one may note immediately a contradiction between price liberalization and the 'heterodox' income policy, as the latter implies that control over an important set of nominal variables is maintained. The issue led to significant controversies, as the incomes policy was strongly criticised by trade unions, managers and liberal economists (in particular, those associated with the Council of Advisors of the President, Lech Walesa, possibly best represented by Jan Winiecki). The government position was that the income policy was critical for disinflation (for Balcerowicz's own account of this discussion, see Balcerowicz 1995: ch. 17, and more details in Balcerowicz 1992). The main efficiency cost of the incomes policy was that it slowed down microeconomic adjustment by making it more difficult for successful firms to rationalize wage structure and attract the best human capital available through offering higher wages. This kind of criticism emerges clearly from the survey of managers reported by Pinto, Belka and Krajewski (1993). The incomes policy was blamed for 'hampering workforce rationalization and flattening the wage structure', and the latter effect was made worse by the replacement of an increase in the wage bill by an increase in the average wage as the tax basis. Human capital-enhancing change in the composition of the workforce was difficult to achieve, as both 'hiring a good worker (who costs more) raises the average wage, while firing a bad worker (who costs less) does exactly the same' (1993: 248). On the other hand, the survey results justified the government position to a degree, as two-thirds of managers admitted that removal of the tax did result in some, albeit limited, wage increases (Pinto, Belka and Krajewski 1993: 248–9).

The third, more general problem results from the fact that both stabilization and liberalization can be introduced quickly, while institutional reforms take longer to implement. In particular this relates to the processes of privatization and demonopolization (breaking up enterprises before or at the time of privatization).

Lack of privatization at the beginning of the programme implies that, in the initial phase, a market environment is introduced while enterprises still operate under the old corporate control structures. Initial concerns related to the expectation that those enterprises which were hit by decline in demand resulting from stabilization and change in relative prices might reduce production, while those facing positive shocks might not compensate with a production increase. While a later interpretation of this phenomenon relies on financial markets imperfections (Calvo and Coricelli 1992, 1993; see also the discussion in Chapter 6), the early exchange of views among the reformers focused on additional dimensions of the problem. The concern was that restructuring and cost-cutting might be difficult to implement for managers with no experience of the market economy. On the other hand, those firms which gained from shifts in demand structure could increase prices instead of production, taking advantage of their dominant market position (Sachs 1993). The gain from privatization would be to bring in new managerial skills and other resources, including finance and access to markets, especially in case of foreign investors. Demonopolization would prevent the cutting back of production to realize monopolistic rents. Thus, this argument goes, without privatization and demonopolization the economic contraction caused by the stabilization (and liberalization) could be amplified (Gomulka 1992; Sachs 1993).

While deep, structural restructuring was indeed impossible to implement quickly, contrary to expectations state firms were, where necessary, able to accept a decrease in real wages, while delaying dismissals and thus slowing down the emergence of unemployment, making an income policy ceiling relevant only in case of the most successful companies (see Pinto, Belka and Krajewski 1993). This behaviour may be consistent with employee control models, as will be discussed in Chapter 5 (and a similar argument can be found in Blanchard *et al.* 1991). While this kind of subsistence strategy (postponing restructuring at a cost of lower wages) is not sustainable in the longer run, in the short run it helped to soften the blow of the structural shock caused by liberalization and stabilization. Paradoxically, from this point of view, the time lag in institutional reform (transfer of corporate control to outsiders) had an (apparent?) positive, not negative effect.

Another concern relates to monopolization of the production structures. While liberalization enables firms to adjust to the market structure of prices to reflect preferences and scarcity, it also enables monopolists to adjust their price and quantity decisions, taking advantage of their dominant market position. While the first process leads to efficient equilibrium, the second may increase inefficiency. In practice, these problems did not materialize where internal liberalization was accompanied by foreign trade liberalization and current account convertibility, as in Poland. Competition from abroad proved to be the most effective disciplining device preventing monopolistic behaviour by domestic producers (Sachs 1993). As a result, the distorted structure inherited from the past was corrected faster by the 'imported' price structure reflecting world prices, and new monopolistic distortions were prevented.

However, there is one further complication here. A necessary condition for the latter effect to work is that the initial devaluation of the domestic currency is not too strong. Thus, we have inconsistency between one of the liberalization objectives (competition) and the aims of macro policy, which were not only orientated on restoring equilibrium, but on restoring external creditworthiness as perceived by foreign suppliers of finance. From the latter point of view, a fast increase in exports was a priority, which was an argument supporting a stronger devaluation. In addition, a strong devaluation was important because the exchange rate was to be used as a nominal anchor and initially fixed. A stronger initial devaluation would diminish the subsequent risk of speculative attacks.[6] In practice, where introduced, external openness and the elimination of trade barriers led to parallel spectacular increases in both imports and exports. The increase in both were thus more complements than alternatives.

Devaluation, stabilization and the fall in output

In this section, we apply the simple framework used by Fischer (1988) to illustrate the empirical regularity noticed in reference to stabilization programmes in transition economies (Christoffersen and Doyle 2000): rapid disinflation under exchange rate-based stabilization programmes was associated with a sharper (albeit temporary) fall in output. A further technical argument demonstrating when exchange rate-based stabilization combined with a restrictive macroeconomic policy may result in a fall in output is presented in Rebelo and Vegh (1995). A critical point to remember is that many exchange-rate based stabilizations (such as Argentina, Chile and Uruguay) produced a boom not a recession immediately after stabilization, so there is nothing deterministic about the outcome, which remains policy-dependent (Rebelo and Vegh 1995). Again, Christoffersen and Doyle's (2000) result suggests that the choice of stabilization design had implications for output paths.

Following the discussion in the previous section, there were two fundamental reasons why the initial devaluation was too strong. Most importantly, given the initial indebtness and lack of external creditworthiness, the main objective of the policy-makers at the beginning of the stabilization programme was to increase exports over imports, thereby leading to an improvement in the current account. That led to a policy bias towards deep initial devaluations. Secondly, the level of domestic reserves was low and the stabilization loan relatively small, which again suggested a larger devaluation to make the foreign exchange rate anchor a credible and working instrument.

However, a strong devaluation led to strong inflationary internal impulses. With a fixed (pegged) exchange rate (and no possibility to calibrate and correct the initial level of nominal exchange rate), the government had no choice but to rely on a restrictive monetary and fiscal policy to counteract the inflationary effects, and achieve disinflation. That had a recessionary impact:

> On this interpretation, output losses are not due to pegs *per se*, but reflect the rate of inflation being stabilised, the rate at which pegs are set, and the supporting policies. (Christoffersen and Doyle 2000: 437)

This effect can be illustrated as follows. Devaluation means that 'the government changes the *nominal exchange rate*, by announcing its willingness to buy and sell foreign currency at a particular price' (Fischer 1988: 118–19, emphasis in the original). However, the key economic variable is not the nominal, but the real exchange rate – 'the change in domestic production costs relative to foreign costs' (Fischer 1988: 119), which in turn affects the price of exports relative to the price of imports. Devaluation makes domestic goods (i.e. non-tradables) cheaper relative to tradable goods, for domestic consumers. Thus, the demand for domestic goods rises. Producers, however, want to shift toward the production of traded goods. There is thus an inflationary impulse on the domestic market (Fischer 1988). It is here that the external surplus (current account) as the objective of the macro policy achieved via devaluation may not be consistent with disinflation.

The strength of the inflationary impulse depends also on the behaviour of the nominal cost of domestic production. Where a fixed exchange rate is adopted after stabilization, it is the level of domestic production costs alone that affects the value of the real exchange rate. That explains the complementarity between adaptation of the fixed exchange rate and the 'heterodox' elements of the stabilization programme. While some domestic costs will be affected via the prices of imported inputs, wages remain the key component and an incomes policy introduced to restrict the adjustment in wages may help. In addition, the consumer price index (CPI) around the time of liberalization is misleading. To allow wages to increase in line with the CPI will in practice mean significant real wage increases. This is because much of the initial price hike is in fact eliminating the 'inflation gap' and adjusting prices which are not reflecting the real availability of goods (see n. 5, p. 63 and further discussion in Sachs 1993). From this point of view, an exchange rate-based programme without 'heterodox' elements could become a worst-case scenario. Drawing from the Latin American experiences in 1980s, this variant was not adapted in the transition economies (Bofinger, Flassbeck and Hoffman 1997).

We can now use Fischer's (1988) current account–aggregate demand diagram to illustrate how the stabilization programme worked. The initial point is represented by *A* on Figure 3.1. The economy is subject to inflationary pressures, while the current account is in deficit. Thus, there is both

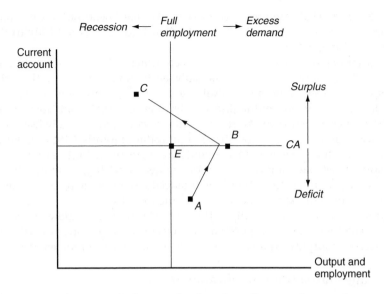

Figure 3.1 Fischer's (1988) framework adapted to illustrate the post-Communist stabilization

internal and external disequilibrium. As a result of a strong devaluation, the demand for domestic products increases. Subsequently, the current account deficit is eliminated, but at the same time the excess demand on the domestic market is strengthened (a move from *A* to *B*).With no possibility of correcting the nominal exchange rate to bring in effective stabilization, devaluation is accompanied by stronger monetary and fiscal measures, as these have to counteract this additional effect of devaluation (implying an adjustment from *B* to the left). A battery of policies reinforces the effect. Wages, and therefore demand, are constrained by incomes policy. Monetary policy results in a credit squeeze. Fiscal policy (liquidating subsidies) results in an additional supply shock. The important point to notice here is that elimination of the 'soft' budget subsidies is a key component of the liberalization programme and the systemic reform, as already discussed. Stabilization is thus difficult to implement without systemic reform, which is another argument for implementing both policies jointly (see also Chapter 2). Reliance on monetary and fiscal policies to bring down inflation with no corrective adjustment in the nominal exchange rate results in point *C* instead of *E* being achieved.

One may also note that, on the external dimension, this adjustment (internal stabilization policy) supports the effect of devaluation even further, creating additional incentives to increase exports, because exporters are 'pushed' from the domestic market (insufficient demand) to actively seek foreign sales. That reinforces the effect of external liberalization on export growth. Thus, the movement from *B* to *C* in Figure 3.1 is not only to the left, but also upwards.

If anything, the policy-makers did underestimate the long-lasting effect of trade liberalization, which was possibly even more significant than the temporary effect of nominal devaluation – i.e. a continuous process of gradual improvement and adjustment leading to a significant increase in exports over several years. Moreover, while devaluation normally leads to a *decrease* in imports, trade liberalization, introduced jointly with a stabiliza-tion programme, resulted in a significant increase in both exports and imports. From the point of view of foreign debt servicing, it is not just the current account, but the ratio of the financial cost of servicing foreign debt to the volume of exports (i.e. the economic capacity to generate funds for payments) which is more critical. The higher both imports and exports are, the smaller level of net exports in the percentage of imports is needed to generate the surplus required to match the financial cost of foreign debt.

Exchange rates: from stabilization to EMU

Possibly, apart from Russia, all the transition economies are 'small open economies' (Buiter and Grafe 2002), for which an irrevocably fixed exchange rate is seen by many economists as a preferred solution. There is a gain from 'predictability': currency pegging would permit the 'import' of policy credi-bility and stability from a low-inflation country. However, the fixed exchange rate alone does not guarantee credibility in the longer term, even if backed by reserves (a stabilization fund) unless it is supported by sound fiscal and financial policies and is seen by the market players as defendable and sustainable. We will discuss fiscal policies in Chapter 7. Below, we consider more specific options that come under the fixed exchange rate label. Cirera and Hölscher (2001) and Corker *et al.* (2000) offer a detailed discussion of exchange rate regimes in the transition economies.

First, abandoning one's own currency may be seen as the most radical form of fixed exchange rate regime. It may come either through membership of a currency union, the EMU in particular, or as a unilateral adaptation of a credible foreign currency. This regime was adopted in both Montenegro and Kosovo, and Gros and Steinherr (2004) make a strong case recommending the solution for those transition economies that have no realistic chance of joining the EU and EMU in the near future. They discuss the long-term experience of Panama and the more recent experience of Equador, the econ-omies that unilaterally adopted the US dollar as their own medium of exchange. Starting from that, they calculate the economic cost of adopting the Euro (loss of seigniorage), which is not high, and present the benefits, in particular of closing the easy channel of a 'soft' budget via central banks operations.

Secondly, the currency board (in Estonia; later on also in Bosnia and Hercegovina, Bulgaria and Lithuania) is akin to the adaptation of foreign currency, but less strict. The monetary authority declares that it is ready to exchange an unlimited amount of foreign currency for domestic currency at the pre-announced rate (see Gros and Steinherr 2004 for a description of this regime). Both adaptation of foreign currency and currency boards are jointly described as 'hard' pegs (Cirera and Hölscher 2001).

Thirdly, some room for flexibility is secured with a 'crawling' peg ('soft' peg). This system was typically introduced in the transition economies by relaxing the initial fixed anchors. The basic idea of a 'crawling' peg is that devaluation is allowed, but instead of taking place at once, it is spread in small percentages over a longer period of time. A parallel concept relates to the exchange rate system, where the exchange rate is not fixed but is allowed to float within pre-determined limits – for instance, 10 per cent from the pre-determined value (a peg with bands). The bands may either be horizontal or a crawling peg; in the latter case, we have a crawling band. The difference between an adjustable peg and some types of floating rate regimes is blurred, as the latter case also includes a managed float, with substantial interventions by the Central Bank.

In Poland, after January 1990, the exchange rate was initially fixed for between three and six months, but eventually remained unchanged for sixteen months. Yet, subsequently, the regime was switched to a crawling peg. Hungary adopted an adjustable peg with a varying frequency of small devaluations. In contrast, in the Czech Republic, the rate was maintained until May 1997, but then devalued by 25 per cent, after the government had spent $3 bn trying to defend the Czech Koruna.

Generally, it is well documented that pegs with formal bands of fluctuations are the regimes most vulnerable to capital flow reversals and therefore to exchange rate crises. This results from the fact that formal bands make them susceptible to speculative attacks and at the same time they lack the credibility of more self-committed forms of fixed exchange rate regimes, currency boards in particular (Cirera and Hölscher 2001). Thus, the peg with bands seems not to be an optimum long-run exchange rate regime (while it may still be useful as a temporary stage). Consistent with this, in the latter stage of transition, one can notice a process of polarization in exchange rate regimes. While a few smaller economies adopted a currency board (see above), quite a few others switched back from a peg towards either an independent float (Poland) or a managed float (the Czech Republic). It can be argued that an independent (free) float is an exchange regime which is conductive to an effective monetary policy, and therefore permits fast disinflation (see the Mundell–Fleming model under the IS-LM framework). That was indeed the experience of Poland, but also of a few other smaller economies with independent float regimes, which also made fast progress fighting inflation around 2000–1 (Albania, Armenia, Georgia).

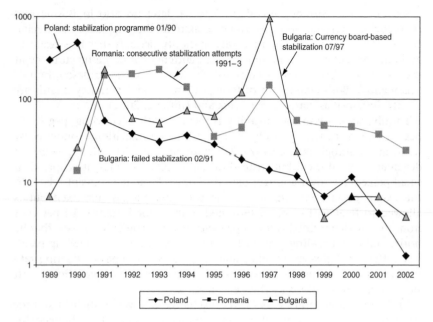

Figure 3.2   Poland, Romania and Bulgaria: annual change in the GDP deflator, 1989–2002
Sources: World Bank; GUS.

The seven main lessons seem to be the following:

(a) In those countries that adopted a fixed exchange rate-based stabilization programme *and* aimed at a quick initial reduction of inflation, the (temporary) output fall was stronger. The primary explanation for this effect is over-devaluation coupled with the policy impossibility of an exchange rate readjustment, with short-term adjustment to a full output equilibrium exchange rate driven by domestic prices being blocked by macroeconomic policies aimed at stabilization of the domestic price level.

(b) Disinflation was typically slower in the countries that adopted floating rate regimes in the initial stage of post-Communist stabilization. Figures 3.2 and 3.3 compare the results of the exchange-rate based stabilization programmes of Poland (January 1990) and Bulgaria (July 1997) with those implemented in the CIS countries and in Romania and Bulgaria in the early 1990s, which were all money-based (please note the different scale of both figures). Fixed exchange rates were thus adopted in a few leading transition economies which achieved sustainable stabilization.

(c) However, maintaining a fixed exchange rate or some form of rigid currency corridors for too long was risky if it was not backed by sound fiscal policies. The Russian crisis in August 1998 (Figure 3.2) and the

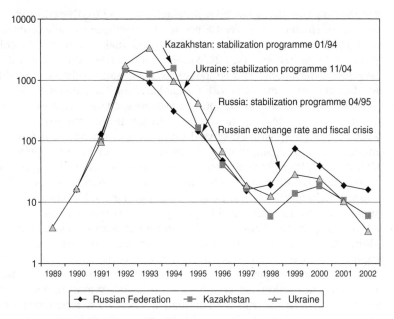

Figure 3.3 CIS economies: annual change of the GDP deflator
Source: World Bank.

experience of the exchange rate crisis in the Czech Republic in July 1997 (see Begg 1998) illustrate the point.

(d) Correspondingly, in a longer-term perspective, the main objective of the exchange rate policy should be to avoid major misalignments in the real exchange rate rather than to defend domestic price stability (the latter task being transferred to monetary and fiscal policies). Foreign exchange rate regimes were typically modified to some types of peg, once the initial inflation had been reduced to manageable levels. This was done in most of the countries that initially adopted exchange rate-based stabilization programmes.

(e) The exchange rate regimes in several countries evolved further towards two polar cases, either floats or (for some some smaller economies) currency boards or adoption of a foreign currency. This polarization in exchange rate regimes is consistent with the global trend, as documented by Fischer (2001). Economies that moved towards a 'hard' peg included the three Baltic states, Bulgaria and some former Yugoslav republics. Economies that moved towards a float during the 1990s were the Czech Republic, Hungary, Poland, Romania, the Slovak Republic and Slovenia (Corker *et al.* 2000).

(f) Eight countries that joined the EU in 2004 are expected to adopt the Euro in the foreseeable future. That is conditional on fulfilling the Maastricht criteria (in particular, a low budget deficit, a low debt/GDP ratio and low inflation). However, the five CE economies continue to have problems achieving fiscal sustainability, which would make Euro membership problematic (Kutan and Yigit 2005). Also, joining the Euro is expected to be preceded by a period of a temporary exchange rate mechanism pegging local currencies to the Euro with formal bands of fluctuations. From this perspective, paradoxically, adopting a floating exchange regime could be a better strategy in preparation for currency union, for two reasons. First, it might help with effective disinflation (see the Mundell–Fleming model assuming, again, that fiscal stabilization is achieved as a prerequisite). Second, it might provide additional information on the right level to fix the exchange rate's. The imposition of a temporary period of pegged exchange rates with bands before joining the Euro may thus be suboptimal, as the regime will be susceptible to currency crises.

(g) Membership in the Euro brings in substantial advantages in terms of elimination of currency risk premium and therefore better access to capital and lower transaction and information costs. Those benefits may be larger than for some present non-core EU members. On the other hand, currency union also entails some costs. Policy tools to respond to asymmetric macro shocks are eliminated, albeit most recent empirical results imply that the significance of this may be small (Buiter and Grafe 2002; Fidrmuc 2003; Gros and Steinherr 2004; Kutan and Yigit 2005). Moreover, it will be difficult for the new member states to fulfil the Maastricht criteria, because of structural inflationary pressures (the Balassa–Samuelson effect and other channels of productivity improvement in the tradable sector, such as the impact of more capital investment driven by a lower cost of capital (see Buiter and Grafe 2002)). Trying to restrain inflation at the Maastricht level may be costly, as it would imply non-structural inflation at a level around zero (as structural inflation may be about 2 per cent), and prices and wages are normally seen as less flexible downwards. The best option would be a relaxation of EMU reference values for the inflation rate and the long-term interest rate up to 2 percentage points; however, that is unlikely to be adopted.

Notes

1. Two other observations blur the distinction between 'fast-reforming' Poland and Czechoslovakia, on the one hand, and 'gradualist' Hungary, on the other. If we focus on micro restructuring, it is Hungary that deserves the 'shock therapy' label, not Czechoslovakia and Poland. At the beginning of 1990, Hungary experienced a wide wave of industrial exit driven by bankruptcies, in contrast to both Czechoslovakia and Poland (Balcerowicz, Gray and Hashi 1998). Also (and not unrelated), as will be discussed in Chapter 9, the scale of employment reduction in Hungary was unprecedented. Thus, it could as well be more appropriate to reverse the stereotype, and label the Hungarian programme a 'big bang'.

2. An interesting account of the second – i.e. Czechoslovakian – stabilization programme is given by Tosovsky (1996), the governor of the Czech National Bank. More analytical discussion of the macroeconomic development in the Czech Republic over several years following stabilization is given by Begg (1998).
3. Arguably, the reason behind the introduction of a flexible exchange rate was not an unconstrained policy choice, but lack of international reserves to back up the fixed exchange rate, similar to the situation in the CIS countries.
4. Here again, the focus is on the Polish programme. Kutan and Brada (2000) compare Poland with the Czech Republic and Hungary. See also Lavigne (1999), who discusses the differences between the programmes of the major reforming economies.
5. A wage–price spiral was unravelling in the late 1980s under the (partly liberalized) command economy. Real wages increased by 14.4 per cent in 1988 and by a further 9 per cent in 1989. This is frequently overlooked when focusing on the apparently dramatic decrease in real wages in the first year of reform. When 1987 is taken as a reference point, real wages in 1990 are lower by 5.7 per cent. The sequence of real wage movement around the time of liberalization is as follows. The peak point can be taken as August 1989. The recorded real wage decline came in two roughly equal waves. The first was in September and October 1989 following a partial liberalization of food prices by the last Communist government (in August, but in the first month its effect on wages was counterbalanced by the wage indexation introduced at the same time). The second wave of decline in the real wage index came in January 1990 following the introduction of complete price liberalization of consumer and producer goods. Subsequently, the real wages index oscillated through 1990 and 1991, but no clear pattern can be detected. Thus, the recorded decrease in real wages coincided with price liberalization, elimination of shortages and a movement towards market equilibrium. Much of the real wage effect is thus spurious, as pre-1990 price indices were based on administrative prices not reflecting scarcity. Generally, the real wage index went up and down during the 1980s due to discrepancies in movements of administrative prices and wages. Again, none of that reflected the real availability of goods and real consumption, due to the initial distortion caused by the administrative control of nominal variables (all GUS data). An English source presenting the same data is Sachs (1993), who provides data on household consumption demonstrating that much of the recorded fall in real incomes was only apparent.
6. On the other hand, a strong devaluation may lead to an inflationary impulse; that was the earlier experience of Brazil and Mexico. An inflationary impulse had already been triggered by price liberalization. The expectations of the policy-makers was that the credibility of the stabilization programme supported by a nominal anchor would affect expectations and therefore increase demand for money, alleviating the problem.

4
Privatization: The Trade-Offs between Speed, Efficiency and Distribution

In Chapter 3, we discussed the introduction of a stabilization and liberalization package which may be seen as equivalent to the beginning of the transition. This chapter is devoted to the key dimension of institutional change: *privatization*. In most countries the process took a long time to implement and is still not complete after fifteen years. In a few others, the initial privatization impulse came fast: yet, at a cost.

The global context and the uniqueness of post-Communist privatization: the trade-off between speed and efficiency

The word 'privatization' relates to the transfer of property to private owners from the state. It is a relatively new term; an earlier one, used before the 1980s, was 'denationalization', implying (correctly) that 'privatization' amounts typically to the reversal of an earlier process of nationalization. Yet, it does not have to be so; especially in the context of the former command economies, much of the property was created as state-owned. Yet, in many other cases, industrial property was confiscated; where it is returned to the (heirs of) the initial owners, we call it 'reprivatization'.

While the transition programme is unique, privatization is not. The corollary is that state ownership of industrial assets has not been confined to the command economy system. The two world wars were associated with the increased role of the state; this is not a historical coincidence. It is war where the elements of a command economy may prove most beneficial – since the system is at its best where economic objectives are few and well defined (maximization of a number of tanks, a well-defined objective of a space programme, etc.), and economic resources have to be 'mobilized' and channelled towards the priorities. That can be achieved with or without formal nationalization (an example of the latter case is the National Socialists in Germany in the 1930s). It highlights the difference between nominal ownership rights and the economic concept of such rights. With key control rights transferred from the legal owners to government administrators or politicians, the economic difference between private and state ownership is narrow. Private owners with restricted rights to (1) use, (2) take benefits from and (3) transfer the assets are nominal private owners, yet no longer 'private owners' in an economic sense. With economic control rights restricted, any claim to residual value may become meaningless, as the latter can no longer be maximized (say, because of restrictions on price-setting or generally on freedom of contract).[1] Nevertheless, the economic role of the government increased significantly in democratic developed countries during the First World War. Some of these policies were abandoned after 1918, but were reinstalled and extended as a policy response to the economic depression of the 1930s and even more so as a necessary element of the war effort during the Second World War. The aftermath of the war saw a wave of nationalization in the industrialized democracies of the West, but the scale was typically limited and confined to a few 'strategic' industries. On the other hand, nationalization of the industrial assets owned by the colonial powers became a trademark for the low- and middle-income countries gaining independence. It was only in the early 1980s that the wave was reversed, producing a worldwide privatization drive (see Megginson and Netter 2001, 2003). Thus, the transition programmes should not be seen out of their global context. Without a change in the intellectual climate around 1980 it is unlikely that the idea of privatization would have gained such a wide popularity among the economists and experts who authored the reform blueprints.[2] And without the drive towards privatization, counterfactually, we could have more post-Communist countries resembling Belarus instead of Estonia (taking as an example two geographically close economies with very different reform outcomes).

Economic policy choices around the world thus had an influence on the policy-makers who prepared the economic transition programmes at the end of the 1980s and the beginning of the 1990s. It is interesting to notice that, only ten years earlier, when the emergence of 'Solidarity' in Poland led to an open and practically unrestricted discussion on economic reform, the independent reform proposals focused on self-government and independence of enterprises, but not on privatization *per se*. Only, in the late 1980s, in both Poland and Russia, were proposals of 'mass privatization' put forward as a key element of reform. These proposals took into account the fact that the task was qualitatively different: not just a small fraction, but the overwhelming majority of the industrial assets were state-owned at the start of the transition. The mass privatization programme later to be put into practice in Czechoslovakia, and subsequently in most other transition countries, was an innovative privatization technique, very different from the British-style privatization practised in the 1980s, which involved initial public offerings (IPOs) on the capital market.

More generally, the key dilemma related to the trade-off between the *speed* and *quality* of the privatization programme. Attempting to privatize rapidly, the policy makers in the post-Communist countries faced a similar problem as the administrators of the French revolution, who attempted to sell (i.e. privatize) the vast amount of landed property (previously confiscated from the Church) and discovered that demand was insufficient to match supply. They were thus forced to lease property. The fundamental problem in both cases was the under-developed market for assets – i.e. the capital market. The market value of any asset is determined by the expected future net income flow, and the ratio of the value of capital to all production generated in the economy (GDP) is typically estimated by the capital markets at somewhere near or above 3:1. Nevertheless, any attempt at a one-off sale of the majority of those assets leads immediately to a liquidity problem. Demand for assets is insufficient, and the prices in privatization sales are depressed to such a degree that the privatization effectively amounts to the free transfer of a vast amount of wealth to a selected group of economic owners. Slow privatization is the alternative. On the other hand, slow privatization would mean that the behaviour of enterprises might remain inconsistent with the market environment created by liberalization, and reforms might not produce positive results.[3]

Privatization objectives: efficiency, finance and political economy

Privatization is more than just an economic policy. A massive transfer of assets is involved and the character of the resulting ownership structures has implications not only for the distribution of income and wealth but also for the shape of the political structure and civic society. We will discuss the privatization objectives under three headings: (1) economic efficiency, (2) short-term economic objectives (related to financial market imperfections) and (3) political economy arguments. The discussion is summarised in Table 4.1.

Table 4.1 Privatization objectives

Objectives	Problem areas	Possible solutions
Economic efficiency		
Tying together residual control rights and claims to residual returns, creating incentives for profit maximization. Creating an efficient match between the resources and endowment of owners and managers and firm assets	To achieve these objectives, post-privatization property rights transfers are critical. However, the transaction costs of the latter may be high, before the adequate institutional and legal framework is implemented, which may take time.	Attention should be paid to the initial distribution of property rights, as subsequent transfers of ownership may be slow

Creating the opportunity to introduce competition	High level of concentration in manufacturing, monopolies in utilities	Competition from imports. Breaking-up large firms before privatization, regulation of natural monopolies
Innovation, adjustment, entreprenership (the latter especially important when the environment is uncertain)	Managers of state-run firms chosen for their ability to implement a plan and conformity, not for innovative skills	*De novo* firms, outside ownership
Optimum wage and employment decisions	Insider interests	*De novo* firms, outside ownership
Financial objectives		
Funds for restructuring/ investment under a 'hard' budget constraint	Insufficient domestic capital	– FDI – Leasing, delayed payments, – Contracts with explicit investment clauses
Raising revenue for the government	'Crowding-out' effect: less money for private investment	Government investment in infrastructure
Political economy arguments		
Reduce government interference in the economy To make lobbying for government support more difficult	Credibility of the declared 'hard' budget constraint	Stable government Commitment Speed
To promote wider share ownership and create political support for reform programmes, and create a foundation for democracy The link between private property and political freedom	Losers (impact of restructuring on employment and wage structure) Corruption, unjustified private gains leading to social dissatisfaction	Social safety net Concessions for insiders Quality of public administration, adequate law and enforcement

Economic efficiency

The first issue relates to economic efficiency. The positive effects follow from tying together residual control rights and claims to residual returns, which create powerful incentives for value maximization (Milgrom and

Roberts 1992). While this is achieved in full only in the entrepreneurial owner-manager firm, even in a modern corporation with separated ownership and management, the link is far stronger than in an SoE.[4] In other words, privatization leads to the reintroduction of a *profit motive* at the enterprise level. However there are some necessary conditions if the positive effects are to materialize in full. First, the inherited economic structures are highly monopolistic; enterprises are big and, in a typical case, all firms operating on the particular product market are clustered together into wider industrial conglomerates. Breaking these monopolies at the time of privatization is an important task if full efficiency gains are to be achieved, but in many cases the simplest and quickest way of reintroducing competition effects is by opening the economy to imports, as already discussed. However, the state sector is monopolized by definition, with one owner and one control structure, so privatization is a prerequisite for competition, not vice versa. Secondly, in industries where external effects are strong, introduction of some regulatory or self-regulatory mechanism is needed. And, last but not least, the owners and the assets are heterogeneous, which implies that achieving an adequate match between them is important. In the longer term, the problem does not exist if property rights are easily transferable – say, via a well-functioning capital market: assets will tend to be transferred to those able to make best use of them. However, this may not be the case in the transition economies, at least at the beginning of the transition period. It implies that the initial identity of the owners may matter and therefore different privatization methods may lead to more or less efficient outcomes.

An important aspect of efficiency follows from *wage and employment decisions*. As will be also discussed in Chapter 5, we may encounter different effects for different categories of emerging private owners. In particular, 'insider ownership' may lead to a low responsiveness of employment, both downwards and upwards.[5] The effects may be transformed from the micro level into general equilibrium effects if 'insider privatization' is the dominant method chosen and the entry of new firms is slow.

'Insider privatization' may also be detrimental to the creation of capital markets as informational asymmetry coupled with potential contractual opportunism problems between the insider owners and outside minority investors may create disincentives for the latter group to acquire equity. In addition, in economies with inadequate protection of minority interests, the potential for the private benefits of control may be high. In some types of privatizations, share transfers may be only internal, and it may be both relatively easy and in the interests of managers actively to prevent the transfer of shares from employees to outsiders. By doing so, they may preserve corporate control and the private benefits linked to it which are not shared with other employee owners; an effect achieved with little capital investment by the managers.[6]

In general, the effects of privatization are conditional on institutional reform, and the existence of protected, enforceable and transferable property rights. Again, 'insider privatization' may not be associated with negative effects, where the institutional environment offers some degree of protection for external minority investors and facilitates transferability.

Where the ownership structures do not evolve after privatization, 'insider privatizations' can fail to overcome another major deficiency of state firms – i.e. problems with attracting external finance. While firms operate in the environment of private financial markets, that may lead to under-investment, due to the informational asymmetry problems perceived by the providers of finance. An alternative is to continue to provide state-sponsored finance, and it may not be a coincidence that in transition economies, where transition programmes were dominated by 'insider privatization', the role of the government in shaping enterprise finance was also important, either by the provision of sponsored finance from state-owned banks, or by variation in the enforcement of tax collection. However, in most cases, informational asymmetry problems between the government and the enterprises are even worse than between the private providers of finance and insiders, the incentives of government officials are inadequate, the quality of administration is low and the likelihood of a 'soft' budget constraint is high.[7] This problem is not unique to transition economies; in both the UK and in other market economies, privatization programmes were typically first initiated for financial reasons. For example, with British Telecom – the archetypical case for many subsequent privatizations – it was practically impossible to raise the amount of debt finance needed to restructure the aging physical capital and introduce modern telecommunication technologies. It could be possible with explicit government guarantees, but with an investment programme of that size that would create significant risk for the state budget.

Short-term economic objectives

Again, both types of privatization and environment characteristics affect access to finance. With capital markets in a nascent state and few savings, there is insufficient supply of funds. Here, we come back to the issue of the *speed–quality* trade-off. Selling fast means not only selling under-priced assets, but also selling to economic agents with no effective opportunity to raise the funds required for restructuring. The limited financial resources of potential buyers imply a trade-off between the price paid for privatized assets and the value of the remaining funds available for investment and restructuring. Leasing and delayed payments may be a solution in this case. Explicit investment clauses may also be introduced as part of privatization contracts. However, in the case of large firms, the best source of finance,[8] but also for the inflow of other tangible and intangible resources, including managerial skills, may be foreign direct investment (FDI). FDI creates more stable links and reduces the risk of speculative flows and the destabilizing impact of changes to the exchange rate, unlike other sources of finance from abroad. However, with excess of asset supply over demand, and high risk premia, the low prices received for assets during a foreign-led privatization may lead to political controversy. Again, where the transaction costs of property rights transfers are relatively low, the initial preference given to domestic players results in subsequent transfer of ownership to foreigners. The only difference is that instead of the state budget, domestic investors cash in on the price premium when selling to foreigners. The Czech Republic may be an example of this kind of ownership evolution.

The issue of FDI leads us to another privatization objective – i.e. raising fiscal revenue for the government. This is no longer an argument based on the efficiency of private firms. Its validity rests on financial market imperfections and the difficulty for the government to smooth its revenue and spending over time. As already discussed, fiscal problems may be particularly acute at the beginning of a transition and this is where privatization revenues can make a difference. In the post-Communist context domestic savings are low and, as already discussed, selling to domestic investors may result in the risk that their funds will be used to pay for privatized assets instead of subsequent investment in privatized firms. From this point of view, the choice of foreign investors, who have access to lower-cost finance available on the foreign financial markets, is attractive. Indeed, there is clear empirical evidence of the link between the amount of government revenue generated from privatization and the involvement of foreign investors in privatization (see EBRD 2000: 84; Hungary is the country with both the highest cumulative privatization revenues *per capita* and the highest cumulative FDI *per capita* over 1989–99; at the other end of the spectrum we find Uzbekistan).

While privatization can generate a substantial amount of fiscal revenue, how these funds are spent by the government is also important. Fiscal policy may be most efficient if the government channels the funds obtained towards productivity-enhancing public infrastructure. Another option is to use temporary privatization revenues to fund a temporary increase in welfare spending resulting from a temporary, restructuring-induced increase in unemployment.

In addition, payments for privatized assets may crowd-out funds that the new owners could spend on investment – this situation has been typical for many employee buyouts, where company funds were channelled as loans to employees to finance the privatization.

A final economic argument relates to a more elusive but nevertheless important effect of privatization on entrepreneurship and innovation.

Managers of state firms were chosen for their ability to implement the plan and their conformity to the regime, not for their innovative skills. Transferring corporate control to outsiders may facilitate a change in management, but nevertheless a more basic problem remains: initially, there is no pool of managers with skills that are fully adequate for a market economy environment. The human and social capital endowment of the new entrants – i.e. entrepreneurs and new firms created from scratch – may be qualitatively different and more relevant for a market-orientated system. Yet on the other hand, different skills are needed to run start-up firms as opposed to large enterprises, so a problem remains. Importing managers from abroad may be a solution; however, the cost is high and they in turn will be hampered by a lack of knowledge of local conditions.

Political economy

In addition to pure economic and finance arguments, privatization objectives may also be defined in terms of political economy. Delimitation of a barrier between the state administration and industry is far easier when firms are privately owned. It makes lobbying more difficult, and therefore improves the overall efficiency of public finance. Here, however, the argument supports faster, not slower, privatization, in direct contradiction to the financial and economic reasons presented above. Leaving many firms in the state sector may result in the subsequent entrenchment of insiders and stagnation.

In a broader sense, there is also a link between the economic and political system. Privatization with many beneficiaries may create political support for market democracy, while an economy dominated by state ownership is difficult to coordinate with political pluralism. With control over economic property, the incumbent government gains an enormous means of economic control over its citizens, including their employment and income. It is not by chance that the command economy was typically mirrored by more or less acute forms of totalitarianism, sometimes hidden behind a façade of democracy.

The political economy argument for fast-paced privatization was evident in Russia in particular. The proponents of this point of view argued that insiders were already endowed with control rights at the onset of the transition, and the formal transfer of ownership to them could lead to a widespread legitimization of private property (Boycko, Shleifer and Vishny 1995; see also Åslund 2002). According to this point of view, the expected positive effects of the reforms on political legitimization outweighed the economic efficiency costs of the chosen privatization strategy.

However, the political results of the programme in Russia were not as positive as expected. The major problems resulted not necessarily from the mass privatization programme, but from the subsequent 'loans-for-equity' privatization scheme, which led to an enormous transfer of wealth to a narrow group of people with strong political connections; this created a class of 'oligarchs', corruption and political capitalism. While the power balance between politicians and business 'oligarchs' evolved over time in Russia, the close relations between the two groups remains a defining feature of Russian capitalism. The problems Russia faces may be seen as an example of a 'political resource curse' – i.e. a situation when a rich endowment in natural resources has negative instead of positive effects on the economy, as it is associated with corruption. Fast privatization may be damaging when the value of assets is very high and involves a non-equivalent transfer of wealth to a narrow group of owners, since it may decrease political support for private property instead of increasing it (we will come back to the political economy issues related to the rich natural resources (especially energy-related) endowment in Chapter 9; empirical evidence on the 'political resource' course is provided by Kronenberg 2004).

Privatization objectives may thus be summarized under three headings: economic efficiency, finance and political economy. The choice of faster, or slower privatization, and the optimum method choice, is conditional on the weights we attach to each category. Economic efficiency and finance arguments suggest that the best method of privatization may be a technically slow privatization to outsiders, with a prominent role played by foreign investors. If political economy arguments imply a fast privatization, then the only feasible solution is either to follow a mass privatization programme (voucher privatizations) or transfer corporate control to insiders.

Trade-offs among privatization methods and secondary ownership transfers

Privatization, as we have seen, may be defined as the transfer of ownership of assets from the government to private owners. From the legal point of view, the situation is clear: firms where over 50 per cent of equity is held by private owners are considered private (i.e. either a privatized or a *de novo* firm). However, it is sometimes not easy to establish this in practice. While state firms were typically prevented from buying assets of other privatized companies, it was not always the case. In reality, the majority equity stakes in 'privatized' companies were sometimes held by some other state companies.

Three main issues matter from the economic point of view: if there is (1) adequate monitoring by owners or their representatives, (2) a positive change in the way a company is managed and (3) access to resources is widened. In this respect, some secondary ownership transfers resulting in majority stakes held by other state companies may not bring negative results, as the company may already be exposed to capital market discipline and a range of minority blockholders can contribute to effective monitoring.

However, a different situation may arise when apparent privatization is in fact a disguised transfer within the state sector. A good example of such a situation is the bank-led restructuring programmes which in some cases led to solutions where debt–equity swaps resulted in majority shares being transferred to state-owned banks, awaiting their own privatization. One well-known example is the Szczecin shipyard in north west Poland, announced as a prominent case of successful restructuring without a dominant role for outside private strategic investors which only a few years later proved to be an example of managerial failure and fraud due to insufficient corporate control by the absent owners. While possibly less spectacular, the results of other firms 'privatized' by bank restructuring programmes were no better (Chudzik 2000).

This example indicates that concern should not be about a formal act of privatization, but about an efficient transfer of *control rights* to investors (owners) capable of imposing a new set of objectives and strategies on the privatized company and also of providing new resources. In this case, the positive effects of privatization may appear even before the nominal transfer of ownership: incumbent managers may improve their performance in order to secure an extension of their contract from the new owners (in addition, they may also receive shares as part of the privatization deal, thus improved performance may be transformed into subsequent wealth increase for them, provided that the price of shares for the privatization sale is not pushed upwards, being based on the accounting value of assets, etc.; see Pinto Belka and Krajewski 1993).

In addition, from the corporate control point of view, it is important to describe the starting point correctly (see Figure 4.1). Dissolution of

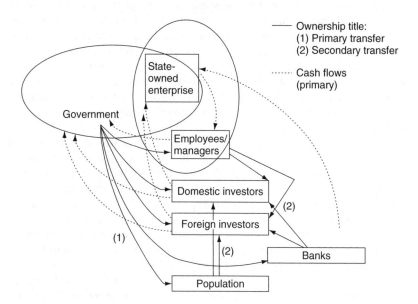

Figure 4.1 Privatization

the central planning administration led to a vacuum, where effective control of thousands of state companies was left to insiders. In different transition countries, the balance of power between managers and workers differed. In Hungary, Poland and Yugoslavia, the role of workers' councils at a time of systemic change was relatively strong, with influence on managerial appointments and the distribution of profits. In countries such as Poland, and later on in Bulgaria, strong independent unions emerged, with well-organized structures able to counterbalance the managers' position. In both cases, due to the initial control void, the impact of trade unions was ambiguous. On the one hand, employment decisions driven by employee interests could work against efficient restructuring; on the other, the unions could provide the only effective mechanism blocking managerial theft, for which incentives had been created by endowing managers with effective control rights without residual claims (and inadequate monitoring and legal enforcement) (Mickiewicz and Baltowski 2003).

The paradoxical feature of the command economy was that the ownership status of the 'state-owned companies' was blurred. Instead of being owned by the treasury, they were ambiguously described as 'socialist enterprises'. Key control rights remained with the economic administration and branch ministries, which were in turn supervized by the Communist party structures. As already mentioned, dismantling of the latter led to insiders being endowed with effective control rights. This left policy-makers with two choices: either accept the status quo and privatize in the form of employee and managerial buyouts (typically based on heavily discounted prices of assets) or 'nationalize' before initiating a privatization aimed at outside owners. The latter option is usually described by the term 'corporatization', where the 'socialist' enterprises were turned into (state-owned) standard limited liability companies by issuing equity shares. The problem with this solution was that the insiders lost important control rights and as compensation they were typically offered minority shares (up to 20 per cent).

One particular issue related to employee buyouts was that even with discounted prices of assets and payments by instalments, it was difficult for employees to raise the necessary finance. The financial sector was not developed enough to participate in the operation. In practice, the only available source of finance was the company cash flow. Paying themselves higher wages was a costly option, given that much of the transfer would be captured by taxes. Thus, a typical scheme consisted of loans offered by the company to the employees, who could (partly) pay with them for the privatized assets. This explains why many employee buyouts left companies with insufficient cash and could result in initial deterioration of performance instead of improvement after privatization. To make things worse, the owner-ship of assets of the privatized companies was typically not transferred to the new private company organized by the employees until more than half of the privatization price had been repaid in subsequent instalments. Thus, the assets were leased and could not serve as a collateral for new finance.[9] In many cases, policy-makers were aware of the potential problems related to 'insider privatization'. For two early reformers (Hungary and Poland), the initial policy choice was to privatize to outsiders via newly created stock exchanges ('capital privatization') using IPOs, a solution copied from standard British and other Western European methods. However, within the first two years of the reform programme only five privatizations were completed via this method in Poland and four in Hungary. The implementation of the programme turned out to be time-consuming, for several reasons. First, the prerequisite for floatation was a mandatory initial valuation. With accounting systems inherited from a command economy, where finance played only a secondary role, valuation by hired international auditors turned out to be very difficult. Secondly, while for political reasons the government agencies were aiming at high prices, the demand for privatized shares was low, given the transitional recession and uncertainty about the future. As a result, a mixture of various privatization methods was adopted in both countries (Frydman, Rapaczynski and Earle, 1993; Mickiewicz and Baltowski 2003; Mihalyi 2000).

In general, where the choice was to privatize to outsiders, policy-makers were left with four major options: domestic investors, foreign (corporate) investors, financial institutions and the population at large. Typically, where financial institutions emerged as dominant owners it was as a result of bad debt problems and debt–equity swaps. Domestic investors played a more important role in the case of small and medium-size firms (SMEs) and a less important role in case of large firms, at least in the initial stages of privatization. There were simply insufficient numbers of domestic investors. Moreover, to chose outside domestic investors was not always the most attractive option from the political point of view. This is because much of the domestic wealth before transition was held by *nomenklatura* members: it was not unusual to see 'red' directors coming back as new private capitalists, provoking public dissatisfaction.[10] In turn, foreign investors were typically capable of paying the highest privatization prices and bringing in financial, managerial and other intangible and tangible resources essential for restructuring. Nevertheless, the dominant role of foreign owners was not always politically expedient, either. That led many policy-makers to adopt another option – to transfer the assets to the population at large. Those schemes, known as 'mass privatization', became a trademark and a unique feature of the transition programmes. First applied in Czechoslovakia in 1991, they were implemented to a different extent in all the transition countries apart from Hungary (Coffee 1996; Estrin and Stone 1996; Takla 1999; Havrda 2003; Mejstrik 2003; Zemplinerova and Machacek 2003).

The basic idea of mass privatization is to issue coupons, available to all citizens, which in the next stage may be exchanged for the equity of privatized companies, typically in auctions, which determine the price of equity in terms of the coupons. The schemes led to the emergence of privatization investment funds, which could make investment decisions on behalf of individual investors.[11] In some cases (in particular, Russia), the mass privatization schemes were combined with 'insider privatization' in such a way that the latter dominated. In effect, these privatizations ended up being 'insider privatizations'.

In terms of control rights, the mass privatization schemes achieved very little in the short term. Dispersed private owners could neither counterbalance the insiders' influence nor were they capable of or willing to provide new finance for restructuring. The investment funds were also not well prepared for efficient monitoring (in contrast to strategic corporate investors), and had no access to new finance. In addition, in Czechoslovakia and in some other cases, specific restrictions were imposed on investment funds so that they did not acquire dominant stakes in the privatized companies. As a result, the control vacuum inherited from the initial point of transition continued for several more years, with protracted stalemates between investment funds and insider managers, and with the rights of minority individual investors neglected altogether. In the longer term, however, the evolution of ownership structures started, with some funds and other investors focusing on the middleman role, specializing in acquiring controlling stakes to sell later to strategic investors.

Table 4.2 summarizes the discussion on the immediate impact of privatization methods. However, there were subsequent transfers between the

Table 4.2 Trade-offs among privatization methods

Objectives Privatization method	Better corporate governance	Speed and feasibility	Widened access to skills and capital	Increase in government revenue	Greater fairness
Sale to outsiders	+	−	+	+	−
Management buyouts	?	+	−	−	−
Employee buyouts (and mass privatization with dominant role of insiders)	−	+	−	−	−
Mass privatization with equal access	−	+	−	−	+

Notes: + = positive effect
    − = negative effect
    ? = ambiguous effect

categories and after a decade of privatization programmes the resulting ownership structures of the CE industries is surprisingly similar, with a dominant role played by foreign capital. On the other hand, much of Russian and CIS enterprises remain controlled by insiders (Filatotchev, Wright and Bleaney 1999; Mickiewicz and Baltowski 2003; Voszka 2003; Zemplinerova and Machacek 2003). From the point of view of capital market efficiency, the subsequent transferability of ownership shares coupled with adequate protection of ownership rights were possibly the two most important conditions if any privatization method was to produce efficient results.

The impact of privatization

The impact of privatization may be considered on both the macro and the micro levels. On the macro level, there are synergies between the different elements of the reforms: the effect of privatization is conditional on other elements of reforms being implemented either first or at the same time. Price-setting, and freedom to export and import are key elements of control rights, without which formal property rights are devoid of economic sense. Where those restrictions were not removed, no changes in the behaviour of economic agents resulted. For instance, rent controls in tenement houses well below equilibrium level led to under-investment and a gradual deterioration of stock and impeded the development of the housing market. In the sectors with technological reasons for entry difficulties, competition policy and anti-monopoly regulation is needed. The major state telecommunication operator may be privatized to a strategic foreign investor without generating fast development of services. Without proper regulation and freedom of entry, the foreign monopolist may remain orientated on maintaining high prices and taking over monopolistic rents.

However, with freedom of decision-making and competitive frameworks, the key issues relate to the improvement in microeconomic efficiency resulting from the transfer of corporate controls to new owners. By now, there is a well-established methodology of empirical studies on the performance of firms after privatization (see especially Megginson and Netter 2001); however, there are caveats to be considered. Five key identification problems can be isolated:

(1) The *period of time may be too short.* Some effects of privatization may emerge with a delay, after a few years. The time path following the restructuring effort may resemble a 'J-curve', with an initial deterioration in financial indicators resulting from reorganization. The issue is not trivial, as can be easily seen by a proliferation of early studies on performance, based on the first–second year after privatization. A lot of attention was given to the results, which may now be justified only

by policy-makers' pressure to have reports on the impact of transition programmes.[12] That leads to the underestimation of privatization effects.

(2) As mentioned earlier, expectations may lead to the *improvement of performance of managers*. As documented by Pinto, Belka and Krajewski (1993), 'managers believe that good performance will be rewarded at the time of privatization and that their reputation, and hence compensation, will depend upon their performance today' (1993: 255) It is not only that they may aim at keeping their jobs after the takeover of control and expect to be rewarded. It is also due to the fact that the emergence of private firms creates a labour market for managerial talent, which has beneficial effects on the performance of those enterprises which remain state owned. Positive incentives for managers appear, because they care for their reputation and career prospect. We may thus have external positive effects of privatization. In each case, the effect will undermine the empirical evidence on the gains from individual privatizations if the latter is based on a comparison between the privatized and non-privatized firms.

(3) However, the opposite effect may take place in the case of 'insider privatizations.' It may be profitable for insiders to hide the good results of their firms before privatization to achieve a *lower privatization price*. The positive effect of 'insider privatizations' may thus be overestimated in empirical studies.

(4) *Reliability of information*. For tax reasons, firms manipulate profit and investment figures. While state firms had incentives to exaggerate their results, private firms, especially those which are not publicly quoted and do not crucially rely on external finance, have an incentive to hide profits and investments, as inflating current cost becomes important where corporate income taxes are high. The quality of accounting and audit improved, but it was particularly poor in the initial period of transition. As a result, privatization results may have been underestimated.

(5) *Selection bias*. This bias may operate in both directions, depending on the circumstances. In companies with high rents and a high value of capital, insiders may block privatization efforts as they may not have sufficient funds for employee buyouts. In badly performing firms, however, insiders may put pressure on the state administration to help them find investors who may save the company. Both those effects can result in inefficient companies being chosen for privatization, especially in the initial phase. On the other hand, external investors, especially foreign investors, may be interested in picking up the best companies; here the resulting bias in empirical estimation of privatization results to foreign investors may be positive. Where a battery of privatization methods is available, it is likely that those firms that cannot attract the interest of strategic investors will be dumped into a wide pool of mass privatization, which may result in the negative selection bias in their case.

The list of performance indicators opens with productivity measures. Total factor productivity (TFP) may be estimated from the production function, although good data on the value of assets is missing, making the estimates problematic. For that reason, many empirical studies focus on labour productivity approximated by the sales/employment ratio. Albeit popular, the measure is misleading. A company (say, a new firm), which increases employment following the increase in sales is recorded as one with deteriorating performance, while another (say, an insider-dominated company) maximizing rents per head and blocking employment increase seems to be more efficient.

With time, the quality of financial information improves, and studies relying on more recent data increasingly use standard financial indicators of performance, such as return on equity (RoE) or asset (RoA). Again, because data on the value of assets is problematic, profits per worker is another statistic often used. Servicing of external financial obligations and no default on debt may be another measure, as are indicators of a 'hard' budget *vis-à-vis* the government (no tax arrears, etc.). Sometimes, an external 'soft' budget may be replaced by a form of internal 'soft' budget in a form of wage arrears, the lack of which may also be included as a performance measure. However, the limited reliability and high volatility of purely financial measures over time led many researchers to rely on simple output (revenues, sales) dynamics, which are typically highly correlated with earnings/profits smoothed over time. Finally, given the short time horizon, studies with access to survey data may rely on some direct indicators of restructuring (quantitative and qualitative). These include indicators of the renovation/ restructuring of capital and machinery, the innovativeness/creation of new products and the employment policies, including the elimination of the excess employment typically present in state firms at the onset of privatization.

Djankov and Murrell (2002) provide an extensive meta analysis, which summarizes existing empirical studies on the performance of privatized companies. Table 4.3 reproduces one of their results: a comparison of the performance change brought about by different forms of privatization – i.e. in comparison with the traditional SoE. It is interesting to note that there is little improvement in firms owned either by insiders or by diffuse corporate owners. The latter seem unable to affect the internal control structures, given the underdeveloped capital markets and inadequate legal protection of minority shareholders. Financial institutions as owners are in the middle range. So are firms, not yet fully privatized, in the initial phase of preparation – that is, 'corporatized'; it seems that the positive impact of the privatization process may already appear prior to the final formal privatization date. Finally, strategic private investors, both domestic and foreign, appear as most effective in imposing the necessary efficiency-enhancing restructuring. One may note that the difference between the domestic and foreign corporate players performing the investment role is not that

Table 4.3   Djankov and Murell results: testing if change of ownership and organizational form brought improvement in performance, as compared with traditional state firms

Category of firm/owners	Significant evidence of improvement	Significance (*t*-statistics) from meta study
Workers	No	–
Diffuse individual owners	No	0.50
Managers	No	0.90
Insiders (as a composite group)	Yes	2.61
Banks	Yes	3.42
Outsiders (as a composite group)	Yes	3.45
State firms after commercialization (corporatization)	Yes	5.69
Investment funds	Yes	7.05
Domestic blockholders	Yes	7.73
Foreign investors	Yes	7.82

Source: Adapted from Djankov and Murrell (2002).

significant. Thus, the important role of foreign investors may result more from the fact that there was a limited number of domestic industrial players that could participate in the privatization process, not that their capacities were lower.

Privatization and the quality of corporate governance: a snapshot

Figure 4.2 presents transition countries' scores plotted on two dimensions: the share of private sector in GDP on the vertical axis and the EBRD measure of corporate governance quality on the horizontal axis. The latter is a composite index, which includes not only the assessment of corporate governance practices, but also the 'hard' budget constraint (lack of production subsidies) and effective bankruptcy procedures protecting providers of credit (EBRD 2004). Other related legal indicators are available from the EBRD, producing a similar pattern. The main theme of this chapter is that the effective legal protection of owners/providers of finance and the transferability of property rights with low transaction costs is more important than the size of the private sector. Transferability reinforces ownership, providing an additional sanction for shareholders; jointly with direct protection, it results in effective corporate governance. Moreover, given that the institutional environment improved, the size of the private sector might not be the most important dimension, as it was the fact that the private sector existed, not its size, that might generate positive external effects on the behaviour of managers of companies prior to privatization, via reputational

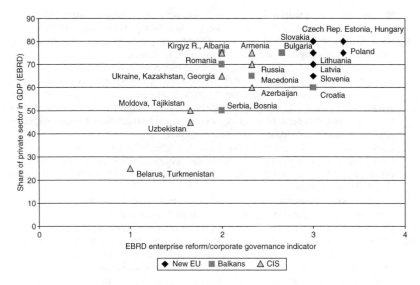

Figure 4.2   Quality of corporate governance and size of the private sector, mid-2004

effects. In this respect, countries with a relatively smaller private sector but good corporate governance (Croatia, Slovenia) were in a far better position than those where the private sector was large but the quality of the institutional environment was low (Albania, Romania).[13]

Notes

1. However, where nominal private owners exist, the systemic change – i.e. a return to a private market economy – is far easier.
2. See Mickiewicz and Baltowski (2003) on the discussion, which preceded the privatization programme's implementation in Poland.
3. However, expectations may play the pivotal role here. There is some evidence that the managers of state firms modified their strategy/as a result of privatization expectations, following 'commercialization' ('corporatization'), which was the first step in the privatization process (Pinto, Belka and Krajewski 1993).
4. It does not follow that the owner–manager firm is always more advantageous than the incorporated company (where control and ownership are typically separated). As always, there are trade-offs. Concentration of risk is one problem (for a more detailed discussion, see Milgrom and Roberts 1992).
5. Hiring new employees implies that they share rents or quasi-rents with incumbents, thus it is against the interests of the latter. Also, reducing employment by more than voluntary outflows means taking collective decisions which would not otherwise be taken by individual employees. It is likely that those affected can build a coalition blocking the move. Combining those two effects, we get a low responsiveness of employment to output shocks. For other possible implications

of employee ownership in the transition context, see Earle and Estrin (1996); for more recent empirical evidence, see Mickiewicz, Gerry and Bishop (2005).

6. See Filatotchev, Wright and Bleaney (1999) for empirical evidence demonstrating that control has been important for managers in Russia.

7. A 'soft' budget is interpreted here as a time inconsistency problem. The government cannot credibly commit itself to bankrupt an enterprise which initiates a negative present value (PV) project, because in the later stage, when some costs are already sunk, the benefits of subsidization will exceed the cost. Knowing that (i.e. expecting future state support), enterprise managers may initiate unprofitable projects (Kornai, Maskin and Roland 2003).

8. Isachenkova and Mickiewicz (2004) provide evidence on this point.

9. For this reason, with prices on asset markets depressed, the first decision of some privatized companies was to acquire more property, as a prerequisite for access to new investment funding.

10. Another equally unattractive source of capital came from the 'underground economy', which thrived in the final phase of Communism.

11. In some countries, all mass privatization was only via funds, as in Poland.

12. Following the classic ('pre-transition') approach (Megginson, Nash and van Randenborgh 1984; Megginson and Netter 2001), three years including the year of privatization are eliminated from pre- and post-privatization comparisons. That research tradition has been typically neglected in the case of transition studies.

13. Ahrend and Martins (2003) discuss privatization in Romania, showing how the large state-owned firms were subsidized both directly and indirectly by the government. Most efficiency gains were limited to the SME sector.

5
Unemployment Paths and Restructuring

This chapter focuses on unemployment. The first section will discuss unemployment in the transition economies, looking into flows between alternative labour market states. Subsequently, we shall use this approach to summarize the main factors that may affect unemployment levels. Finally, we shall offer a brief overview of the empirical econometric results on the differences between the labour market characteristics of the 'old' and 'new' EU member states.

'Transitional unemployment' and the flows between labour market states

As previously discussed, the Central and Eastern European (CEE) labour markets have been subject to far-reaching transformation since 1989. The introduction of market principles to the allocation of labour has had positive results, accompanied by negative side-effects, of which unemployment is the most important. The repercussions for the labour markets of the region were serious. Dealing with unemployment, poverty and social exclusion for some vulnerable social groups is one of the most important challenges that emerged after the transition. However, it seems that the transition policy-makers were not able to find a satisfactory solution to all these problems and then to implement them. As a consequence, the majority of the countries of the region are confronted by serious labour market problems reflected in both high unemployment figures and popular dissatisfaction (Figure 5.1).

Unemployment was not easy to avoid and an optimum policy response was difficult to design. The transition/liberalization programmes in the region were introduced as a response to the economic crisis and the meltdown of the command economy system and to the collapse of the Communist political regime. Reforms led to enormous shifts in the production structures of these countries and to corresponding adjustments in employment. Moreover, the systemic features of all these economies implied that at the initial starting

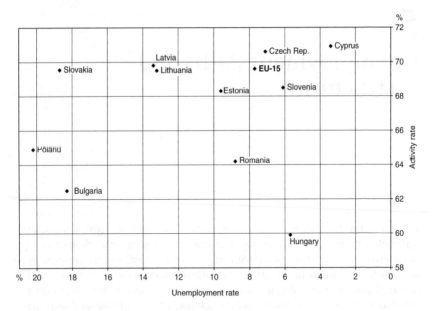

Figure 5.1   Unemployment and activity rate, 2002
Source: European Commission.

point (typically taken as 1989), they were characterized by a significant level of 'labour hoarding' (i.e. employment above the technically efficient level) in their industrial enterprises. Existing estimates of 'labour hoarding' suggested levels in a range of 15 per cent–20 per cent for the USSR, 18 per cent for Czechoslovakia and between 20 per cent–25 per cent for Poland (see Porket 1984; Brada 1989; Rutkowski 1990, 1995, respectively). Both *labour reallocation* and '*labour shedding*' implied the emergence of high unemployment levels.

Indeed, the countries that implemented a coherent reform programme experienced a faster and more dramatic initial increase in unemployment. With some simplification, this may be exemplified by the difference between the pattern typical for CE economies (i.e. the eight countries from the region which joined the EU in 2004) and that which characterizes the CIS economies. Two South East European (SEE) economies – Bulgaria and Romania – lie in between, as they were characterized by an erratic path of 'stop–go' reforms. The Czech Republic – with a combination of advanced reforms and low unemployment for most of the 1990 – has been an interesting exception, which we will discuss below.

The differences in unemployment correspond to differences in production paths. In the CE economies, implementation of coherent reform programmes led to both a rapid emergence of unemployment and an immediate 'transformational recession'. Yet, in those countries, the period of recession was relatively short and, following recovery, growth was relatively strong (see Chapter 6). In the CIS countries, the recession was more protracted and while the initial increase in unemployment was slower, it rose to levels similar to those observed in CE economies. There is thus no empirical evidence of any sustainable social gains from delaying the reforms. One should also note that – where implemented – the coherent reform packages not only introduced market liberalization measures but also relatively well-functioning welfare systems. Paradoxically, under the old command economy regimes social welfare systems were underdeveloped, as social benefits were typically associated with employment status, and enterprises performed strong social functions (on this see, for instance, Rein, Friedman and Wörgötter 1997). Another way of interpreting the slower emergence of unemployment in the CIS countries is to note that where the level of social welfare protection remains inadequate workers may stick to their jobs in spite of dramatic wage decreases and wage arrears. Open unemployment may still therefore be a socially better outcome (Mickiewicz and Bell 2000).

This leads us to a more general question. Given the initial level of labour hoarding (in the region of 20 per cent), why did unemployment not reach that level in transition countries? The mean/median values of unemployment rates in the transition countries remained far closer to 10 per cent than to 20 per cent.

To answer this question it is useful to look at unemployment issues directly from a flow perspective. In accordance with the transition economic literature (Blanchard 1997; Roland 2000), the basic framework splits employment into two categories: the 'old' and the 'new' sector. This distinction may be given more than one empirical interpretation. It may relate to the ownership dimension, where 'old' means state and 'new' means private. Yet in this case a more relevant distinction may relate to the contrast between (1) the firms controlled by *insiders* (including typically state firms at the starting point of transition and also 'insider privatizations') and (2) those where corporate control was transferred to *outsiders* (either as a result of privatization or in new companies). In both cases, the 'new' sector is the one where economic restructuring and adjustment in firms' objectives consistent with a new market environment took place. Apart from ownership, 'new' and 'old' sectors may also be identified in purely structural terms. 'New' (i.e. expanding) sectors are in services and in consumer products while 'old' (shrinking) sectors relate to heavy industry and mining. The distinction is highly correlated with the ownership cross-section: from the very beginning of the transition, the service sector was dominated by private firms, as a result of rapidly implemented 'small privatization' programmes and new start-ups and, on the other hand, the privatization process was slowest in heavy industry and mining so those sectors remained dominated by state companies.

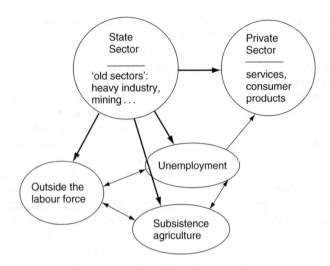

Figure 5.2   Labour market flows during the economic transition

Taking these distinctions into account, the underlying idea of labour market flows during the transition is illustrated by Figure 5.2, where the thickness of the arrows representing flows corresponds to the empirical data on transition countries.

The first explanation of the observed unemployment rates may relate to the slower inflows into unemployment. In particular, as already mentioned, in slow-reform countries inadequate provision of social welfare created disincentives to enter unemployment. Workers in the CIS countries preferred to accept a dramatic decrease in wages and face wage arrears rather than quit their jobs. Parallel to that, in slow-reform countries some sections of industry were still operating under 'soft' budget constraints: various fiscal and financial channels were used to support employment in the 'old' (unrestructured) sectors. In the longer run, this policy of postponed restructuring turned out to be self-defeating as the prolonged recession associated with a lack of efficient restructuring and crises in public finance made high employment levels unsustainable.

A parallel explanation relates to the differences in privatization programmes. Unlike Central Europe, the dominant privatization methods applied in the CIS countries, and in Russia in particular, were equivalent to an 'insider privatization'. As is well documented in the employee ownership literature, this form of ownership is typically associated with higher wage flexibility and lower employment flexibility (both downwards and upwards). It follows that expected inflows to unemployment are lower.

The second explanation relates to the outflows from employment outside the labour force instead of to unemployment. Some of those flows represent positive social phenomena resulting from adjustment to the new market conditions, but some follow from misguided policies.

One factor decreasing activity rate, among younger people in particular, relates to inflows into higher education. Under the command system returns to education were low, and so were incentives to study. Liberalization of wage systems led to an increase in relative returns to education and following that, to a significant increase in the number of students. The inflow to education was also partly responding to a mismatch of skills resulting from a change in the economic environment. Programmes in business studies (finance, marketing, management), economics and information technology (IT) experienced the largest increases, responding to a change in the structure of labour demand.

Arguably, a parallel and more general development reflected a 'natural' adjustment in activity rate consistent with preferences, following the dismantling of the command economy system. The argument relies on the fact that the activity rates in Central Europe at the beginning of the transition process were much higher than those in the economies with a similar level of income *per capita* in different parts of the world. The command economy operated in a way which, on the one hand, guaranteed employment but on the other had built-in penalties for those not working. Thus, employment was both a right and an obligation. As mentioned earlier, without employment, access to social benefits was difficult. Moreover, people not in employment could find themselves directly persecuted as social parasites, albeit the official policy became relatively more relaxed in this respect in most countries in the late Communist period. Employment and labour was strongly promoted as a key social virtue by official propaganda. Thus, after liberalization, some downward adjustment in activity rate was to be expected: in middle-income countries, the value-added from households' occupations outside formal employment might in some cases be higher as compared with wage earning. Thus, when people became free to choose their lifestyle, some adjustment followed.

Some other outflows into inactivity resulted from questionable policies. A visible decrease in child care provision pushed many women with children outside employment. Yet, generally, women's participation rates remained high in CE countries, thanks to two counterbalancing factors: new employment creation was in services, where female employment is typically higher and – last but not least – because of the fact that the women in the region scored highly in terms of educational endowment, quite different to the position in comparator middle-income countries outside Central Europe (Figure 5.3).

Another channel of outflow into inactivity resulted from a policy which substituted open unemployment with early retirement programmes. The problem with this approach results from rather naïve view of employment as a zero-sum game, where the removal of older people from employment releases jobs for younger people. In fact, the resulting pattern may be a

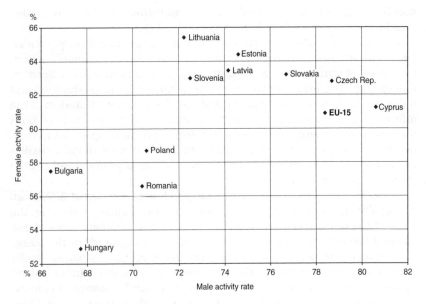

Figure 5.3   Male and female activity rate, 2002
Source: European Commission.

mismatch between the supply of released jobs and the skill and experience characteristics of the labour supply. Arguably, the departure of some skilled older workers might have an overall negative effect on average productivity, creating negative results for employment.

Looking more closely into CE statistics, one can see easily that Slovenia is an outlier in terms of having a very low employment rate in the oldest age group (55–64), in sharp contrast to its overall employment rate (i.e. 15–64) (Figure 5.4). This corresponds to over–reliance on early retirement programmes.

Similarly, Hungary is an example of a country where unemployment rates remained low, but at the cost of a significant decrease in the activity rate and a low employment rate (Figures 5.1, 5.4).

The third explanation of observed unemployment levels below these expected initially relates to inflows into new employment. Job creation in new sectors remained a most efficient channel of suppressing unemployment. In the sectoral perspective, *restructuring by job creation* may be defined as job creation consistent with a structural change converging towards the employment structure in high-income EU economies. In this respect, in the second half of the 1990s, Poland was the best performer in Central Europe, followed by Slovenia. Interestingly, fast structural change in that period was also observed in some EU economies. Spain, in particular, scored as highly

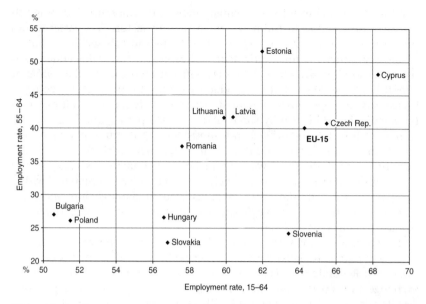

Figure 5.4 Employment rate: aggregate (15–64) and in the oldest age group (55–64), 2002
Source: European Commission.

as Poland on this measure of restructuring by new job creation, in contrast to both Portugal and Greece (for computational details, see Mickiewicz 2003). The process of job creation was parallel to the rate of creation of new enterprises, where Poland again scored high during the 1990s among other transition countries. The process could be partly fuelled by social attitudes: a cross-country study by Blanchflower, Oswald and Stutzer (2001) found that the willingness to become self-employed in Poland was matched only by Italian respondents (with East Germany and Russia located at the opposite end of the spectrum). Nevertheless, the combination of tax policies, an increase in bureaucratic barriers and the possible impact of macro policies resulted in a considerable slowdown in the dynamics of the Polish entrepreneurship sector around 2000, matched by a considerable increase in unemployment.

The share of self-employment in total employment can be taken as a proxy for the size of the entrepreneurial sector. However, when using this measure we have to control for the size of the agricultural sector, as the two dimensions are closely correlated. It therefore makes sense to compare economies with a similar size of agricultural sector. Both Lithuania and Poland have a much larger entrepreneurial sector than Latvia, even if the three economies are characterized by a similar size of agricultural sector. Similarly, the Czech Republic may be favourably compared with the Slovak Republic in terms of its entrepreneurial sector.

While discussing inflows into employment, it is important to distinguish between job creation in the new and in the old sectors. The latter relates primarily to (subsistence) agriculture. Jobs created in this sector are only a temporary buffer for unemployment and represent low value-added, and the corresponding structural change is inefficient in the sense that sooner or later it has to be reversed, if the productivity and income levels are going to increase. Again, open unemployment may be socially superior as it may be a temporary stage followed by some labour market participants finding jobs in new sectors. On the other hand, subsistence agriculture may be associated with a fast erosion of skills or their replacement with skills which are not consistent with the new economic system. Romania is an economy which exemplifies the case of relatively low unemployment matched with a dramatic increase in the share of agriculture in employment and poor performance in terms of aggregate productivity and income dynamics (compare Figures 5.1 and 5.5).[1]

Finally, the outflows from unemployment into employment may be enhanced thanks to active labour market policies (ALMP). In this context, the Czech Republic is a very interesting case. Until mid-1997 (the Koruna exchange rate crisis), the unemployment levels were exceptionally low, despite the fact that the country had been regarded as one of the leading

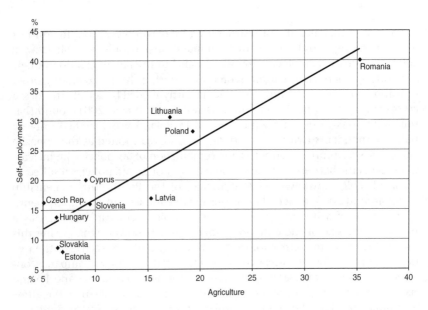

Figure 5.5 Employment in agriculture (per cent of total) and self-employment (per cent of total), 2002
Source: European Commission.

reformers. At the same time, spending on labour market policies was high and existing evidence showed that the programmes had made some difference. One of the most telling indicators was the number of registered unemployed per staff member. In the early transition period (1993) it was 675 persons per staff member in Romania, 270 in Bulgaria, 235 in Poland, 162 in Hungary, 123 in the Slovak Republic and only 30 in the Czech Republic. The Czech ratio was even lower than in the Scandinavian countries, where ALMP traditionally play a significant role (data from Boeri 1997). Unfortunately, ALMP alone can never solve the unemployment problem and in this respect, without other complementary policies, may even be ineffective in the longer run. The Czech case exemplifies that. The main problem was that in the Czech case, despite some formal institutions of tripartite wage bargaining, the wage-setting mechanisms did not result in sustainable labour market equilibria for both low unemployment and wage dynamics consistent with changes in labour productivity. In the period of low unemployment – i.e. between 1991 and 1997 – Czech wages (as measured in US dollars) increased dramatically from the lowest level in the Visegrad Group (which includes the Czech Republic, Hungary, Poland and the Slovak Republic) to the highest among those four economies. That alone would not have had serious implications, had it not been for the insufficient increase in labour productivity, which might be linked to the chosen privatization methods (the mass privatization programme and a correspondingly low inflow of foreign capital, see Chapter 4). As a result, the combination of a strong increase in labour costs, inadequate pace of industrial restructuring and productivity enhancement, the fixed exchange rate regime and lack of adjustment in fiscal policy triggered an exchange rate crisis in mid-1997. Unemployment started to grow, with spending on passive labour market policy crowding-out spending on ALMP. The ratio of ALMP spending per unemployed person decreased quickly and the Czech labour market moved from a 'good' labour market equilibrium to a 'bad' one, no longer dissimilar from neighbouring economies. The Czech Republic is still characterized by one of the more efficient labour markets in Europe (see Figures 5.1, 5.4), but is no longer the outlier it used to be in the early 1990s. Again, the basic lesson is that that ALMP alone are not capable of guaranteeing 'good' equilibrium in longer term if wage-setting produces inefficient outcomes (Mickiewicz and Bell 2000).

This stylized account of labour market development in the Czech Republic is not intended to question the importance of ALMP. They may have an important role to play in particular in combating long-term unemployment. Decreasing long-term unemployment rates and rising labour turnover are improving the performance of the labour market, regardless of its impact on the aggregate unemployment level. Active measures in the labour market are designed to introduce an early identification of the needs of unemployed persons and to promote programmes leading to the improvement of human resources quality (training courses, practical vocational training, subsidized employment) (Sztanderska and Piotrowski 1999). Yet CE countries continue to devote scarce amounts of budgetary resources to this aim. EU average resources destined for labour market policies are 3 per cent of GDP, while in the CE countries they are less than 1 per cent. In Poland, for example, expenditure on passive labour market policies such as unemployment benefits in the 1990s constituted around 2 per cent of GDP and were approximately three times larger than the expenditure on ALMP (Sztanderska and Piotrowski 1999).

Post-transition labour market equilibria?

We may now summarize the factors affecting unemployment rates in the (post-) transition countries.

First, the inflows from employment into unemployment resulted from the elimination of the initial 'labour hoarding' and the unprecedented scale of restructuring. While there is some microeconomic evidence that 'labour hoarding' is now over (Mickiewicz, Gerry and Bishop 2005), the restructuring process is still far from complete, and will continue to affect the labour market.

Second, the outflow from unemployment into jobs, in particular to jobs in the 'new' sectors (see pp. 88–90), remains a key factor. This outflow may be negatively affected by a range of factors. Wages may not be flexible and wage growth may be too strong in relation to changes in productivity, due to inadequate wage-setting/wage-bargaining mechanisms. The taxes on wages may be too large, as the structure of taxes relies too much on labour taxation in these countries. The financial system and legal protection for the providers of finance may be inadequate, slowing down investment related to new job creation (see Chapter 8). General uncertainty in the business environment may not create the incentives for growth. Bureaucratic barriers and corruption may severely diminish the benefits from the creation and expansion of new enterprises (Aidis and Mickiewicz 2005).

These last two factors may play a more serious role in SEE (such as Romania) and CIS countries (especially Ukraine) than in Central Europe. For the CE economies, the tax burden on labour may play a significant negative role hampering employment. The European Commission (2003) reports the heavy burden of labour taxation for low-wage earners (below 67 per cent of the average wage), a group which is particularly vulnerable in terms of unemployment. When measured as a share of the total tax cost (income tax on gross wage earnings plus employer and employee social insurance contributions) in labour costs, the CE percentage (38 per cent) is higher than the EU average, apart from Estonia, which is at the EU average level.

On the other hand, there is no strong evidence that labour market outcomes can be linked to the role of CE trade unions. When the position of trade unions is approximated by union density, CE economies score between 15 per cent for Estonia and Poland and 41 per cent for Slovenia, which corresponds to the lower part of the EU spectrum (European Commission 2003). CE Union density levels decreased significantly over the 1990s (compare European Commission 2003 with Riboud, Sanchez-Paramo and Silva-Jauregui (2002), who present data on an earlier period). If there are problems resulting from inadequate patterns of industrial relations, they tend to be restricted to few sectors in some countries only. The mining sector in Bulgaria, Poland and Romania may be one of those cases. Miners in these three countries enjoy large wage premia, much higher than in any other EU country apart from the Neitherlands (59 per cent of the country-average wage for Bulgaria, 68 per cent for Poland and 65 per cent for Romania, as of 2000 – see European Commission 2003). Meanwhile ineffective restructuring programmes in the mining sector and the cost of implicit subsidies affect public finance and indirectly other sectors (see Driffill and Mickiewicz 2003 and also Chapter 7).

Outflows from unemployment may be hampered by the mismatch between the structure of the labour supply and that of job offers. That is, the Beveridge curve (unemployment–vacancies) may be positioned unfavourably high. This mismatch has several dimensions. One is that *occupational mobility* is negatively affected by the major mismatch in skills, as the 'old' structure of skills is not consistent with a market environment and this heritage has not yet been overcome. Another relates to low *spatial mobility*, which is – among other things – related to badly functioning housing markets. The role of migration in adjusting the labour market mechanism is small, as confirmed by Gacs and Huber (2003a). The resulting problems would be less serious if the quality and density of transport infrastructure were high. But it is not.

Finally, a careful reader may notice that three factors are missing from our analysis.

First, so far we have not mentioned the level of unemployment benefits and social welfare provision as a factor affecting unemployment rates in these countries. The first reason is that there is no evidence that the replacement rates in those countries are particularly high. And, more importantly, we need to assess the unemployment problem in the wider context of economic efficiency. As we have argued, from that point of view while adequate provision of benefits may increase unemployment in the short term, in the longer term it may facilitate job quits and subsequent matching with new jobs, therefore leading to reduced unemployment later. The dynamic perspective may thus lead to different conclusions than the static one and suggest that an adequate level of unemployment benefits may be advantageous.

Second, the level of the minimum wage is unlikely to have much impact in Central Europe. It is in the range of 25 per cent–40 per cent of the average wage for the accession countries, similar to the three south European 'old'

EU members: Greece, Portugal and Spain, and lower than other EU countries, which are in the range of 40 per cent–60 per cent.

Third, CE employment protection indicators are not high as compared with the 'old' EU member states. Data for the Czech Republic, Hungary and Poland show that employment protection is focused on collective dismissals in particular, being particularly high in the Czech Republic, assessed as second only to Sweden across the enlarged EU. Yet, it is the Czech Republic where labour market indicators are still relatively favourable. Employment protection is not generally considered now as an important factor affecting the unemployment level (see European Commission 2003 and the further references there).

Empirical econometric evidence

In an assessment of the unemployment rates across the CEE regions and the 'old' EU member states, Gacs and Huber (2003b) found three key characteristics of CE labour markets, using standard econometric tests. CE labour markets are characterized by the following significant differences, as compared with the 'old' EU member states:

(1) *Unemployment rates are higher* than in the 'old' EU member states; 78 per cent of the 'new' member states' population live in regions with unemployment rates in excess of 10 per cent, the corresponding figure for the 'old' EU regions is only 34 per cent.

(2) Both *long-term unemployment* and *youth unemployment is higher*. This is consistent with (1), as both long-term and youth unemployment typically respond more than proportionately to the increase in the base unemployment rate. Here, Gacs and Huber's (2003b) results may be supplemented by those of Góra and Schmidt (1998) and Lehmann (1998): those who dominate long-term unemployment are 'individuals with unfavourable demographic and skill characteristics, i.e. workers who are old and have obsolete skills.'

(3) The 'new' member states are characterized by significantly lower *gender-based differences* along the labour market dimension, including unemployment rates, than the 'old' member states.

(4) There is more *polarization among the regions* of the 'new' EU states than in the 'old' members' group. This relates to both unemployment rates and participation rates. An obvious implication is that the new members create a serious challenge for EU regional policies.

(5) In Central Europe, factors on a *national* level affect unemployment relatively more than factors on a regional level, as compared with the relative importance of these factors in the 'old' EU member states.

(6) *Industrial patterns* are more important in explaining unemployment in the CE than in the 'old' member states.

Point (6) relates closely to the issue of transition-related restructuring shocks, as discussed above. Gacs and Huber's (2003b) results corroborate findings by Newell and Pastore (2000), who demonstrated that regions with higher unemployment were those experiencing greater change in industrial structure. A corollary is that high-unemployment regions are those with higher inflow rates to unemployment.

At the outset of the transition, big and typically inefficient SOEs dominated not only in industry but also in agriculture, which was particularly resistant to the command economy method of coordination. Apart from Poland, the private sector in agriculture was practically non-existent, or played only a limited role. A decrease in agricultural employment was one of the main dimensions of structural change. The restructuring of the agriculture sector caused a situation where the highest unemployment was reported in rural, economically backward, mainly agricultural areas (see Gacs and Huber 2003b for evidence). Because of ownership transformations a great number of former state-owned farms' employees became unemployed. These were mostly people with low skills, for whom the opportunities of finding jobs, both within and outside their area of residence, were particularly limited. Mickiewicz and Bell (2000) show that the initial percentage of state-owned farms in agricultural land was a significant predictor of decrease in both employment and participation rates across the Polish regions. In contrast with agriculture, services remained the sector, which was mostly associated with job creation. Rutkowski and Przybyla (2002) found a strong correlation between regional specialization in services (a high percentage share of services in total employment) and the hiring rate.

Conclusion

If the analysis of the economic transition in Central and Eastern Europe has contributed to our general understanding of labour market processes, it is largely due to a renewed interest in the link between structural change and labour market outcomes. A low level of unemployment is not desirable when it comes at the cost of a large agricultural sector with subsistence farming being a substitute for social welfare. Similarly, jobs in the 'old' industrial sectors may be preserved by a combination of inadequate social welfare provision and industrial subsidies, typically of an implicit nature. That route turned out to be self-defeating, and is more typical of those East European countries which were not able to gain a place in the first (2004) round of EU enlargement. The distinction between 'old' and 'new' sectors is thus important. Sustainable jobs are created in services and 'modern' branches of industry, which is why the unemployment problem is related to structural change.

Focus on structural change is connected to the analytical approach which stresses flows and dynamics. The key labour market questions relate to factors affecting inflows and outflows from unemployment. The lesson from Central and Eastern Europe is that policies to slow down the inflow into unemployment turned out to be inefficient. The main challenge is thus how to remove the constraints which hamper outflow to employment. Our one preferred recommendation for Central Europe would be to look closer into the issue of *tax structure*, and the level of labour taxation in particular. However, a full list of policy recommendations is longer, and not uniform across the region. High unemployment levels and the continued process of structural change remain a challenge, one becoming more and more similar to that faced by the 'old' EU members.

Note

1. The share of agriculture in employment is 35.2 per cent in Romania. The next country in this group is Poland with 19.3 per cent. However, the Polish figure masks an important difference with respect to other transition countries. It was the only command economy with a dominant private sector in agriculture, consisting of small farms, as larger farms were banned under Communism. And, unlike Romania, the share of agriculture in Poland shrank dramatically as compared with the pre-reform starting point (i.e. 1989).

Part II
Why? New Empirical Results

6
Post-Communist Recessions Re-Examined

Recessions examined

In this chapter, we wish to explore the determinants of the post-Communist recessions – i.e. the recessions experienced during the 1990s by the twenty-seven countries that emerged from the Soviet Bloc. As will be discussed in this chapter (and again in Chapter 10), most of transition theory focuses on the related but different concept of 'transitional recession'[1] – i.e. the recession following the implementation of the liberalization programme.

Empirically, this 'transitional recession' is a part, but only a part, of the experience of post-Communist economies. From empirical studies on economic growth in the region we know that the 'transitional recession' was a real phenomenon; however, it corresponded to the 'J-curve' path of output – i.e. it was relatively short and led to subsequent higher growth (see also Chapter 10). In some countries, this short transitional recession was the only recession that was experienced. In Poland, the recession was two years long; in neighbouring Ukraine (and in Moldova), it took ten years for economic growth to recover.

Moreover, the timing of recessions did not always coincide with the introduction of the core liberalization programme. Out of twenty-seven former command economies in Central Eastern Europe and the FSU, twelve went into recession in 1989, twelve more joined in 1990 and virtually all the post-Communist economies were in recession in 1991 (see Table 6A.1, pp. 113–14). More importantly, these were not 'transitional' recessions: twenty-five economies went into recession *before* the stabilization or liberalization programmes had been implemented. The only two exceptions were Hungary and Poland. In Hungary, GDP growth reported for 1989 was close to zero (i.e. 0.4 per cent). The stabilization programme was introduced in March 1990 and the economy went into recession in the same year. However, the level of liberalization corresponding to the Polish reforms of 1990 was reached in Hungary only two years after the recession started (i.e. in 1992).[2] That leaves us with Poland as the only example where the beginning of the recession coincided with introduction of the full liberalization and stabilization programmes. Indeed, in 1989, Polish GDP seemed still to be growing at a rate of 2.8 per cent,[3] albeit inflation was soaring and it is disputable how long the growth could last. The stabilization and liberalization programmes were introduced in January 1990, and the economy immediately went into recession, which lasted for just over two years: as it turned out later, the shortest period as compared with any other transition economy (see also Chapter 3). This account is intended to reiterate what was already discussed in Chapter 1. The command economies were already in crisis in the late 1980s. The liberalization introduced in early 1990s was a *response* to this crisis. While it made recession worse for a short time, it also led to faster recovery.

The empirical literature

Two lessons emerge from the empirical literature on economic growth in the region: both transitional reform and stabilization was conducive to economic growth in the longer run; however, the reforms resulted in J-curve short-term output paths, as did some (but not all) types of stabilization policies. We shall discuss these two results in turn.

Econometric evidence on the output response to reforms can be found in seven published studies on economic growth in the region based on panel data: Loungani and Sheets (1997), Selowsky and Martin (1997), Christoffersen and Doyle (2000), De Melo *et al.* (2001), Falcetti, Raiser and Sanfey (2002), Havrylyshyn and van Rooden (2003) and Merlevede (2003). All these studies are consistent in finding that the overall impact of reform on economic growth (as measured by EBRD indicators) is positive. At the same time, the reform resulted in a temporary output slump in the year of implementation, which was counterbalanced by lagged effects. In the six studies which allow for lagged effects (i.e. except for Loungani and Sheets 1997), we have the same, consistent pattern of a J-curve-type response of output to reforms.

The second set of results relates to the link between macroeconomic stabilization and output. In the studies quoted above, empirical results show that macroeconomic instability (measured as either high inflation or a low (negative) government budget balance) affects growth negatively. There is no indication of a short-term positive correlation between inflation and growth (and of a negative impact of disinflation on growth). Campos and Corricelli (2002) summarize the existing evidence in the light of theoretical insights, noting that:

> based on the experience of programmes implemented in developing market economies, stabilization *per se* should not have caused a sharp fall in output. (Campos and Coricelli 2002: 819)

All this evidence still does not exclude the possibility that *some* types of stabilization programmes could have had a negative impact on growth. As far as we know, the only published econometric evidence on the impact of stabilization programmes which distinguishes between different types and is based on a cross-country panel of transition economies comes from Christoffersen and Doyle (2000). They did not find any systematic, general impact of stabilization on output (other than a positive one via disinflation). This can be easily corroborated by the evidence provided in Table 6A.1 (pp. 113–14). The only two countries where the beginning of recession coincided with stabilization were again Hungary and Poland. However, Christoffersen and Doyle (2000) found one significant effect: where sharp disinflation (inflation more than halved in one year) was implemented under the presence of a pegged exchange rate regime, the policy had a negative effect on growth (see Chapter 3). Even in this case, however, the longer-run impact of these programmes should be positive, as short-term negative effects may be counterbalanced by the subsequent positive effect of macroeconomic stabilization on growth.

In the next section, we shall consider theoretical explanations for the link between systemic reforms and the output path. In the subsequent section, we wish to focus on the empirical analysis: which set of factors explains the length and depth of recessions experienced by the group of post-command economy countries? Because those recessions did not necessary coincide with 'transitional' recessions proper (i.e. those resulting from the systemic reforms, which have short-lived negative impacts on growth), a better name to use would be 'post-Communist' recessions. As will be argued, it is not transition and stabilization, but the absence of them, that imposed the most serious economic costs on the group of countries we consider.

The theoretical literature on 'transitional recession'

As already discussed, the 'transitional recession' triggered by liberalization, even if short-lived, was a real phenomenon and of considerable interest from the economic theory point of view. It is not often that a large group of countries decides to dismantle a command economy. Again, the timing of this systemic transition is best represented by liberalization. Institutional reforms took longer to implement (see Chapter 2) and, empirically, it was typically liberalization which coincided with a large one-off decrease in output (even if, as already discussed, the recession started earlier).

Before discussing the explanations for the 'transitional recessions', it is worth noting two themes which feature frequently in the literature, where the term 'transition' does not necessarily apply.

First, the evidence discussed already shows that *some* types of stabilization programmes had a temporary negative impact on GDP growth. However, the experience of the transition economies does not differ here from that of other middle-income market economies, Latin America in particular. The transition countries inherited monetary overhangs resulting from initial price controls, which implies that liberalization could result in a one-off price jump which could trigger a policy response in the form of stabilization programmes. However, the macro disequilibria to be addressed were more deeply rooted than simply the effects of price liberalization. Whatever the initial reason, the stabilization programmes were addressing macro disequilibria which were qualitatively not very different from those in any other market-type economy. The issue has already been discussed in Chapter 3, and generally, it is not in macro policy where the transition experience has some unique features.

Secondly, the foreign trade shock was real, but should not be related to *individual* liberalization programmes. The disappearance of trade structures coordinated by the Soviet Council of Mutual Economic Assistance (CMEA) and the disruption of intra-Soviet trade within the FSU (fifteen out of the twenty-seven transition countries were Soviet republics in 1989) led to trade shocks. This explanation is consistent with the empirical results, which we shall discuss again in Chapter 10: the more trade-dependent countries were more affected by recessions. A possible link to liberalization is that the old administrative foreign trade links were disrupted before they could be substituted by new ones based on international market mechanisms. However, there are two problems with this line of argument. First, the effects appeared regardless of liberalization in a given country – it was sufficient that the neighbouring countries liberalized. And, secondly, a more important effect is not that the old coordinating mechanism was replaced by market structures. In fact, trade openness was associated with better trade and output performance, as exemplified by Estonia and several other CE countries. The problem was rather that the old coordinating mechanism was not replaced by international market arrangements but by new set of barriers and inefficient exchange rate mechanisms, in particular in the CIS countries (see Gros and Steinherr 2004).

This leaves us with explanations for 'transitional' recessions that may be grouped under two main headings although they may be seen more as complementary than as alternatives:

(1) *Shocks in relative prices* resulting from price liberalization. These are typically exemplified by two channels. The first relates to the elimination of the 'soft' budget constraint (i.e. introducing 'hard' credits and the reduction/elimination of budgetary subsidies to enterprises), which results in a different set of producer prices (Blanchard 1997). The second relates to the direct shift of prices of energy (and energy-intensive products) towards world prices (even if energy prices were not liberalized fully, prices were at least partially adjusted upwards) (McKinnon 1993). There are two possible mechanisms linking a change in producer prices

with recession. First, financial market imperfections may imply that firms with good projects have no resources to expand quickly, while firms with bad projects are immediately hit and reduce output. Recession follows (Calvo and Coricelli 1992). Secondly, firms hit by price shocks are unable to adjust their labour costs downwards. A reduction in both employment and production follows (Blanchard 1997).

(2) *Disorganization.* Dismantling of the command economy mechanism leaves individual firms with a large set of bargaining problems with their suppliers and customers. In some areas, market equilibrium prices may quickly emerge, but in some informational barriers may lead to strategic behaviour and inefficient outcomes, where some productive links will be broken. In short, while a new coordination mechanism based on prices ultimately emerges, it may take time to establish it, and an output fall is more likely in industries with a large number of rigid connections between producers of intermediate goods. This empirical prediction is confirmed by Blanchard and Kremer (1997).

In Blanchard's (1997) version, the first model (under the name of 'reallocation') relies on labour market mechanisms, not on financial sector imperfections. It starts with the distinction between those firms which lost out from the shift in relative prices, and those which gained. In the first category we find firms that were subsidized under the old system, in the second those which had to pay the cost of it in terms of higher taxes. The losers (the 'old' sector) may be identified with the state sector, and the gainers with the new private sector or with firms restructured after privatization (the 'new' sector). Alternative categorizations are possible: the 'old-sector' label may be attributed to firms controlled by insiders (both 'old' state and privatized to insiders) and the 'new sector' label to firms where either outsiders or owners-managers (entrepreneurs in the case of small firms) are in control. The key economic distinction relates to the fact that the 'new' sector is *more productive* – in Blanchard's model, the quality of a representative consumer good produced is higher and the old equilibrium was supported by fiscal distortions (subsidies and taxes) and resulting price distortions.

Elimination of fiscal intervention makes the prices of the goods produced by both sectors equal, and the consumer demand shifts towards the 'new' sector due to the positive quality differential. If wages in the 'old' sector adjust downwards, there are no negative effects on employment and production, otherwise the transition leads to an initial increase in unemployment and a slump in production.

In Calvo and Coricelli's version (1992, 1993) companies face a shift in costs resulting either from the removal of subsidies or the higher prices of energy-related products. 'Bad' firms (those for which command economy distortions were favourable) are hit immediately and reduce production while good firms cannot adjust quickly, as they face credit constraints (and investment processes take time). A recession follows:

> Over time, firms can accumulate monetary balances and converge to the optimal level of output that would have been reached in the presence of perfect credit markets. Accordingly, the implied behaviour of output would follow a U-shaped pattern. An implication of this view is that output decline should be accompanied by a decline in productivity. Moreover, real wages would drop as well, as enterprises attempt to generate liquidity to purchase inputs. (Campos and Coricelli 2002: 820)

There is thus a direct link between credit market and labour market explanations. However, Blanchard's model imposes stronger labour market rigidity assumptions than Calvo and Coricelli's model. In the latter, wages can adjust downwards, and in fact this is to be expected along the lines quoted above: the credit constraint implies that it is in the interest not only of producers of 'bad' products, but also of 'good' producers to cut wages temporarily. However, wages can neither go down to zero nor become negative (so that firms could borrow from their employees). Workers are restricted by their access to credit and by their risk preference, and have some non-negative reservation wage. There are thus limits as to how far the internal finance can be generated by a drop in real wages.[4] That explains why firms producing 'good' products cannot accumulate the financial resources quickly enough to expand production. However, the recession also results from the fact that wages in firms producing 'bad' products cannot cut wages deeply enough to match the impact of the slump in product prices, and the latter effect is parallel to Blanchard's model.

The second model (disorganization) has been presented by Blanchard and Kremer (1997) and Blanchard (1997) in two related versions, describing either a representative production chain or a representative firm facing a number of suppliers. In both cases, previous to liberalization, coordination was imposed by the economic administration of the command economy system. Liberalization leads to outside opportunities being open to all parties involved. The possible inefficiency results from the fact that the suppliers and purchasers of intermediate products have to negotiate prices. Bargaining under informational asymmetries may lead to inefficient outcomes, where efficient links are broken, as the suppliers may chose alternative trade partners even if the real opportunity cost exceeds the benefit.

With the benefit of hindsight, what can we say about the empirical explanatory power of the alternative 'transitional recession' models? The first issue to consider is *wage flexibility*. Contrary to some expectations, wages turned out to be flexible downwards, at least during the 'transitional recessions' (see Chapter 5). That is consistent with the model stressing financial constraints and inconsistent with the model stressing labour market rigidities. However, additional theoretical insights may be gained from a reference to the labour-controlled model of enterprise, of which state firms at the onset of transition would be a clear example. An expected result is that while employment is less flexible, wages may in fact be more flexible in state firms during the recession. Here, the first argument hinges on the impossibility of a complete intertemporal contract between owners (or managers) and employees in private firms. In the latter, workers may be unwilling to accept wage cuts because they cannot be guaranteed to participate in future rents resulting from a successful restructuring. The problem may be easier to overcome in worker-owned companies. Secondly, insider ownership may be seen as equivalent to the 'efficient contract' solution, where not only wages but also employment is taken into account in firms' optimization decisions and the employment effects of higher wages are taken into account, in contrast to no-coordination, 'right to manage' models. The third argument, which highlights a counterbalancing negative effect, however, is that the worker may discount the future gains more than the private investor, and therefore may opt for higher wages now at the cost of future gains. This, again, assumes imperfect financial markets, demonstrating how strong the link is between the finance and labour perspectives. In general, however, wage flexibility turned out to be high, either due to financial reasons (as presented by Campos and Coricelli 2002), or due to the implications of effective employee control in the state sector (with the first two effects outweighing the third).[5]

Secondly, the additional empirical support for financial explanations of the 'transitional recession' comes from the well-documented fact that underdeveloped financial intermediation was one of the most characteristic features distinguishing the transition economies from others (Gros and Suhrcke 2000; Gros and Steinherr 2004). We shall discuss this further in Chapter 8.

Before that, we now turn to the empirical tests.

New empirical results: initial conditions, wars, stabilization, liberalization and the post-Communist slump in output

Explaining recessions

We intend to look for a possible set of factors that can explain the recessions experienced by the post-Communist economies during the 1990s. There is more than one way of measuring the economic cost of recession. Moreover, the presence of serious measurement errors (Åslund 2001) calls for the use of a battery of alternative indicators to check the robustness of results. We propose to focus on four alternative measures:

- The first is the *depth of the recession*, as measured by the ratio of the lowest value of output to its 1989 value. For most countries, the indicator was provided directly by the EBRD (1999, table 3.1: 63); however, here it was verified for the two countries which were still in recession in 1999 (Ukraine and Moldova) and supplemented for the missing countries (Bosnia and Hercegovina, Serbia and Montenegro) using EBRD and World Bank statistics. The indicator shows that the recession had been most shallow in the Czech Republic and the most dramatic in war-torn Bosnia and Hercegovina.

• The second relates to the *length of the recession*. Here, the range of outcomes varies between two years for Poland and ten years for neighbouring Ukraine and also Moldova.

• The third is a close correlate. Instead of length, it measures the time span between 1989 and the *exit from recession*. Thus, while the former measure shows lower values for countries that entered recession later, the latter is defined by the timing of the final entry on the post-Communist positive growth path. The indicator can be easily computed from the fifth column of Table 6A.1 (pp. 113–14). It has some advantage over the previous one, if we take into account that the early output statistics may be more problematic for some of the transition economies while in contrast there is little measurement error related to timing of exit from recession.

• Finally, the fourth is a crude proxy for the overall *cost of the recession*, as measured by a combination of both depth and length. It is calculated as a product of the depth of output slump at the lowest point and the length of the recession.[6]

The set of explanatory variables used is based on information provided in Tables 6A.1 and 6A.2 (pp. 113–14, 115–16).

We follow the existing research tradition, where the timing of the beginning of a transition is interpreted as equivalent to the introduction of some basic set of liberalization measures. This approach is used in the more recent empirical studies quoted above, in particular in De Melo *et al.* (2001), Falcetti, Raiser and Sanfey (2002) and Merlevede (2003), where the time dimension is adjusted taking the starting point to be when the basic set of liberalization measures was implemented. A similar approach is presented by Blanchard (1997). However, the most explicit discussion of measurement and empirical applications of the threshold level of reforms can be found in earlier work by De Melo and Gelb (1997). We follow this tradition, additionally motivated by our own results in Chapter 2, where PCA resulted in reforms split along two latent dimensions: liberalization and institutional reforms. However, for the sake of comparability, instead of a latent variable we opt for a measure used in the empirical studies discussed above and based on the same set of indicators; namely on a simple average of the three EBRD indicators, measuring (1) Internal price liberalization, (2) External liberalization and (3) Small-scale privatization and freedom of entry. The 'liberalization threshold' is defined as the time when this average reaches 3 (which is equivalent to the Polish score in 1990). The data comes from Falcetti, Raiser and Sanfey (2002) and EBRD (1994–2005), taking into account the fact that the price liberalization indicator was re-defined by the EBRD from 2003 onwards, with new value of 4 being equivalent to the old value of 3 (we rely on the old definition). One may note that, using this criterion, at the time of writing there was no liberalization in Belarus, Turkmenistan and Uzbekistan. The EBRD indicators cover institutional reforms as well. However, unlike liberalization, these were spread over a longer period of time. Moreover, the theoretical arguments linking output slumps with reforms relate to components of liberalization.

Stabilization dates are taken from EBRD (1999). However in a few cases, where repeated attempts at stabilizations were undertaken (i.e. the first programme was unsuccessful), the date of the latest programme is used.

The timing of both liberalization and stabilization programmes is measured in the following way. In both cases, we divided the observations roughly into two halves, creating dummy variables which represent 'early' and 'late' implementation of the liberalization and stabilization programmes, respectively. The resulting cut-off point divides stabilization programmes into those introduced in 1992 or earlier and those implemented after 1992. For liberalization, the corresponding year is 1994. Our motivation in constructing the variables this way is to minimize the problem of endogeneity of reforms. We intend to explore how the early implementation of liberalization and stabilization measures affected recessions over the long term. In contrast, any measure based on subsequent paths of reform may be endogenous – i.e. affected by economic growth. Indeed, we shall provide direct evidence of that being the case in Chapter 9.

Next, we have a set of variables corresponding to the initial conditions.[7] First, we have 'Years under communism', an indicator based on the assumption that the longer the time span under the old regime, the more distortions were introduced and the more difficult would be the return to a market economy. With this measure, some degree of arbitrariness is unavoidable; for consistency, we follow figures by Fisher and Sahay (2000), being fully aware that there may be reason to modify some of their entries. The next measure – an indicator of the rich (natural) resource base – is also based on the same source, but measurement appears less problematic. The next three indicators of initial conditions are based on De Melo *et al.* (1997). The first two are measures of repressed inflation and the 'black market' exchange premium at the onset of reforms. Unfortunately, these cannot distinguish between half of the observations in our sample – i.e. the reported value is exactly the same for the fifteen countries emerging from the FSU. For this reason, both measures may be strongly correlated with some other omitted variables and therefore remain problematic. The third indicator – a measure of trade dependence on other command economies – is better in this respect, as it distinguishes between the former Soviet republics based on data on intra-Soviet trade.

Finally, we wish to explore if formerly being in a federation counts; the corresponding indicator takes a value of one for countries emerging from Czechoslovakia, the Soviet Union and Yugoslavia, and zero otherwise. We also investigate if the narrower dummy, for the CIS only, captures any specific influences.

Results

Most of the indicators correlate with recession measures with the expected sign. The strongest effect links war with the depth of recession (correlation between the war dummy and the lowest/1989 output ratio is –67 per cent).[8] Similarly, both time spent under communism and inherited disequilibrium (repressed inflation, 'black market' exchange rate premium) correlate well with recession. Initial trade dependency made things worse, as more open economies were more exposed to the initial disruptions in trade. Being in a federation does not have such a clear impact on recessions, due to the fact that the indicator includes three successful economies: the Czech Republic, Slovakia and Slovenia. Being a CIS country, on the other hand, is significantly linked with recession. Possibly the most interesting results relate to the timing of liberalization and stabilization programmes. First, following the argument presented in Chapter 2, the time discrepancy between stabilization and liberalization correlates with the recession indicators. When we take the absolute value of the time difference between the stabilization and liberalization programmes, and correlate it with the lowest/1989 ratio of output, the correlation coefficient is –29 per cent. However, the effect is dominated by simple measures of the timing of both programmes. The correlation coefficient between early stabilization (as defined above) and the lowest/1989 ratio of output is a hefty 54 per cent; for early liberalization it is almost the same, at 53 per cent. The unambiguous result is that the early introduction of both liberalization and stabilization programmes correlates with less serious recession.

Things become more challenging, however, as soon as we move from bivariate correlations to multivariate regression models. The sample is small, and does not allow for models with a larger number of variables. Moreover, results are sensitive to specification due to multicollinearity. What emerges from the regression analysis is that war remains a single variable with a clear and robust impact on the depth of recession and therefore on the overall cost of recession, but not on the length of recession. Next in the ranking come three factors: timing of stabilization, timing of liberalization and initial trade dependence. However, here multicollinearity between liberalization and stabilization measures becomes a problem. While, when measured by simple correlation, the link between the timing of liberalization and recession was almost as strong as the link between the timing of stabilization and recession, as soon as we move to the multivariate regression settings the effect of early liberalization becomes dominated by early stabilization.

Why is the positive impact of early stabilization so strong? Delay in successful stabilization programmes was itself an indicator of the more fundamental problems with the fiscal side – i.e. problems with tax collection, tax structure and control over public expenditures. All these reflect the most important aspects of inadequate institutional reforms, an issue to which we shall return in more detail in Chapter 7. One may also note that those issues are not captured by the EBRD indicators of institutional reforms, as those do not cover fiscal issues (apart from one important dimension, i.e. the 'soft' budget constraints for firms).

Table 6A.3 (p. 117) presents regression results. The reported models are only those corresponding to the set of explanatory variables which prove most significant and robust to specification. As mentioned, the effect of timing of liberalization tends to be dominated by other variables for the depth of recession, where the impact of war and initial conditions (initial trade dependence on other command economies) is most critical.

However, as one would expect, initial conditions have a smaller impact on the length of recession, which is clearly dominated by stabilization ((3) and (5) in Table 6A.3) and less clearly by liberalization ((4) in Table 6A.3). The impact of initial conflicts (war) on the length of recession is highly insignificant (in contrast to its impact on the depth of recession) and the corresponding variable is not included in the reported specifications. Once we combine both dimensions into one proxy of the cost of recession, the timing of both stabilization and liberalization seems to dominate the impact of initial conditions, with the negative impact of war remaining significant.

Generally, early stabilization comes across as the significant predictor associated negatively with both the length and the depth of recession. We did additional checks, constructing a continuous variable representing the exact timing of stabilization, and it worked equally well. Early liberalization also has a positive impact in making a recession shorter, but does not come across as a significant predictor of the depth of recession. In contrast, initial conditions count for the depth of recession, and far less for the length of recession. Specifically, the more open a given economy was to its Communist trade partners, the more serious was the effect of initial disruption in the trade patterns and contamination coming from neighbouring economies facing their own crises. This effect was particularly serious for smaller post-Soviet Union republics affected by the initial slump in Russia, as demonstrated by Christoffersen and and Doyle (2000). Again, the effect of initial trade patterns on the depth of recession is robust and significant. Finally, the last dimension that emerges as a very robust predictor of the depth of recession is the war indicator. It also has a significant impact on the aggregate measure of the cost of recession.

Finally, in Table 6A.4 (p. 118), we present an alternative approach, where direct interdependence between the depth and length of recession is taken into account in a seemingly unrelated regression model. In this context, we return to the liberalization indicator, whose significance was slashed due to multicollinearity in the OLS regression models. The specification presented includes indicators of early stabilization, early liberalization and the war dummy. Here, early stabilization seems to make the recession shorter by 2.4 years, and the effect is significant. It has no significant effect on the depth of recession. On the other hand, early liberalization reduces the depth of the slump in output by 13 per cent on average, but has no significant impact on the length of recession. Again, war leads to a more serious slump, but its impact on the length of recession is highly insignificant (with the wrong sign).

To conclude: we know from the empirical literature on the GDP dynamics in transition economies that both liberalization and some types of stabilization programmes led to a contemporaneous dip in output followed by a strong recovery (J-curve effects). This is consistent with the results presented here. Economies which introduced effective stabilization and liberalization programmes early suffered less from the post-Communist recessions. However, the initial conditions were also important. More open, smaller economies suffered more, as they were more affected by the initial disruption in trade patterns after the Soviet Bloc disintegrated. And, finally, war is not good for growth. Czechs and Slovaks, who decided to separate without a single shot being fired, did much better than the former Yugoslavia republics (apart from Slovenia) and some of the former Soviet republics.

Evaluation of recessions

We intend to make a link between our results and the theoretical literature on recessions. Out focus will be on Blanchard and Kremer (1997). The first thing, however, is to consider the empirical evidence provided by these authors.

Based on input–output tables for nine transition economies, Blanchard and Kremer construct an index of complexity of production structures and find that it correlates with recession, controlling for an appropriate set of other variables. However, the problem with the estimations provided by Blanchard and Kremer (1997) is that we are unable to distinguish between the effects of full liberalization and those of some partial reforms. In fact, their sample (Albania, Armenia, Azerbaijan, Belarus, Georgia, Kirghizstan, Macedonia, Moldova, Russia) relates to economies which were not in the group of 'fast reformers' at the time the data was collected.

Blanchard and Kremer (1997) note the difference between the group of countries in the dataset used for econometric estimations and the CE economies. They present additional OECD data showing that shortages of materials were no longer the major constraint for producers in Central Europe (the Czech Republic, Hungary, Poland) in contrast to economies such as Bulgaria, or Russia which still experienced serious problems.

However, their provisional explanation is that the differences between the two groups of countries result from initial conditions, not from differences in economic policies and reforms. The two initial conditions they mention relate to the degree of centralization in industrial structures and enterprises (and therefore more specialization leading to the negative impact of disorganization) and to the further distance to the main EU markets and volume of trade, which decrease a possibility to alleviate the problems of specificity (1997: 1122).

The first argument (centralization) may be valid, the second (trade links) seems to be partly invalid, as demonstrated by the estimates reported earlier: more open economies suffered more not less from recessions – initially, the negative effect of breaking the existing trade links was stronger than the positive effect of overcoming specificity. More importantly, however, the main contribution of our results may be to show that it is not the difference in initial conditions but in the timing of the basic set of liberalization measures and stabilization that may be the key dimension explaining the post-Communist recessions. From the SUR regression reported earlier, we may see that early introduction of full liberalization was linked to a shallower output slump (with the estimated difference being 13 per cent of the 1989 GDP value).

All this does not invalidate the Blanchard and Kremer (1997) model; it may suggest, however, that instead of being a general model of 'transitional recession' it may in fact be a more narrow model of disorganization under partial liberalization conditions. There are two possible lines of argument here.

First, one may note that liberalization accompanied by private sector growth has two dimensions. The first is that the set of available transactions for existing suppliers expands, which may lead to a breakdown of existing production chains and decrease in the old sector output and recession, along the lines discussed above. The second effect, however, is the creation of new suppliers, which is likely to work the other way round: the increase in the number of suppliers is likely to decrease specificity and hold-up problems, provide alternative opportunities for producers and thus increase output. In fact, Blanchard and Kremer (1997) note a major important channel that may operate in this way – i.e. the availability of external options provided by foreign trade. However, the issue links more to liberalization than to initial conditions. While initial trade dependence had a negative effect (the breaking down of old links), it is trade liberalization and openness which led to new connections being established in place of old ones. More generally, to the extent that the entry of new suppliers takes time, the first (negative) dimension could still dominate early in the transition; the second, however, may prevail later on (provided there is sufficient freedom of entry). From this perspective, the recovery is created not just by the efficient completion of the search and bargaining process aimed at the new equilibrium set of prices, but also – or even more importantly – by the entry of new suppliers. A second argument which would link the model to incomplete liberalization is slightly different. Some prices along the production chain may be still controlled, while freedom of contract may be introduced early. That makes outside options more attractive – another words, the disrupting effect of partial liberalization may be more serious than that of full liberalization. For that reason, incomplete liberalization may lead to the outcomes that a combination of selective price controls and new outside options (including in the 'underground' economy) leads to long-lasting disruption. A good example of that may be the situation which developed in the CIS area with underpriced energy coupled with inadequate control over the sale decisions of enterprises, including illegal exports (see Gros and Steinherr 2004).

In general, it is likely that the disorganization mechanism was one of the sources of 'transitional recessions', but had even more serious negative effects in the case of partial liberalizations and incomplete transitions. To reiterate the empirical result: 'transitional recessions' caused by liberalization were J-curve-type phenomena. Slow liberalizations (i.e. partial liberalizations) and late stabilizations led to more prolonged and deeper slumps in output.

Notes

1. The term may be attributed to Kornai (1995).
2. This delay led to a (now mostly obsolete) discussion of 'gradualism' versus 'big bang', where Hungary was taken as an example of the former, and Poland of the latter. A sampling of that early discussion can be found in Portes (1993).
3. For both Hungary and Poland, the output statistics are as reported by the corresponding Central Statistical Offices for GDP, not for the net material product (NMP). The latter measure, standard under the old regime, excludes a major part of the service sector. The difference is not trivial. For both countries, the use of NMP would show a recession in 1989 (the latter statistic is sometimes confused with GDP and makes its way into some Western reports, in disguise).
4. Here, wage cuts is one mechanism and wage arrears is another. Wage arrears can be seen as equivalent to borrowing from workers. Modelling of this issue is provided by Earle and Sabirianova (2000). See also Desai and Idson (2000, ch. 8).
5. For a general discussion of employee control during the transition, see Earle and Estrin (1996).
6. When divided by two, it gives a rough measure of the area of output loss, but this additional transformation is spurious – it is just a linear transformation, not affecting the estimation results in any other way.
7. The list of the indicators is not complete. See Campos and Coricelli (2002) for a further discussion.
8. However, a word of caution is needed. Åslund (2001) argues that countries experiencing wars were not only affected by the collapse of output, but also by the collapse of output statistics.

Appendix Data and estimation results

Table 6A.1 Timing of recession, liberalization and stabilization programmes

Country	Liberalization date[a]	Stabilization programme date[b]	Beginning of recession[c]	Last year of recession	Length of recession	Lowest output/ 1989 value[d]
Central Europe and South East Europe						
Albania	1993	1992	1990	1992	3	0.604
Bosnia	1998	1997	1989	1994	6	0.120
Bulgaria	1994	1997	1990	1997	8	0.632
Croatia	1991	1993	1989	1993	5	0.595
Czech Rep.	1991	1991	1990	1992	3	0.846
Estonia	1993	1992	1989	1994	6	0.608
FYR Macedonia	1991	1994	1989	1995	7	0.551
Hungary	1992	1990	1990	1993	4	0.819
Latvia	1993	1992	1991	1995	5	0.510
Lithuania	1993	1992	1990	1994	5	0.533
Poland	1990	1990	1990	1991	2	0.822
Romania	1994	1993	1989	1992	4	0.750
Serbia	2001	1993	1989	1993	5	0.400
Slovakia	1991	1991	1990	1993	4	0.750
Slovenia	1991	1992	1989	1992	4	0.820

Table 6A.1 (Continued)

Country	Liberalization date[a]	Stabilization programme date[b]	Beginning of recession[c]	Last year of recession	Length of recession	Lowest output/ 1989 value[d]
CIS						
Armenia	1996	1994	1990	1993	4	0.310
Azerbaijan	1998	1995	1989	1995	7	0.370
Belarus	not yet	1994	1990	1995	6	0.627
Georgia	1996	1994	1989	1994	6	0.254
Kazakhstan	1995	1994	1989	1995	7	0.612
Kirghizstan	1994	1993	1991	1995	5	0.504
Moldova	1995	1993	1990	1999	10	0.317
Russia	1993	1995	1990	1998	9	0.553
Tajikistan	2000	1995	1989	1996	8	0.392
Turkmenistan	not yet	1997	1989	1997	9	0.420
Ukraine	1996	1994	1990	1999	10	0.365
Uzbekistan	not yet	1994	1991	1995	5	0.834

Notes:

[a] Liberalization: year when the average of the three EBRD liberalization indicators (price liberalization, external liberalization and small privatization) takes value of 3 or higher (with the price liberalization indicator based on the pre-2003 EBRD definition, adjusted where necessary to preserve compatibility). *Source:* EBRD (1995–2005) and Falcetti, Raiser and Sanfey (2002).

[b] Stabilization: year when successful stabilization programme was introduced (i.e. for countries with recurring high-inflation episodes, the second date is reported, cf. Bulgaria). *Source* EBRD (1999–2005).

[c] Timing of recession: based on EBRD (1995–2005) and World Bank, *World Development Indicators* (2001 dataset).

[d] Lowest value of output (depth of recession): based on EBRD (1995–2005).

FYR = Former Yugoslav Republic.

Table 6A.2 More explanatory variables

Country	War[a]	Years under Communism[b]	Rich resource base[b]	Repressed inflation (1987–9)	'Black market' exchange rate premium (1990) (%)[c]	Trade dependence (1990) (%)[d]	Formerly part of federation (USSR, Yugoslavia, CSSR)
Central Europe and South East Europe							
Albania	0	45	0	4.3	434	6.6	0
Bosnia	1	44	0	12	27	6	0
Bulgaria	0	43	0	18	981	16.1	0
Croatia	1	44	0	12	27	6	1
Czech Rep.	0	43	0	-7.1	185	6	1
Estonia	0	51	0	25.7	1828	30.2	1
FYR Macedonia	0	44	0	12	27	6	1
Hungary	0	41	0	-7.7	46.7	13.7	0
Latvia	0	51	0	25.7	1828	36.7	1
Lithuania	0	51	0	25.7	1828	40.9	1
Poland	0	42	1	13.6	277	8.4	0
Romania	0	43	1	16.8	728	3.7	0
Serbia	1	44	0	12	27	6	1
Slovakia	0	43	0	-7.1	185	6	1
Slovenia	0	44	0	12	27	4	1

Table 6A.2 (Continued)

Country	War[a]	Years under Communism[b]	Rich resource base[b]	Repressed inflation (1987–9)	'Black market' exchange rate premium (1990) (%)[c]	Trade dependence (1990) (%)[d]	Formerly part of federation (USSR, Yugoslavia, CSSR)
CIS							
Armenia	1	74	0	25.7	1828	25.6	1
Azerbaijan	1	75	2	25.7	1828	29.8	1
Belarus	0	75	0	25.7	1828	41	1
Georgia	1	70	2	25.7	1828	24.8	1
Kazakhstan	0	75	0	25.7	1828	20.8	1
Kirghizstan	0	75	0	25.7	1828	27.7	1
Moldova	1	52	0	25.7	1828	28.9	1
Russia	1	74	2	25.7	1828	11.1	1
Tajikistan	1	75	0	25.7	1828	31	1
Turkmenistan	0	75	2	25.7	1828	33	1
Ukraine	0	75	1	25.7	1828	23.8	1
Uzbekistan	0	75	1	25.7	1828	25.5	1

Notes:

[a] War: a military conflict, either internal or with neighbouring countries (based on author's assessment)

[b] Number of years a country spent under Communism and indicator of rich resource base: both based on Fischer and Sahay (2000).

[c] Black market exchange rate premium and trade dependence, both based on De Melo et al. (1997).

[d] Trade dependence defined as the average of exports and imports divided by GDP.

CSSR = Czechoslovak Soviet Socialist Republic.

Table 6A.3 Determinants of post-Communist recessions[a,c]

Dependent variable / Explanatory variables	Depth of recession: lowest value of output/1989 value of output		Length of recession in years		Time recession ended relative to 1989 (year of lowest output 1–1989)		Cost of recession; a proxy calculated as: [1–(lowest output/ 1989 output)]* (length of recession)	
	(1)	(2)	(3)	(4)	(5)	(6)	(7)	(8)
Stabilization before 1993 (dummy variable)	0.088 (0.063)[b]		-2.536*** (0.673)		-2.143** (0.674)		-1.456* (0.623)	
Liberalization before 1995 (dummy variable)		0.100 (0.065)		-1.576† (0.809)		-1.039 (0.797)		-1.265† (0.672)
Initial trade dependence (def. as in Table 6A.2)	-0.005* (0.002)	-0.004 (0.002)	0.054* (0.026)	0.042 (0.033)	0.072* (0.026)	0.066† (0.032)	0.049* (0.021)	0.036 (0.024)
War dummy (def. as in Table 6A.2)	-0.236*** (0.062)	-0.229** (0.062)					1.350* (0.618)	1.437* (0.649)
Constant	0.699*** (0.063)	0.648*** (0.084)	5.618*** (0.655)	5.891*** (0.98)	5.819*** (0.656)	5.796*** (0.97)	1.907** (0.632)	2.346* (0.877)
Number of observations	27	27	27	27	27	27	27	27
F-statistics	12.02***	12.37***	10.51***	4.37*	10.16***	4.70*	9.35***	8.21***
R^2	0.611	0.617	0.467	0.267	0.459	0.282	0.550	0.517
Adjusted R^2	0.560	0.567	0.422	0.206	0.414	0.222	0.491	0.454

Notes:
[a] Estimator: OLS.
[b] Standard errors in parentheses.
[c] Significance levels: *** 0.001; ** 0.01; * 0.05; † 0.1.

Table 6A.4 Determinants of post-Communist recessions: seemingly unrelated regression model[a, b, e]

Explanatory variables	Dependent variables	Depth of recession: lowest value of output/ 1989 value of output	Length of recession in years
Stabilization before 1993 (dummy variable)		0.040 (0.075)[c]	-2.418* (0.989)
Liberalization before 1993 (dummy variable)		0.131[td] (0.070)	-0.647 (0.923)
War dummy (def. as in Table 6A.2)		-0.191** (0.066)	-0.255 (0.870)
Constant		0.530*** (0.055)	7.065*** (0.725)
Number of observations		27	27
F-statistics		10.42***	4.78**
R^2		0.576	0.384

Notes:
[a] Estimator: Zellner's seemingly unrelated regression model.
[b] Covariance matrix for the residuals computed with a small sample adjustment.
[c] Standard errors in parentheses.
[d] Significance levels (for coefficients, based on *t*-statistics): *** 0.001; ** 0.01; * 0.05; † 0.1.
[e] Correlation of residuals from the two equations: −0.367; $\chi^2(1) = 3.629$ (10% significance level).

7
Liberalization and Public Finance

While both liberalization and stabilization were relatively easy to implement (provided the commitment of policy-makers was present), the same cannot be said about fiscal reform. Yet, in the longer run, stabilization is not sustainable without fiscal transformation. And with recurring fiscal destabilization, the positive impact of liberalization is also dampened.

This makes fiscal issues a key to the overall success of the transition programme. However, with fiscal reorganization we are moving into the area of *institutional reforms*, which are slower and more difficult to implement, as they require changes in the law and implementation. The latter relies on the adequate functioning of the public administration, which in turn implies an improvement in human and social capital, a change in attitudes and practices – a new pattern of behaviour.

Moreover, the reforms, liberalization in particular, may lead to a temporary fiscal tension. These *feedback effects* may potentially cause a threat to the overall success and pace of the reform programme.

We first look briefly at the inheritance from the old regime. We then sketch the key issues related to fiscal reform. Subsequently, we test empirically if and how the fiscal balance was affected by the components of the liberalization programme and contrast the results with transition theory. Finally, in an Appendix (pp. 131–41) we look at Poland, to discuss how the interplay of institutional and structural issues may affect the fiscal balance of the government.

The inheritance

Under the old regime, tax collection was a simple task. The state administration was not restricted by legislative process, courts, nor media, and arbitrary decisions were commonplace. One could even argue that in the era of the command economy it was not meaningful to speak of 'fiscal policy' and 'public finance', because:

> The existence of *public* finance presupposes that of *private* finance. The countries did not need market-type tax systems to raize public revenue because the government could simply appropriate the share of total, and mostly public, production for its own needs. (Tanzi and Tsibouris 2000: 3–4, emphasis in the original)

Before the transformation began, all was, in a way, public. Moreover, many fiscal functions, as these are defined in market economies, were not carried out by the government but by state enterprises.

In particular, most taxes were collected directly from the SOEs, and the process was largely not visible to the general public – i.e. to the ultimate individual taxpayers. The flows between the state-owned firms and the treasury were all within the state sector; they caused relatively little friction and did not require any level of the sophisticated tax administration one finds in developed market economies. Explicit taxation consisted of wage taxes, national insurance contributions (paid by enterprises on behalf of the workers) and a turnover tax levied on final consumption. The latter was a primary source of income and (unlike value added tax (VAT)) its rates varied for different categories of products, with the number of categories running into hundreds or even thousands. For that reason, it had highly distortionary effects (Gregory and Stuart 1995).

The explicit taxes were complemented by implicit taxes. Administrative transfer prices resulted in taxing profits away from some enterprises and redirecting them towards firms which would have been loss-making had market prices and 'hard' budgeting prevailed. As wages were under administrative control, simply keeping them at a low level was equivalent to the taxation of income, as the value-added retained within the enterprise could be easily transferred elsewhere by economic administrative decision. This implicit tax collection at the enterprise level was supplemented by related additional mechanisms. First, savings were implicitly taxed by maintaining negative real deposit rates within the monobank system (and, again, on the other hand, some firms were subsidized via the low cost of finance). Second, the shortage of consumer goods at prevailing administrative prices was another characteristic which supported implicit taxation via negative interest rates, since it forced many individuals to save.

While serious problems existed on the revenue side of public finance, the expenditure side was no better. The SOEs were not only production units; they were also providers of welfare. Somewhat paradoxically, some elements of the specialized institutions of the modern welfare state were therefore underdeveloped under Communism. They were substituted by the provision offered to workers and their families by state-owned companies, including housing, health care, child care, recreational facilities and various benefits in kind. Rein, Friedman and Wörgötter (1997) report that the share of these in labour costs ranged between 10 per cent in Hungary and a staggering 35 per cent in Russia. This pattern of welfare provision was both inefficient and incompatible with the new market environment. Yet, creating the new institutions of a specialized governmental welfare system was a challenge, compounded by the emergence of open unemployment and growing income inequality. The increase of spending on welfare had to be matched by a decrease in enterprise subsidies if a fiscal crisis was to be avoided.

In general, the measured, explicit levels of taxation and public spending were both very high, especially when the transition economies are compared with the middle-income group of countries to which they belong. For several economies (Bulgaria, Czechoslovakia, Hungary and Romania), the ratio of government revenue to GDP exceeded 50 per cent at the onset of the reforms.[1] The overall level of transfers, implicit spending and taxation included, was even higher, in particular if we take into account the social and fiscal roles of the state enterprises which substituted the government: some redistribution had already occurred at the enterprise level, where social welfare provision was financed via lower wages.

Reforms and fiscal imbalance during the transition

The setting up of tax systems broadly similar to those prevailing in Western Europe was a common goal of the transition economies. This benchmark system relied on (1) individual personal taxation which included both income tax and social security contributions/payroll taxes collected from both employers and employees; (2) taxation of enterprises (corporate income tax); (3) indirect taxation in the form of VAT and some excise taxes; and (4) some taxation of wealth (property taxes and inheritance taxes; both were typically limited in the transition economies). To transform the old system based on the direct taxation of wages and on a turnover tax in the new system required new legislation – the enactment of the many rules and regulations that accompany a modern tax system and that make the administration of that system possible, and the setting up of an appropriate tax administration.

Application of these laws requires skills in both compliance and enforcement, and these skills were slowly enhanced during the transition. The task was further complicated in comparison with the Western economies, where tax systems operate in a relatively unchanging environment (stable inflation, small fluctuation of output, stable structures of production). In general, a well-functioning tax administration requires adequate staffing, computerization and adequate software including the establishment of a modern taxpayer and national insurance identification system and master files, modern registration and collection procedures, information systems for tax payers, internal monitoring and audit, limited arbitrariness, transparency and other anti-corruption measures (Tanzi and Tsibouris 2000). Introduction of all these elements requires time, knowledge and specialized resources.

In those countries which faced the most dramatic decrease in revenues, poor tax collection often had its roots in the poor design and administration of taxes. The definition of tax bases remained problematic throughout the CIS, taxes also tended to change frequently without due notification, and were sometimes applied retroactively. The tax law was complicated and unclear, some of the marginal rates very high, but were hardly ever applied due to widespread exemptions and tax credits that eroded the tax base. The end result was widespread arbitrariness by tax administrators and a lot of management time dedicated to the avoidance or evasion of taxes. Continued use of barter exchange and the accumulation of payment arrears (whereby a large share of transactions and income effectively escaped taxation) was partly associated with tax evasion and remained a major cause of poor tax revenues, particularly in the CIS throughout the 1990s.

The ratio of effective to statutory taxation offered an aggregate indicator of the distortions in the tax structure and its overall quality. As shown by Schaffer and Turley (2001), in the late 1990s the rates were generally lower for the CIS and higher for Central Europe, ranging between 9 per cent for the non-reformed economy of Tajikistan, where tax decisions were clearly left almost entirely to the discretion of the government administration, and 68 per cent for Estonia, with consistent and transparent tax rules on a par with some of the best instances of the high-income non-transition economies.

On the expenditure side, the critical issues were to introduce unemployment benefits and strengthen the social safety net; to reduce and streamline social expenditure for some occupational groups, privileged under the former regime; to eliminate the system of direct subsidization of loss-making enterprises; to reduce military expenditure; to create an efficient balance between central government, specialized government agencies and local government; to reform the pension system and the educational system.

Those issues are relatively well covered in the transition literature, and a good account can be found in Barr (1994, 2001) and Funck and Pizzati (2002). Since we have no real hope of adding anything new on these topics, we turn our attention to another issue: the interplay between liberalization and fiscal balance.

Liberalization, fiscal revenue and expenditure: some econometric results

Liberalization and fiscal balance

The removal of subsidies was an integral part of the price liberalization, and as a result many large SOEs moved into a period of low or negative profit. On the other hand, the emerging small enterprises in the new private sector were paying no corporate income tax, as they also went through an initial period of zero or low profits, albeit for different reasons, consistent with the early stage of the 'lifecycle' pattern of companies. This combination implied an initial negative shock to government revenues, as the tax base for 'old' taxes was shrinking, without being counterbalanced by the 'new' sector. Similarly, foreign trade liberalization led to increased competition, and the price shocks faced by the 'old' sector were enhanced. The immediate impact on tax revenue was to be negative, parallel to internal price liberalization. Yet, the negative effect of price liberalization on tax revenues was likely to be matched by its dampening effect on expenditure, as the removal of subsidies led to smaller government budgets. Price liberalization was thus likely to result in an immediate scaling down of the government budget, with its effect on the budget balance remaining ambiguous and dependent on the relative magnitude of the balancing revenue and expenditure effects.

Unlike immediate effects, subsequently, the effect of the reforms on expenditure was likely to change from negative to positive. All three elements of liberalization – internal prices, external liberalization and freedom of entry – led to an increase in income inequality and unemployment.[2] With the social functions of SOEs scaled down, the social safety net system had to be developed as a response, leading to an increase in government expenditure. Thus, it was not the case that the overall level of government expenditure was reduced, but rather that its structure changed, with subsidization of loss-making state enterprises being replaced by increased direct social transfers.[3]

Changes in revenues and expenditure can be also interpreted in a manner consistent with a traditional cyclical pattern – while economies shrank during the prolonged post-Communist recessions, parts of the tax base (such as profit and income taxes) were eroded. On the other hand, growing unemployment could result in a countercyclical increase in expenditure.

The interesting empirical question is to see if the direct impact of reforms on taxes, expenditure and fiscal balance can be disentangled from the effects working through both GDP and the unemployment path. This is an issue we shall investigate next.

Reference point: results by Pirttilä (2001)

The analysis that follows builds on the model developed by Pirttilä (2001), who examines the determinants of the government balance using panel data for twenty-five transition countries for the period 1990–7. The set of explanatory variables includes both standard macroeconomic variables – GDP growth and the unemployment rate – and the three EBRD measures assessing the components of liberalization: (1) Internal price liberalization, (2) External liberalization and (3) Freedom of entry and small-scale privatization. The main extension we offer is that in addition to the fiscal balance, separate models for both expenditure and revenues are estimated. As follows from the discussion in the previous section, we expect that the reforms may result in parallel shifts of both revenues and expenditure, making interpretation of the resulting impact on the fiscal position difficult to understand without looking at the two sides of the budget statement separately.

Another important modification in our design relates to the fact that we do not change the time identification of the observations in our panel. In contrast, Pirttilä (2001) shifts his observation ordering. Instead of real time, his panel is compiled according to 'years of transition', assumed to start in 1990 for Hungary and Poland, in 1991 for all the other CEE economies and in 1992 for all the former Soviet republics. The motivation for the change is not obvious to us. While for most countries the chosen dates for the beginning of the transition correspond to the time when the main components of liberalization were implemented, this is not true for several CIS countries, which either introduced their main reform packages later than 1992 or did not introduce radical liberalization at all (see Chapter 6 for details). Furthermore, the model includes the dummy variables controlling for 'transition years', which by construction are likely to be highly correlated with the reform indicators and this multicollinearity problem may be the underlying reason why the models estimated by Pirttilä (2001) are sensitive to specification. In contrast, any shocks which were real-time specific are not adequately controlled for, including the impact of the disintegration of the CMEA trade area.[4] Another important drawback is that observations prior to the main liberalization programme are eliminated. This excludes important control observations, as we are unable to compare fiscal dynamics in countries which introduced reforms early on with those that did not. It seems to us that the overall impact of the chosen design is to make the results reported by Pirttilä (2001) less stable. Nevertheless, the main results stand the test of time – i.e. the impact of differences in specification is not decisive.

In practice, the difference that is more important is possibly the simple fact that we have at our disposal a far longer time series, which is 1987–2002. The chosen end-year is implied by the availability of macroeconomic data at the time of writing. The extension of the time window frame backwards is motivated by the observation that some economies (former Yugoslavia, Hungary and Poland) were already partly liberalized prior to 1990 and taking that into account provides us with better measurement and timing of reforms. In addition, we can extend the sample from twenty-five to twenty-seven countries, as data for both Bosnia and Hercegovina and for Serbia and Montenegro are now available, at least for part of the period. The primary source of data is EBRD (EBRD 1995–2005 and Falcetti Raiser and Sanfey 2002), supplemented in some cases (especially for the early period) by information drawn from World Bank (*World Development Indicators* 2004, CD ROM edition). As a result, the number of observations we have at our disposal now is more than twice that used by Pirttilä (2001): between 255 and 268 depending on specification, as compared with 106–136 for the (2001) study.

Appropriate estimator

There are several characteristics of our panel dataset that have to be taken into account in the choice of an appropriate estimator. These are: the dynamic nature of the fiscal relationship, an absence of any strictly exogenous explanatory variables or instruments, the time dimension, the unbalanced nature of the panel and the presence of unobservable country-specific effects. Reforms could be taken as exogenous; however, the prevailing view in the recent literature is that they are not (Falcetti, Raiser and Sanfey 2002; see also Roland 2000 for a theoretical analysis). For instance, in our context, it is possible to think that a better fiscal position of the government makes it more likely to undertake risky reforms and accommodate the negative fiscal shock that may emerge as an immediate result.

Our chosen estimation technique, which takes into account these issues, is a version of the Generalized Method of Moments (GMM) estimator, developed by Arellano and Bond (1991). Here, the variables are first-differenced to eliminate unobserved individual-specific effects, and lagged values of the endogenous or predetermined variables (in levels) are used as instruments. The GMM estimator is robust in that it does not require information on the exact distribution of the disturbances and is instrumental in combating the problems associated with potential endogenity of the explanatory variables. This estimator is related to the earlier Anderson–Hsiao method (Anderson and Hsiao 1981), but uses a larger number of instruments (the Anderson–Hsiao estimator relies on either $y_{i,\,t-2}$ or $(y_{i,\,t-2}-y_{i,\,t-3})$). We follow standard practice and use one-step GMM. The one-step estimator is superior to the two-step version, as the latter technique offers very modest efficiency gains and, more importantly, the asymptotic distribution is less reliable under the two-step method (Arellano and Bond 1991; Bond 2002). The estimator consistency relies on the orthogonality conditions between lagged values of $y_{i,\,t}$ and disturbances, and also on the assumption:

$$E(\Delta v_{i,\,t}\,\Delta v_{i,\,t-2}) = 0$$

A null hypothesis of no second-order serial correlation for the disturbances (of the first-differenced equation) accordingly is tested.

Judson and Owen (1999) performed Monte Carlo experiments comparing four estimators: a standard least squares dummy variable estimator, a corrected version of that estimator introduced by Kiviet (1995), the Anderson–Hsiao method (1981) and Arrelano and Bond's (1991) GMM estimator. For balanced panels, the Kiviet method is possibly the best choice. For long, unbalanced panels, both Anderson–Hsiao and Arrelano–Bond perform well, and the latter has a clear advantage for the panels with a short time dimension ($T \le 10$).

Model specification

We report nine specifications in Tables 7.1–7.3. We explored longer lag structures for all explanatory variables, and found that for individual reform indicators all variables lagged more than one period were consistently insignificant, so the corresponding models are not reported.

Models (1)–(3) (Table 7.1) estimate the determinants of government expenditure, revenue and balance, all as a percentage of GDP. The set of explanatory variables follows Pirtillä (2001) and includes GDP growth rate, the unemployment rate and three indicators of liberalization: (1) internal (price), (2) external, and (3) freedom of entry and small privatization, plus annual control dummies. However, the model is augmented by the use of a lagged dependent variable and by longer lag structures for GDP and unemployment. Models (4)–(6) (Table 7.2) are similar, except that now only one-year lags are used for all variables to make the specification more compatible with Pirtillä (2001) and also to see if the results are sensitive to a change in specification. Finally, in models (7)–(9) (Table 7.3) one composite liberalization indicator (as defined by Falcetti, Raiser and Sanfey 2002) is used instead of three separate indices. The three elements of the reforms are correlated and, using the aggregate measure, we may get some intuitions on the overall impact of liberalization; in addition, a longer lag structure is applied here.

Table 7.1   Estimation results: models (1)–(3) with separate reform indicators[b]

Dependent variable[a]	(1) Government expenditure as % of GDP	(2) Government revenue as % of GDP	(3) Government balance as % of GDP
Dependent variable			
1 y lag	0.37 (0.06)[c, d, e]***	0.19 (0.07)**	0.40 (0.06)***
GDP rate of growth	− 0.32 (0.06)***	− 0.00 (0.05)	0.24 (0.07)***
1 y lag	− 0.13 (0.06)*	0.04 (0.04)	0.18 (0.06)**
2 y lag	0.13 (0.06)*	− 0.01 (0.04)	− 0.15 (0.05)**
Unemployment rate	0.11 (0.16)	− 0.08 (0.12)	− 0.24 (0.15)
1 y lag	− 0.00 (0.18)	0.28 (0.13)*	0.45 (0.17)**
2 y lag	0.18 (0.15)	− 0.20 (0.11)†	− 0.43 (0.16)**
Price liberalization	− 2.27 (1.43)	− 2.37 (1.10)*	− 0.73 (1.36)
1 y lag	1.01 (1.26)	0.90 (0.95)	2.15 (1.15)†
External liberalization	− 1.31 (0.98)	− 1.35 (0.76)†	− 0.40 (0.96)
1 y lag	1.73 (0.91)†	0.74 (0.70)	− 1.07 (0.88)
Free entry and small privat.	1.37 (1.14)	1.13 (0.86)	− 0.26 (1.10)
1 y lag	2.21 (1.03)*	1.05 (0.79)	− 0.79 (1.02)
Constant	− 2.57 (5.38)	2.06 (4.08)	3.65 (3.57)
No. of observations	258	255	262
Second-order autocorrelation: z	− 0.90	− 0.24	1.37
Sargan test for over-identifying restrictions: χ^2	94.03	90.33	100.28

Notes:
[a] All variables in first differences. Estimator: Arellano–Bond one-step GMM. Unbalanced panel for twenty-seven transition economies, 1987–2002, using all available data points.
[b] Data sources: EBRD, *Transition Reports* 1995–2005; World Bank, *World Development Indicators* 2004.
[c] Standard errors in parentheses.
[d] Time controls (annual dummies) included but not reported.
[e] *** significant at 0.001; ** significant at 0.01; * significant at 0.05; † significant at 0.1.
1 y = One-year.

Table 7.2   Estimation results: models (4)–(6) with separate reform indicators[b]

Dependent variable[a]	(4) Government expenditure as % of GDP	(5) Government revenue as % of GDP	(6) Government balance as % of GDP
Dependent variable			
1 y lag	0.36 (0.06)[c,d,e]***	0.19 (0.06)**	0.36 (0.06)***
GDP rate of growth	– 0.30 (0.07)***	0.01 (0.05)	0.22 (0.07)***
1 y lag	– 0.10 (0.06)†	0.02 (0.04)	0.13 (0.06)*
Unemployment rate	0.11 (0.16)	– 0.08 (0.12)	– 0.21 (0.16)
1 y lag	– 0.04 (0.15)	0.17 (0.12)	0.47 (0.16)**
Price liberalization	– 2.88 (1.37)*	– 2.35 (1.06)*	0.43 (1.32)
1 y lag	0.09 (1.24)	1.01 (0.93)	3.11 (1.14)**
External liberalization	– 1.19 (0.96)	– 1.06 (0.73)	– 0.74 (0.96)
1 y lag	2.13 (0.90)*	0.60 (0.69)	– 1.80 (0.87)*
Free entry and small privat.	1.29 (1.12)	0.74 (0.85)	– 0.13 (1.09)
1 y lag	2.33 (1.04)*	1.18 (0.79)	– 0.44 (1.02)
Constant	– 0.50 (5.32)	1.52 (3.99)	1.13 (2.13)
No. of observations	262	259	268
Second-order autocorrelation: z	– 0.96	– 0.08	1.29
Sargan test for over-identifying restrictions: χ²	101.91	100.32	99.07

Notes:
[a] All variables in first differences. Estimator: Arellano–Bond one-step GMM. Unbalanced panel for twenty-seven transition economies, 1987–2002, using all available data points.
[b] Data sources: EBRD, *Transition Reports* 1995–2005; World Bank, *World Development Indicators* 2004.
[c] Standard errors in parentheses.
[d] Time controls (annual dummies) included but not reported.
[e] *** significant at 0.001; ** significant at 0.01; * significant at 0.05; † significant at 0.1.
1 y = One-year.

Results and discussion

We shall start with expenditure, then fiscal revenue and finally the government balance.

First, with coefficient estimates for the lagged dependent variable varying between 0.36 and 0.42 (specifications: (1), (4) and (7)), we may note considerable and significant persistence in the government expenditure share in GDP. Next, GDP growth dominates the impact of all the other explanatory variables. All specifications detect a strong contemporaneous negative effect of GDP growth on the share of expenditure in GDP. This negative effect is still significant, but weaker, after one year; however, it changes sign after two years, where it turns into weak positive effect. Given that expenditure is measured as a ratio to GDP and that not all expenditure items adjust automatically to GDP, the clear-cut negative effects – both contemporaneous

Table 7.3   Estimation results: models (7)–(9) with the aggregate reform index[b]

Dependent variable[a]	(7) Government expenditure as % of GDP	(8) Government revenue as % of GDP	(9) Government balance as % of GDP
Dependent variable			
1 y lag	0.42 (0.06)[c,d,e]***	0.21 (0.07)**	0.44 (0.06)***
GDP rate of growth	– 0.31 (0.06)***	0.02 (0.05)	0.27 (0.06)***
1 y lag	– 0.11 (0.06)†	0.04 (0.05)	0.14 (0.06)*
2 y lag	0.15 (0.05)**	0.01 (0.04)	– 0.17 (0.05)***
Unemployment rate	0.05 (0.16)	– 0.16 (0.13)	– 0.28 (0.15)†
1 y lag	– 0.10 (0.18)	0.21 (0.13)	0.47 (0.17)**
2 y lag	0.24 (0.15)	– 0.23 (0.12)†	– 0.47 (0.15)**
Liberalization index	– 1.02 (1.65)	– 1.36 (1.22)	– 1.38 (1.64)
1 y lag	3.14 (1.56)*	0.47 (1.19)	– 0.98 (1.43)
2 y lag	1.08 (1.39)	2.23 (1.01)*	0.94 (1.33)
Constant	– 3.49 (5.59)	0.14 (4.24)	– 3.41 (4.02)
Number of observations	259	256	262
Second-order autocorrelation: z	– 0.69	0.89	1.35
Sargan test for over-identifying restrictions: χ^2	76.50	92.75	88.21

Notes:
[a] All variables in first differences. Estimator: Arellano–Bond one-step GMM. Unbalanced panel for twenty-seven transition economies, 1987–2002, using all available data points.
[b] Data sources: EBRD, *Transition Reports* 1995–2005; World Bank, World Development Indicators, 2004. Liberalization (Reform) Index: defined as in Falcetti, Raiser and Sanfey (2002), as a simple average of the three transition indicators: for price liberalization, foreign trade liberalization and for entry and small-scale privatization.
[c] Standard errors in parentheses.
[d] Time controls (annual dummies) included but not reported.
[e] *** significant at 0.001; ** significant at 0.01; * significant at 0.05; † significant at 0.1.

and with a one-year lag – are not surprising. It seems, however, that sustainable growth triggers policy response and a small upward adjustment in expenditure, typically after a delay of two years.

On the other hand, the effects of unemployment are all insignificant. This may be seen as an important result when compared with theoretical models of the transition based on the interaction between fiscal variables and unemployment (see especially the seminal paper by Aghion and Blanchard 1994). The discrepancy between the theory and the empirical results may be explained by the relatively modest role of social support for the unemployed in many transition countries (Mickiewicz and Bell 2000; see also the data on unemployment benefits compiled by Golinowska 2001). In fact, Aghion and Blanchard (1994) declare that their model applies to CE economies where the responsiveness of expenditure to unemployment may be stronger. Our empirical results are based on the sample of all twenty-seven transition economies. And last but not least, while in the theoretical model all the social effects of restructuring are captured by unemployment, in practice outflows into economic inactivity or subsistence agriculture makes unemployment a very imperfect proxy of the increase in social spending triggered by the liberalization.

The components of the liberalization programme have some significant impact on government expenditure, as expected. First, price liberalization leads to a contemporaneous decrease in government expenditure, even if the magnitude of the corresponding effect varies from significant ((4)) to marginally insignificant ((1)). The result is consistent with the expected impact of removal of subsidies and, generally, with 'hardening' of the budget constraint, which is a defining element of price liberalization and equalization. External liberalization is also associated with a contemporaneous decrease in expenditure; however, the effect changes sign (significant) after one year, similarly to internal price liberalization (insignificant). Similarly, reforms related to the freedom of entry produce a significant increase in expenditure with a one-year lag, and we obtain the same result when the aggregate measure of liberalization replaces individual components ((7)).

Thus, a J-curve pattern emerges, on which we may impose the following speculative interpretation.[5] Liberalization leads to an immediate reduction in government spending due to the elimination of subsidies and a general 'hardening' of the budget constraint (which also includes items such as subsidization of bank credit). At the same time, liberalization increases pressure on the 'old' sector, restructuring is triggered, factories start to shed excessive labour, wage dispersion increases and enterprises are forced to cut down the provision of social benefits and concentrate on their core activities. All that leads to an increase in government spending, which we clearly detect as emerging with a one-year lag. Thus, in this wider interpretation, the link between reforms and government spending is restored, consistent with Aghion and Blanchard (1994) and Blanchard (1997). Yet, an important new detail derived from the empirical analysis is *timing*: the positive and negative effects of reforms on government spending are not yet synchronized. Reforms imply an immediate reduction in government spending, an effect which is reversed later, being triggered by the impact of restructuring working through the economic system.

We may now turn to the determinants of government revenue. The first thing to note is that there is less persistence in government revenue: the coefficients on the lagged dependent variable are less significant and the values are about twice as small as for expenditure, ranging from 0.19 to 0.21 (specifications (2), (5), (8)). In addition, the share of revenues in GDP does not respond to GDP growth, and the corresponding coefficients are close to zero. And the impact of unemployment is ambiguous: generally, the negative effects prevail, but some of the lagged effects appear to be positive. As the results are ambiguous, we abstain from imposing our interpretation here.

In contrast, we have some clear-cut and stable results related to the liberalization indicators. The contemporaneous impact of both internal and external liberalization on government revenue is negative and significant. Interestingly, however, when we allow for a longer lag structure, liberalization has a strong positive impact on revenue, emerging with a two-year lag; taken together, the positive effects clearly more than counterbalance the initial negative effects. This result may be combined with the findings on the impact of reform on the dynamics of expenditure. If the reform implies that the protection of the 'old' sector (in terms of a 'soft' budget, foreign trade barriers and entry barriers) is removed, that may produce a sequence of a fall in both expenditure and revenue first, an increase in expenditure next and finally an increase in revenue. The time pattern detected is consistent with the following stylized interpretation. First, the 'old' sector firms face a negative shock affecting their revenues and a decrease in government revenue appears. Second, after a while, continuing competitive pressure results in an employment reduction, the cutting of the enterprise-level social spending and other adjustment measures. All that calls for a response from the government, and spending increases. Finally, after about two years, the positive effects on government revenue start to prevail, as the taxes from the emerging 'new' sector finally counterbalance the decrease in revenue from the 'old' sector. Government revenue increases again. Taken together, we can observe a clear J-curve time pattern in government revenue.

An alternative interpretation could be offered in the spirit of Aghion and Blanchard's (1994) paper. In their model, restructuring triggered by the reform leads to an increase in social expenditure, which has a subsequent impact on the increase in taxation, as the government is forced to match expenditure with taxation, facing a limited possibility of debt financing.

What makes this interpretation marginally less convincing is the fact that we should see a parallel effect on economic growth. Yet, as may be seen from the results in Chapter 6, faster and more radical reforms result in shorter recessions. Thus, it is more likely that the empirically observed increase in revenues comes from the 'new' sector firms, instead of being a sign of bad equilibrium resulting from too much liberalization.

Where our empirical results may contribute to the discussion is to demonstrate that the fiscal effects are never instantaneous and that there are important time lags built into both the response of enterprises and the response of the government to liberalization shocks.

Finally, we may look at the estimates of the budget balance, which enable us to compare some of the results with those obtained by Pirttilä (2001). First, similar to expenditures, but unlike revenue, the government balance exhibits a relatively strong persistence: the coefficient on the lagged dependent variable varies between 0.36 and 0.44 (specifications (3), (6), (9)). The growth of GDP improves the government's fiscal position (both a contemporaneous positive effect, as in Pirttilä 2001, and also with a one-year lag), but later on tends to have some correcting, weak negative effect on the fiscal balance (two years after economic growth appears). The latter effect is clearly driven by the increase in expenditure, as may be seen from both specifications (1) and (7). Some speculative political economic arguments may be applied here. Economic growth may ease the government budget constraint and lead to more expenditure, an effect which is not only transition-specific, but likely to have a more universal character.

Again, similarly to Pirttilä (2001), the effects of unemployment on the fiscal balance are ambiguous; in the case of the longer lag structure ((3) and (9)), adding up all the corresponding coefficients the net impact is negative – i.e. on balance, higher unemployment results in a deterioration in the fiscal position. The effect with a two-year lag is unambiguously negative; the mixed results for the contemporaneous and one-year impact may be attributed to the fact that unemployment may be a proxy for efficient restructuring and elimination of 'soft' budget government financing, as indicated by consistently positive (albeit insignificant) contemporaneous sign of unemployment in (1), (4), (7).

Looking at the impact of the reforms on the fiscal balance, two main results emerge. First, we have a strong and robust positive effect of price liberalization on the government balance after a one-year lag. This may be contrasted with the ambiguous contemporaneous effect. A closer inspection reveals that after a one-year lag, price liberalization results in an increase in expenditure, but revenues also start to recover. Clearly, the positive effect of revenue on the fiscal balance dominates.

We may also look at the coefficients in (9), where an aggregate reform index with a two-year lag structure is included. While the results are not significant, they indicate again the J-curve-type response of the government balance to liberalization: negative initially and turning positive later on, when the positive effects of increased revenue prevail.

Appendix   The interplay between institutional reforms and fiscal balance: Poland – a case study

There is always a trade-off between the stronger but narrower results of econometric analysis and the richer but less conclusive insights of a narrative account. In this Appendix we turn to the latter, to discuss a case study in the interplay between reform and the government budget. The case relates to the budget tensions that followed a package of institutional reforms introduced in Poland in the late 1990s.

Macroeconomic developments

As already discussed in Chapters 3 and 6, Poland emerged from a short transitional recession quicker than any other transition economy and experienced a unique period of fast GDP growth in the mid-1990s, ranging between 6 per cent and 7 per cent in 1995–7. However, growth weakened to 4 per cent in 1998–9 and subsequently to around 1 per cent in 2000–1, before increasing again from 2003 onwards (GUS, EBRD data). The slowdown and near-recession was possibly affected by an external development in the export market, in particular by the collapse of the Russian rouble in August 1998 and the slowdown in the economy of Euroland. The current account changed from + $5 bn in 1995 to –$12 bn in 1999 and the merchandise balance from –$2 bn to –$15 bn, mostly covered by capital inflows (EBRD, CASE data). The exchange rate was floated in April 2000 and monetary policy tightened (until the end of 2001), which possibly contributed to a temporary decline in domestic demand. Since 2000, Poland's government budget deficit has been steadily increasing, from below 1 per cent to 5.7 per cent in 2004 and at the time of writing there is still a risk that the debt/GDP ratio may approach the 60 per cent mark (EBRD, OECD data), the constitutionally imposed barrier, which legally binds the government to radical adjustment – i.e. to balance the budget in the two subsequent years. The financial imbalances have serious structural roots. That makes Poland an interesting case study.

Tax reforms

First it is useful to eliminate some unlikely explanations. Fiscal imbalances emerged in spite of a solid track record of fiscal reform introduced during the 1990s. The three pillars of modern taxation – personal income tax, corporate income tax and VAT – were all introduced promptly. Decentralization was introduced, with more independence allowed at the local government level. Major tax reforms were launched in 2000: corporate income tax was decreased from 34 per cent in 1999 to 30 per cent in 2000, 28 per cent in 2002 and 19 per cent in 2004. At the same time, the VAT tax base was broadened, and in 2000 the parliament approved the introduction of VAT for agrarian produce for the first time (at a reduced 3 per cent rate), making a dent in the opposition from a strong political lobby. As of 2003, indirect taxes played a dominant role in government revenues (62.3 per cent), shared between VAT (39.7 per cent) and excise taxes on fuel, tobacco products and alcohol (22.6 per cent). The direct taxes share was 26.2 per cent, with 16.9 per cent collected from personal income tax and 9.3 per cent from corporate income tax (GUS data). This reminder is important, as it demonstrates that the sources of the problem have to be sought on the *expenditure* side.

Public spending

Inefficient institutional structure of public spending

As of 2001, 40 per cent of public spending (150 bn zł) had been channelled via numerous state funds located outside the government budget. While the situation in some sections of this system improved as a result of reform (see below), the financial discipline of many of the funds continued to be weak, particularly in the smaller ones. The proliferation of funds and special agencies proved an attractive way of realising political gains for virtually all political parties in Poland. The deteriorating fiscal situation triggered the interest of the Polish media and a public investigation by the Ministry of Finance in 2001, which unearthed many fiscal anomalies. One notorious example was the Fund of Guaranteed Employee Benefits which once collected a high 1 per cent of the wage bill from employers (more recently reduced to 0.08 per cent) to 'counteract the employment implications of industrial restructuring'. Its balance sheet for 2000 demonstrated that it should have had sufficient reserves to finance its legal obligations for forty-four years. In spite of that, it faced liquidity problems because its funds had been used to offer loans with a high credit risk. Another example relates to the Fund for the Rehabilitation of the Disabled, which pursued a different strategy: a policy of profitable financial investments, which could pay the large cost of an overgrown administration, with spending on assistance for the disabled remaining inadequate. Most of the Ministry of Agriculture spending had been channelled via specialized funds and agencies, and lack of proper monitoring brought criticism by the EU Commission over alleged irregularities in the spending of EU assistance funds. In addition, some activities of the funds remained semi-independent from the budget, as they were financed not by direct subsidies but from initial endowments. These enabled the funds to generate revenues to sustain their administration, even if their initially intended functional task had been completed. Two prominent examples of these included the Agricultural Property Agency and the Military Housing Agency.

Extra budgetary funds have always been far easier to create than to liquidate. One outstanding example is the Fund for the the Service of the External Debt, once involved under Communism in the illegal purchase of discounted Polish debt on international financial markets. The undercover nature of those operations created extensive opportunities for fraud. The Fund was placed in liquidation shortly after the transition started, but could not be closed due to a prolonged and complicated criminal financial inquiry which is likely to be concluded by the courts in 2005, after more than ten years of costly investigation.

In terms of the volume of financial flows, however, the Social Insurance Fund remained the major extra-budgetary source (channelling two-thirds of all extra-budgetary funds), and possibly the only fund which had been successfully reformed through the pension reform (see below), achieving a visible improvement in insurance contributions and a more aggressive collection of debts via the initiation of bankruptcy procedures, the use of property registers and public prosecutions in cases of fraud.

The second largest recipient and distributor of extra-budgetary funds was a network of regional health funds, created as part of the health care reform. The latter led to a temporary improvement in financial discipline. However, the health care reform proved to be unpopular, stemming partly from imperfections in implementation and the fact that this sphere was highly sensitive to voters, who associated reforms with more risk and uncertainty. One of the objectives of the health care reform was to strengthen the patient's position and her choice with respect to the system. This was not entirely accomplished and the medical profession remained a sphere of widespread corruption where the position of the patients was weak. After the change of government in autumn 2001, the reform was stalled and competition (in the form of private health funds) was not introduced. Subsequently, in 2003 the reform was partly reversed by a recentralization, bringing the regional health funds back under the central umbrella of the Ministry of Health. The irony is that the health care reform stalled before all the elements were in place to prove it viable. The unpopularity of the reform among voters may be largely attributable not to the characteristics of the institutional design, but to the fact that the previous government had failed to provide an adequate level of spending on health care. If we take into account that the share of health care in the budget systematically declined throughout the 1990s, including the post-reform years, then the fact that there was no adequate improvement in health care is not particularly surprising, yet this is precisely why public opinion turned against the reform. As a result, the budget in health care remains 'soft' at the time of writing. However, a new element in the health care system relates to the new opportunities which opened up to the medical profession due to EU accession (May 2004) and possible migration. This created a pressure to increase relative wages in health care, which in the longer term will help to rationalize the system and combat corruption. Wages have already been adjusted in the neighbouring Czech Republic, and it may just be a question of time before a similar development is adopted in Poland.

Overall, one major source of fiscal problems relates to the inheritance of opaque patterns of revenues and spending on extra-budgetary funds. The future development will be determined by two conflicting tendencies: imposing more fiscal discipline on the remaining funds or bowing to special interests and dismantling the reforms (health care in particular). In theory, no funds are supposed to go into deficit. However, recurrent borrowing has been extended from both the central budget and banks, 'softening' the budget constraints.

Cost of restructuring programmes and impact of continuous low fiscal discipline of the largest state enterprises (coal mining, metallurgy, rail transport)

The official estimated value of public support for industry was 1.2 per cent of GDP for 1998 and 1.5 per cent for 1999. More than 50 per cent of the transfers related to deferrals and remissions from payments of taxes and other obligations towards public institutions. However, according to Anna Fornalczyk, the former chair of the Anti-Monopoly Commission, the figure could still exclude about 80 per cent of support disguised under additional deferrals of various miscellaneous payments.

The overdue obligations of Polish State Rail amounted to zł 3 bn in 2001. It remains to be seen whether the current reorganization of State Rail into several companies (freight/cargo, passenger transport, maintenance, infrastructure storage, etc.) will improve the situation. Similarly to rail, over zł 4 bn were spent on the mining sector restructuring programme, with an exceptionally generous allowance for any miners willing to quit their jobs. Yet, after significant downsizing, the sector had still paid only 86 per cent of VAT due and 65 per cent of local taxes in 2001. Current national insurance contributions were paid in full, but coalmines made no effort to repay any older overdue payments. The metallurgy sector had zł 1.2 bn in overdue payments in taxes in 2001. The restructuring programme in the sector implemented in 2001 included state guarantees for investment credits for zł 1 bn . Another sector that benefited from support was sugar refineries. To this, one should add the value of public guarantees for credits for all these sectors.

Yet, hope for a more stringent fiscal discipline results from implementation of the law on public support for enterprises, which became operational in September 2001. The law demands that information on all forms of explicit and implicit subsidization be made public, it determines the upper limits of assistance, asks for impact assessment studies and takes into account the implications for market competition. In addition, EU accession (May 2004) imposed additional legal constraints on governmental support. And last but not least, a recent surge in demand on the world market is helping the ailing primary sector, easing pressure on government assistance.

The issue of governmental aid and the interplay between restructuring, enterprise finance and tax revenues to industry may be illustrated by the controversy over the rescue package proposed in 2002. The issue was brought to the forefront of public discussion by Grzegorz Kolodko (Minister of Finance in 2002), who proposed a rescue package for the largest Polish companies. The programme was focused on 399 companies with employment over 1,000 facing financial difficulties. They could apply to the government for cancellation of debts, under the condition that they reached an agreement with all other creditors on rescheduling obligations and paid an upfront 'restructuring fee' corresponding to 1.5 per cent of their obligations. In return, the creditors would be able to count the overdue liabilities as costs, resulting in tax credits that would lower their corporate income tax payments. Participation in the programme was conditional on providing a restructuring plan. In addition, some financial assistance was offered to finance the retraining of employees.

To some extent, the programme resembled an earlier bank-led restructuring scheme. The latter had induced a positive change in the banking sector, forcing banks to identify bad debts and to arrest their growth. It also enabled the privatization of a few major banks. However, the existing evidence demonstrates that the programme had little positive effect on the manufacturing firms involved. The programme offered temporary financial relief and improved liquidity but induced little real restructuring. In the majority of the participating companies the problems re-emerged. The flagship case, the Szczecin shipyard, went bankrupt again after few years, in spite of gaining broad access to finance from both domestic banks and the EBRD.

The general problem, in the case of 'restructuring programmes', is that there is little evidence of effective restructuring without the entry of a strategic private investor. Thus, the programmes cure only some symptoms, postponing the crisis. At the same time, the fiscal cost is paid by other companies, which instead of generating employment and growth strive to pay their tax obligations. Generally, there is clear evidence that financial results deteriorate most in those companies and branches that remain state-owned. The weighted average ratio of earnings before taxes to sales was 1.2 per cent in private enterprises and –0.8 per cent in state enterprises (2001). Given these results, a natural way of adjustment would be to dispose of some assets of state companies, which would be equivalent to privatization. Such a rescue method was used successfully at the beginning of the transition. However, in the remaining part of the state sector, the process has virtually stalled, due to several factors. First, the managers of state-owned companies are reluctant to risk accusations of underpricing, which may lead to public prosecution. Second, the trade unions in those companies are also typically against such a process, assuming that the assets would significantly contribute to the value of shares transferred to employees when the firm was ultimately privatized (that expectation may be myopic). Third, the tax office, which uses a procedure that permits swapping assets for some tax arrears, is very slow to process applications. The opportunity cost of idle assets (real estate, in particular) also includes the costs of administration and relevant tax obligations generated by the property. Ironically, in some instances, the latter taxes became an important factor contributing to the financial crisis in state enterprises. Financial disarray and low liquidity in the state sector is typically accompanied by low tax discipline (in the case of the largest state enterprises, in particular).[6] The share of liabilities from taxes and social security obligations in the total short-term liabilities of enterprises is much higher for the state sector, and the difference between state-owned and private firms has been growing. These data confirm the view that part of the state sector continues to operate under a 'soft' budget constraint and uses deferred tax obligations as a source of finance. The aggregate share of deferred tax obligations in liabilities (i.e. for all enterprises, in both sectors) has remained at around 7 per cent.

In general, it is easier to collect taxes from smaller companies, while large companies in a poor financial condition may have some leverage against the treasury, as potential bankruptcies and reductions in employment are costly from a political point of view (for a general argument, see Shleifer and Vishny 1994).

To summarize, at the beginning of the transition, Polish policy-makers were relatively successful in imposing fiscal discipline and eliminating the 'soft' budget – in banking, in particular. However, later on, the residual state-enterprise sector was able to strengthen its lobbying position and in some cases found a new way of avoiding facing a 'hard' budget constraint via relatively lax tax enforcement. Large state companies in key sectors had sufficient political bargaining power to obtain substitute finance in the form of unpaid tax obligations.

The retired, pensioners and public sector employees

Between 1990 and 2000, the number of retired and pensioners (recipients of disability benefits) increased from 5.5 m to 7.5 m. While part of this increase might be explained by demographics, most of the additional 2 m resulted from treating early retirement as a policy tool to mitigate the impact of industrial restructuring and from lax control over disability benefit entitlement. It is far from obvious if the policy generated any real gains, as people with relatively high skills were needlessly pushed outside the labour force (see also Chapter 5). Moreover, 7.5 m pensioners represents a major lobby, which was able to make significant gains in their income position in relation to other income recipients in the economy. The ratio of the average retirement pension to the average net wage increased from below 50 per cent before the transition (1989) to just below 70 per cent in the late 1990s. Public perception of this is blunted by vivid images of pockets of poverty among the elderly and disabled, which could be more adequately addressed by targeted social assistance than by the indiscriminate protection of average incomes for the whole group.

Other privileged income groups are located in some segments of the so-called 'budgetary sphere' – i.e. occupational groups whose wages and salaries are paid directly from the state budget. Here, the situation varies immensely, as it is related to the lobbying power of different groups. Teachers in elementary and secondary education were particularly effective in protecting their branch privileges, short work time, generous vacation and retirement regulations, and also their wage levels. Successful countrywide protests by nurses were characteristic of some years, but were less successful. On balance, the wage level in the public sector was 16 per cent higher than in the private sector (1999),[7] while the private sector was a driving force behind new job creation throughout 1990s.

Fiscal implications of institutional reform

Paradoxically, one of the reasons for the deterioration in the fiscal balance since the late 1990s was the ambitious programme of reforms introduced in a span of two years between the end of 1997 and January 1999. The government introduced four major reforms almost simultaneously – of the educational system, local administration, health care and the pension system. Of those four, the last, a three-tier pension system introduced in January 1999, was probably the most important from the fiscal point of view.

While beneficial in the medium/long term, the reforms proved to be more costly than expected in the short run, adding to fiscal tensions. The reasons for the increase in a social security financing deficit were the inefficiencies in transitional legislation and the incompetence of the public administration, including significant delays in the implementation of the required new software, which was not fully operational at the time the reform was introduced. In addition, there was a continuing problem of loopholes leading to fraud in the sickness benefit system (prior to and at the beginning of the reform) and collection of national insurance contributions was poor, especially in large state enterprises. The reform alleviated the latter problem only after a delay, by creating individual pension accounts and motivating employees to monitor their contributions.

Health care reform introduced specialized 'Regional Sickness Funds', which negotiated health service provision with all relevant medical institutions. The reform was intended to introduce some financial discipline into the sector affected by a 'soft' budget constraint and inefficiency; however, the immediate results were mixed, at best. In 1999, the central budget was forced to lend zł 847 m to the regional funds, the debt being cancelled subsequently. In 2000, a new loan of zł 1 bn was offered and the government was forced to accept a delay in repayment for the next two years. The longer-term response was to increase contributions marginally on an annual basis, starting from an increase of 0.25 per cent in 2002.

The Pension Fund borrowed even more: zł 4 bn from the central budget in 1999 and zł 2 bn in 2000. In addition to this, the Pension Fund borrowed implicitly from both banks and (private) Open Pension Funds, by postponing due payments. At the time the reforms were introduced, in 2000, the limit for bank credit was zł 3 bn while the debt of the Open Pension Funds amounted to zł 3.5 bn. However, unlike the health care system, the reform of pensons gradually saw an improvement. The collection of national insurance contributions improved significantly after 2000, following two years of disarray.

Structural problems and EU accession: agriculture

In 2002, 16.9 per cent of the labour force was in agriculture (GUS data). The shrinkage of the agricultural sector accelerated in the late 1990s, following the collapse in external demand after the Russian exchange rate crisis in late 1998 and the decline in internal market prices due to large production surpluses. While before accession, the Polish government had spent more on support for agriculture in relation to GDP than the EU countries (2.6 per cent, including subsidies to the Agricultural Social Insurance Fund in 2002), the support was thinly spread over an unsustainable number of producers. Strong downward pressure on agricultural incomes resulted in social protest, including road blockades, and led to the adoption by the government of some short-term temporary protectionist measures in 2001. New import levies were added for milk, wheat products and sugar. However, it is not only that employment in agriculture is declining, but also that a wide-scale product restructuring has occurred in many farms, producing a more concentrated set of agricultural products. In the 1990s, the number of farms producing sugar beet fell four times, the number of commercial milk producers fell three times and the number of suppliers of swine fell by 35 per cent. Similarly, the number of tobacco and hop growers is declining, following downward trends in demand. On the other hand, production of both fruit and vegetables is increasing. These structural changes are radical. There are also widening regional differences, since the north of Poland never recovered from the collapse of the once-heavily subsidized state farms. In 2004, the more efficient farms started to benefit from EU transfers. About 700,000 farms – less than half the number of existing farms – qualify. EU accession helped to ease fiscal tensions via more than one channel. The direct effect of the transfer of EU funds is the most obvious. However, a second factor is that, in the longer term, the assistance is targeting larger and more efficient producers, inducing structural change. And last but not least, agriculture and the food industry were the sectors which benefited most from the final removal of trade barriers between the old EU and the new member states. Exports to the EU of several main food products surged after May 2004, injecting new financial flows into a sector with high restructuring needs.

Structural problems and EU accession: the environment

While Poland has succeeded in achieving a reasonable level of alignment with the *acquis communautaire*, it still does not have a full comprehensive environmental policy. In order to implement the *acquis* to a greater degree, such a policy must be developed, along with a detailed financing plan and a timetable for expenditure. Where environment protection legislation has been completed, compliance is quite poor. However, these remaining problems mask a significant increase in investment outlays – in both the water

Table 7A.1   Investment outlays on environment and water protection, 1990–2003

	1990	1996	2000	2003
Share in total investment outlays (%)				
Environmental protection	3.6	9.4	4.9	4.6
Water management	2.2	2.2	1.2	1.5
Share in GDP (%)				
Environmental protection	0.7	1.6	0.9	0.6
Water management	0.4	0.4	0.2	0.2

Source: Central Statistical Office (GUS).

and waste sectors, in particular. Environmental protection investment as a percentage of the national economy increased markedly, peaking around 1996 and reaching almost 10 per cent of all investment outlays (see Table 7A.1). Since then, the share of spending on environmental protection has decreased, but with EU accession one may expect it to increase again in line with the implications of EU norms. The issue is also important for regional development and for job creation to substitute for the shrinking employment in agriculture. Lack of environment-related infrastructure, such as sewage systems, is one of the major obstacles to investment in some areas. Poland has increased its investment in environmental protection via its National Fund, yet implementation of EU directives will demand still higher investment, even where governmental funds are matched by EU transfers.

In short, the improvement of environmental standards had visible fiscal implications for Poland, especially in the second half of the 1990s. With EU accession, the transfer of funds may facilitate investment, but will still require matching funds from the government.

Conclusion

While tax reform is important, the main source of the current problems remains on the expenditure side. The underlying reason for an increase in fiscal pressure in Poland, visible in recent years, is the inability of subsequent governments to reform the structure of public expenditure. In the near future the impact of inefficient institutions and policies will be exacerbated by external factors.[8] The structure of payments on the Polish external debt, inherited from the Communist past, implies repaying the so-called 'Paris Club' $23 bn until 2010. The significant increase in the burden relates to 2005–7, where payments amount respectively to $3.3 bn, $3.7 bn and $4 bn. In addition, some of the EU-related income remains uncertain and conditional on the efficiency of the government to handle EU-sponsored projects (albeit in early 2005 the assessment was positive in this respect).

Expenditure will include co-financing of structural funds and other projects paid directly from the Polish budget. Meanwhile, Poland is expected to spend between $3.2 and $3.7 bn annually on environmental protection. Jointly, EU-related expenditure could amount to $10.7 bn in 2005, $12.0 bn in 2006 and $13.3 bn in 2007. Needless to say, this challenge is not related only to Poland.

One key point related to expenditure is the inefficient institutional structure of public spending, as discussed above. Around 40 per cent of public spending is channelled via numerous state funds, which are formally located outside the government budget. The financial discipline of many of the funds remains weak. Additional factors include the fiscal implications of expanding spending during a period of fast economic growth (a more universal phenomenon, see p. 127–8), and from the fiscal costs of postponing the restructuring of several important industries that remain under state ownership. A visible slowdown in the privatization process works against efficient restructuring, which is typically induced by strategic investors. Thus, at time of writing, many difficult decisions related to fiscal adjustment lie ahead, but a recovery in economic growth may make the implementation easier.

Notes

1. The record belongs to Czechoslovakia, one of the most centralized command economies, where the ratio of revenue to GDP peaked at close to 62 per cent in 1989. Hungary comes next, with 55 per cent in the same year. Three reform laggards – Belarus, Tajikistan and Turkmenistan – still recorded government revenues above 50 per cent for some years during the 1990s (EBRD 1995–2005).
2. Here, we deal with time paths resulting from the reform process. It is worth reminding ourselves that negative social costs in the reforming countries were counterbalanced later by beneficial results from economic growth. In other words, the most dramatic social costs in terms of poverty were experienced by those countries which did not reform (see Milanovic 1998 for evidence). In general, when GDP declines, the poor lose more than the rich (Milanovic 1998: 132). The length and depth of the transitional recession (see Chapter 6) is thus closely associated with the incidence of poverty, and the former was clearly negatively affected by slow reform.
3. In many cases, an increase in expenditure was also linked to the costs of bailout of the banking sector. While a system of direct subsidies to the 'old' sector was relatively easy to dismantle, the 'soft' budget constraint associated with bank lending was far more difficult to eliminate. Given the latter phenomenon, the negative effects of liberalization on enterprise financial positions could trigger banking crises (with some delay).
4. While any real-time shocks confined to the FSU are accounted for by construction (for these economies, the chosen timing of transition coincides), any other effects common to all transition countries are distorted.
5. A word of caution. The magnitude of the contemporaneus negative effect is most likely to be inflated in a spurious way, due to the phenomenon discussed in Rzońca and Ciżkowicz (2003). See also the discussion in Chapter 10.

6. The remaining part of the discussion on pp. 136–7 draws from Driffill and Mickiewicz (2003). See that source for an extended discussion.
7. In addition, the job security has been higher in the public sector.
8. The figures in the remaining part of this section are drawn from Kamela-Sowinska (2003: B3).

8
The Order of Financial Liberalization

This chapter begins with an overview of the functions of financial intermediation and possible sources of inefficiency in the context of economic transition. We refer to the optimum order of financial liberalization, discussed by McKinnon (1993). We next move to an empirical analysis. First, we test how the transition economies in general, and the two main regions within this group (CIS and non-CIS), differ from other comparator economies along basic financial dimensions. Second, we test how the reforms implemented in the transition countries affected the characteristics of their financial systems, distinguishing between immediate effects and those that came with a time lag. We then draw some brief conclusions.

Financial intermediation and transition

Financial Intermediation

It may be useful to start our discussion with the basics. Reforms introduced in Central and Eastern Europe and Central Asia aimed at rebuilding the basic functions of financial intermediation, most of which were simply not performed under the old regime. Thus, borrowing from Stiglitz (1992) and expanding, we may distinguish five key roles of financial intermediation:

- First, the financial sector facilitates the transfer of 'resources (capital) from those who have it (savers) to those who can make use of it (borrowers, or investors)' (Stiglitz 1992: 163). This is possible due to *credible financial contracting*: the investors expect future returns, with NPV no smaller than the invested funds. Finance is always thus linked to intertemporal choice and to the willingness of some economic agents to trade present for future consumption. In addition to transfers, the financial institutions facilitate cooperation between individual investors in agglomerating capital for a given investment project. This is important, as many projects 'require more capital than that of any of one saver or any small set of savers' (Stiglitz 1992: 163).

- This links to the next point – i.e. *risk management*. Because all financial transactions involve time, they also involve risk, as the future is always uncertain. The risk varies between one project and another, and the financial sector creates a possibility to match alternative projects with investors characterized by different preferences towards risk. Moreover, financial intermediation reduces the overall level of risk for any investor, by creating opportunities for pooling risks and creating diversified investment portfolios for which the idiosyncratic risks of individual projects balance each other.

- Financial institutions are also responsible for selecting the projects and choosing the structure of *financial contracts* that maximizes efficiency for a given type of project. It is not always the case that individual borrowers have sufficient knowledge to arrive at a realistic assessment of the value of their projects. Moreover, they may be motivated to misrepresent the information they offer to the providers of finance (pre-contractual opportunism or the adverse selection problem, Stiglitz and Weiss 1981). The incentive to do so results from the fact that in many financial contracts we see an asymmetry of benefits and costs from possible outcomes of the project. If the financial contract is based on fixed claims (such as an ordinary bank loan), the borrower may be tempted to chose a risky project which may yield high returns in the case of success. The (mean) expected PV of the project could be negative, but it may still be attractive to the borrower, who will get all the residual value (after paying fixed returns to the lender) in the case of a positive outcome, but will be limited in her losses to her initial share if things go wrong. An alternative category of financial contract is equity. Here, the provider of the finance shares the residual value. That may reduce pre-contractual opportunism, but can increase post-contractual opportunism (the agency problem). The latter issue stems from the fact that while residual claims are shared between insiders and outsiders, much of the effective control rights remain with insiders (managers). As a result, the value of the project (the firm) is no longer fixed. It depends on the actions of managers, who may pursue some private benefits of control (Jensen and Meckling 1976; see also Hart 2001).

- That leads us to the next point. The efficient outcome will be achieved by combining an *adequate financial contract and monitoring* (which ensures that funds are used in the way the receivers of finance committed themselves to, i.e. counteract post-contractual opportunism – the agency problem). Thus, efficiency is increased via both the expertise of the financial sector in monitoring and via effective financial regulations, which make monitoring more easy.

- And, finally, contracts have to be *enforceable*, so that those who have obtained the funds transfer back the resources in the way specified by the contract. Effective bankruptcy procedures are part of the solution here.

Institutional and legal environment

These last comments indicate that the efficiency of financial contracts is affected not only by the actions of the parties directly involved, but also by the institutional and legal environment. Some of those common arrangements result from self-regulation (for instance, on some major stock exchanges), and in many cases reputation may be the strongest single mechanism enforcing compliance. However, in the transition environment waiting for the natural 'bottom-up' construction of self-regulatory mechanisms by market participants may be an unrealistic option, as reputational effects may be slow to build and incentives to free ride may remain strong. Relevant behavioural mechanisms may take decades to build, as exemplified by the history of self-regulatory financial institutions. It is typically thus the government administration – an institution endowed with the right of coercion – which plays an important role in preventing fraud and deception and building a institutional framework for the financial sector. An important function of efficient regulation is to increase the amount of information available to the relevant parties. That comes in the form of disclosure laws, in particular, so that investors can adequately assess risk. Because of the large number of dispersed investors, a free rider problem may arise, and there is thus a need for centralized monitoring and regulation of financial institutions. Moreover, the government may increase the overall efficiency of the financial sector by competition policies, as in other sectors of the economic system.

The importance of the involvement of government for the financial sector is enhanced by the fact that the financial sector is strongly affected by the macroeconomic performance of the economy, and vice versa – problems in the financial sector may have detrimental effects on the rest of the economy.

The first issue leads to the simple observation that maintaining overall macroeconomic stability may decrease the cost of finance, expanding the volume of financial intermediation and leading to more investment and growth. A high inflation rate is typically associated with more variation and more risk with a detrimental effect on any long-term investments. Later in this chapter, we shall test the link between macroeconomic instability and finance cost empirically.

On the other hand, financial crises and the collapse of financial intermediation have a strong negative effect on economic activity – i.e. they may lead to recession and prolonged slump. For that reason, the government typically plays the role of the lender of last resort (LOLR), using deposit insurance and guarantee funds. However, such public insurance may again result in opportunistic behaviour (moral hazard). Insurance may decrease the monitoring effort by the ultimate providers of finance. It thus works only if some public agency offers an efficient replacement for monitoring, which leads us back to the issue of public regulation. The government needs to impose a system which minimises the risk of financial meltdown, in particular by imposing adequate reserves requirements on banks. However, while important, such reserve requirements, and other forms of 'financial repression', increase the cost of finance, as they lead to a larger wedge between the loan and the deposit rate (McKinnon 1993). This is a second theme we shall focus on in the empirical section.

Finance in the transition economies

The quality of financial market regulation correlates with the general level of economic development.[1] Djankov, McLiesh and Shleifer (2005) demonstrate a clear-cut link between the level of GDP *per capita* and the index of creditors' rights.[2] In the same paper, the authors also distinguish between five legal traditions: English, French, German, Nordic and Socialist. In the French and Nordic legal traditions, creditors' rights are protected less than in the English one. The comparison of the latter with both German and Socialist legal traditions is less clear-cut. It is interesting to note that the transition economies are not included in one legal tradition category. While all twelve CIS countries, for which the Communist period lasted for about seventy years, are included in the 'Socialist' legal tradition category, the remaining fifteen transition economies are not. In the latter group, the Communist system was imposed within the timespan of a few years after the Second Word War and lasted for about forty years. Even more importantly, it overlapped with only the few final years of the Stalinist era, when the process of eradication of market institutions was most radical. More importantly, all economies in the latter group (non-CIS) were able to reinstall their pre-1939 legal regulations, without the necessity of creating or importing their business law from abroad. That gave them a clear advantage in terms of financial markets regulation and meant that they could introduce more advanced reforms faster. In the empirical section, we shall examine the differences between both groups; before that, however, it is worthwhile making few comments on the appropriate order of financial reforms.

Before transition, the banks merely executed the plan, and never exercized any monitoring or risk assessment role. Thus, at the beginning of the transition, the banks had to develop monitoring skills, build up information on their customers and learn how to assess risk. To complicate the task even further, the past performance of the clients was not relevant for the assessment of future performance, as firms were operating under a very different set of incentives, and different skills were rewarded (Chapter 1). Even if the banks had had long-term relationships with some firms, the nature of economic change made this past knowledge mostly redundant from the point of view of financial assessment. Neither was present performance a good indicator of future performance, due to the high level of economic instability. According to Colombo and Driffill (2003), initial imperfections in the credit financial market particularly affected three aspects of the transition processes:

- Restructuring of the state-owned and privatized companies
- Growth of the new entrepreneurial firms
- Privatizing those companies – i.e. pricing the firms and channelling the demand for assets.

We have already discussed the first two issues in the context of the explanation of 'transitional recessions' (Chapter 6). The third was discussed in Chapter 4.[3]

The theme we focus on in this chapter is the *policy trade-off* between expanding finance (which may facilitate both restructuring and expansion of the new sector) and minimizing the risk of financial crisis, likely when the pace of financial liberalization is faster than the related creation of a regulatory environment. This issue is discussed in detail in a seminal book by McKinnon (1993: first edn, 1991; see also his 1992 paper) and while there is no no need to reproduce the whole argument, the main line of reasoning is worth bearing in mind.

McKinnon (1992, 1993) draws attention to the *interdependence* between financial sector reforms, macroeconomic stabilization and privatization. He argues that there is an *appropriate order* of financial liberalization, and that more advanced steps should not be implemented before the previous ones are in place. This is not necessarily an argument for gradualism and sequencing. Subsequent elements can be introduced faster or even contemporaneously, as long as we are sure that the most fundamental elements are already in place.

The first issue to note is that *macroeconomic stabilization* is a fundamental prerequisite, a necessary condition for both financial and fiscal reform. Persistent high inflation may result in a high real cost of credit (see p. 152). McKinnon (1993) argues that, in turn, the high cost of credit provides a strong motivation for the government to subsidize enterprises. The financial source comes typically in the form of an inflation tax (imposed on the banking sector in particular) and a vicious circle of 'non-reform' is created. That leads us naturally to the reform of *government finances* (both removal of 'soft' budgeting and tax reform) as a second necessary condition for a sustainable expansion of the financial sector and macroeconomic stabilization.

In the sequencing of bank reforms McKinnon (1993) accentuates the role of *positive real interest rates* triggered by their early liberalization, and argues that an initial high relative cost of finance may be less harmful than it appears, as long as high lending rates are accompanied by an increase in deposit rates. The first argument is that much of enterprise finance for development relies on retained earnings, which are deposited within the banking sector; positive rates on deposit therefore play a critical role in encouraging financial accumulation in successful companies. Second, high deposit rates are instrumental in rebuilding domestic savings, and increasing the supply of credit for good projects.

McKinnon (1993) argues that high lending rates and a large spread between lending and deposit interest rates in the early period of reform may be a necessary price to pay for the preservation of financial system stability. If moral hazard in bank lending is significant (so that past loans are not repaid), it is better to force banks to create reserves to protect against bad debts and impose a regulatory regime which will increase the cost and supply of credit than to risk financial meltdown.

However, while an efficient regulatory regime may arrest the development of bad debts and prevent banking crises, it cannot by itself guarantee that the process of financial intermediation is efficient. For the latter, both the objective function of the financial institutions and their technical capacities have to change. Adequate privatization may result in the objectives of the banks becoming consistent with economic efficiency and may provide the know-how, human capital and managerial skills and resources for investment. The most realistic opportunity for such investment relates to the inflow of foreign capital and the takeover of banks by foreign owners. Fries, Neven and Seabright (2004) demonstrate that the foreign-owned banks initially had a cost advantage in the transition, albeit the effect vanished in the latter stages, possibly due to spillover learning effects. Yet, privatization must be accompanied by a competition policy, which is again particularly important to ensure the critical effect of positive deposit rates.

Empirical analysis

Transition economies in comparative perspective

Gros and Steinherr (2004)[4] compare the transition economies with other countries, using a 1997 cross-section of countries. Their methodology relies on regressing an indicator of interest on GDP *per capita*, GDP *per capita*^{2} and dummies representing three subgroups of the transition economies: twelve CIS countries, eight economies that joined the EU in 2004 (CE8) and the remaining group of transition economies, all in South Eastern Europe (SEE, the Balkans). They report results for the following three financial indicators:

(1) *The ratio of broad money (M2) to GDP.* This indicator approximates the size of the banking sector. The results are that the dummy for the CIS is negative and significant; for the CE8, it is negative and insignificant.

(2) *Credit to the private sector as a percentage of GDP.* This is the same measure as used by Djankov, McLiesh and Shleifer (2005). It may be a better measure of the financial sector as it excludes the financing of the government, which adds nothing to the task of financial intermediation. On the other hand, it does not distinguish between two effects: the size of the financial sector and the size of the private sector.The results were that all three groups of transition countries were significantly different from comparator countries in 1997.

(3) *The spread between lending and deposit rates,* an indicator which measures the efficiency of the financial system (a high spread may be caused by monopolistic banking structures, but also by an unstable macroeconomic environment and high inflation (see McKinnon 1993). The results are that the CIS dummy is highly significant, and the dummies for the two other groups are insignificant, due to a large variation within those groups. In particular, Hungary was identified as a positive outlier.

The results of a similar exercise based on more recent data with a slight variation in methodology are reported in Tables 8A.1–8A.3 (pp. 154–6). Instead of one-year cross-sections, all estimations are based on 1998–2002 five-year averages, to suppress the econometric 'noise' attributed to annual variation linked to changes in macroeconomic parameters. The non-linear GDP *per capita* variable is estimated using both two-term quadratic approximation (apart from the interest-spread regression, where the non-linear term was highly insignificant and therefore dropped) and one-term logarithmic transformation.

The 1997 groupings of transition economies (CIS, CE8, remaining SEE) is no longer adequate in the subsequent period. In general, we face further polarization of the transition economies. Out of the residual group, two more economies are likely to join the EU in 2007–8 (Bulgaria and Romania), which reflects the advanced level of reform and adjustment in the more recent period. Similarly, Croatia is advanced in its reforms, and at the time of writing the EU accession negotiations had not started, for political reasons. Thus, the SEE group shrinks once Bulgaria, Romania and Croatia are moved to a 'new and prospective EU' group. In addition, reforms are progressing in the other Balkan countries.

We asked two questions: (1) Is the group of transition countries as a whole still distinguishable from the rest of the world in terms of finance; (2) How much of this result is driven by the results of the CIS group?

From Table 8A.1 we may see that with respect to private credit, the answer to question (1) is 'yes', and the answer to question (2) is ambiguous. With CIS dummy not included, the transition dummy is clearly highly significant – the size of private financing still remains significantly lower in the transition economies than in the comparator countries, after about ten years of transition. On the other hand, the result for the CIS is sensitive to the way the GDP *per capita* variable is modelled. When quadratic approximation is used (as in Gros and Steinherr 2004), the CIS effect clearly dominates over the transition effect, rendering the latter insignificant (Table 8A.1, (8)). With logarithmic approximation, the difference between the CIS and the rest of the group is less clear-cut, albeit the size of the financial sector appears still smaller in the CIS.

The CIS effect is strong when M2 is used as a proxy for the size of the financial sector. It dominates over any transition dummy effect, in both logarithmic and quadratic approximation, albeit in the second case the transition effect is still significant, even if the difference between the CIS and non-CIS transition economies is about ten times larger then the difference between the latter and the comparator group.

Finally, in Table 8A.3, we have a different result. For both versions of GDP *per capita* approximations, the effects for the non-CIS transition economies have a different sign than for the CIS economies. For the first group, the financial system seems more efficient than for the comparator group! This is obviously an optimistic result.

Combining the results on the size and efficiency of the financial sector, we may say the following: after ten years of reforms, the transition economies have not had sufficient time to build a sufficiently wide financial sector. However, in those economies which were more successful in their reforms in terms of the efficiency of the financial sector, the results were already better than for a comparator group of countries with similar level of GDP *per capita*. Quality turned out to be easier to achieve than quantity.[5]

The differences between the CIS and other transition economies in their financial systems are consistent with the analysis offered by Berglof and Bolton (2002), who offer more detail on differences in financial systems, and discuss the possible factors that could affect what they label as 'the great divide'. Interestingly, one of the key points they make concerns the link between the likelihood of reforms and the different political balance of power within these economies, an issue to which we intend to return in Chapter 9.

Determinants of financial characteristics: dynamic panel specification

After establishing results on the differences between the transition countries and others, our next step is to investigate the links between the reforms, the macroeconomic environment and our proxies of size and efficiency of the financial system. The design of the model is driven by the intuitions derived from the discussion on pp. 146–8.

First, we expect that both macroeconomic instability and lax public finance may exert a negative impact on the financial sector. We approximate the former by the inflation rate and the latter by the government balance (expecting a negative sign of the coefficient).

Secondly, following McKinnon (1993), we expect that the initial 'hardening' of the budget constraint may be accompanied by 'financial repression' – higher interest rates, higher reserve requirements and other measures that may lead to a shrinkage in the volume of credit and finance. Again, however, following the appropriate order of financial liberalization, the effect should be temporary and after establishing some rudimentary financial control, the expansion of finance may again follow. As in the previous chapters, our primary proxy of this initial financial 'hardening' is the EBRD liberalization index, which includes measures of the 'soft' budget control.

Thirdly, the structural reforms in the banking system should be expected to bring positive results. A better corporate governance legal framework should result in lower agency problems and lead to an increase in supply of finance. The proxies are the EBRD indicators for 'Bank reform' and 'Governance and enterprise restructuring'. In addition, EBRD data permits us to investigate the impact of both the ownership composition of the banking sector and the number of banks operating in a given economy. The latter may be used as an (imperfect) proxy for competition in the banking sector. The measure is very crude – as, for instance, a situation with one dominant bank and large number of very small banks is clearly not equivalent to a competitive structure – however, we have no better indicator. Regarding ownership, the share of the state sector in the banking sector may be a proxy for less advanced reforms associated with a smaller size of financial sector. The opposite may be true in relation to the share of foreign banks. Finally, we expect the number of banks to be positively related to the size of the financial sector, albeit the relationship may be non-linear: a very large number of small banks may be an indicator of lax regulations, with counter-productive effects on the financial system.

In addition to the variables discussed above, in the models of the size of the financial sector (private credit/GDP ratio and M2 over GDP), we control for the size of GDP, to take into account the same effects as those estimated in the previous section. For the interest rate spread, GDP growth rate may be a more appropriate control variable (we tried GDP level as an alternative, with no impact on results). In addition, the EBRD publishes the estimates of the private sector share in GDP. This is convenient, as we may control directly for the obvious effect on private credit of the size of private sector.

To our best knowledge, the only empirical study which could offer us empirical guidance is Fries and Taci (2002). The authors estimate the growth of credit offered by banks, using a combination of economy-level characteristics and individual bank characteristics. Fries and Taci (2002) estimate separate models for high-reform and low-reform economies. The results are stronger for the first group and the impact of economy-level variables dominates. GDP growth is associated with the expansion of credit and the budget deficit and inflation have the opposite effect. For low-reform countries, only the negative effect of inflation is significant.

We use the same method as in Chapter 7, i.e. the Arrelano–Bond GMM dynamic panel estimator; see the methodological discussion there. All data are taken from World Bank, *World Development Indicators* 2004 and EBRD *Transition Reports* 1995–2005, supplemented by Falcetti, Raiser and Sanfey (2002) in regard to reform indicators.

The results are presented in Tables 8B.1(p. 157)((25)–(26); determinants of private credit), 8B.2 (pp. 157–8) ((27)–(28); determinants of interest rate spread) and 8B.3 (p. 158) ((29)–(31) determinants of broad money). Where alternative models are presented, the differences result from slight variations in lag structure and/or dropping insignificant variables to explore robustness. The only difference is in regard to the determinants of broad money, where possible strong multicollinearity makes the choice of variables ambiguous, and different combinations of indicators of reforms are presented.

For the determinants of private credit, we obtained the following results. Not surprisingly, both the size of GDP and the size of the private sector in GDP are positive and significant. The impact of the government balance on the size of the financial sector is significant and positive, as expected (Table 8B.1 (26)). Inflation has a negative impact, again as expected, but the coefficient is insignificant. Generally, we are able to confirm our initial intuitions regarding the negative influence of macroeconomic instability on the size of finance.

An interesting pattern emerges in relation to reform. Price liberalization (which may also serve as a proxy for the cluster of most fundamental reforms) has a mild immediate negative impact on the volume of credit. This effect is more than counterbalanced by the far stronger positive influence that comes with a one-year delay.[6] Interestingly, a similar pattern appears with relation to the EBRD measure of bank reforms and interest rate liberalization. As described by McKinnon (1993), interest rate liberalization leads to an initial restriction in credit, as lending rates adjust up to higher levels, which are positive in real terms. Later on, there is a weak positive response of credit to reforms, but it is not significant.

The results relating to private credit are corroborated by estimates of broad money (M2). The macroeconomic variables turn out to be highly insignificant and the corresponding specifications are not reported. On the other hand, we find again the J-curve-type response to reform. Price liberalization, which includes elimination of state procurement at non-market prices, affects broad money first negatively and then positively with a one-year lag. Both effects remain highly significant. On the other hand, the impact of banking reforms seems dominated by an 'enterprise reform' indicator, which measures improvement in corporate governance framework and elimination of 'soft' budgeting at the enterprise level. There is a clear-cut positive and significant effect, which appears with a one-year lag. The result implies that legal framework which alleviates agency problems is conducive to the expansion of the financial sector.

In addition, in Table 8B.3 (29), we introduce both the share of the state sector in total bank assets and the number of banks (in natural logarithms) – two direct measures of structural change available from the EBRD. The share of the state sector has a negative impact on the size of the financial sector, but the coefficient is marginally insignificant. The number of banks is positively associated with the size of the financial sector, but the impact is non-linear – i.e. when the number of banks grows, the marginal effects becomes negligible.[7]

Finally, we estimated the determinants of interest rate spread, which may be seen as a proxy for banking sector efficiency. Here, faster GDP growth is associated with a lower spread, but the effect is marginally insignificant. On the other hand, inflation is clearly associated with a wider spread – i.e. it leads to lower efficiency of financial intermediation.

The impact of reforms is as follows: again, the basic reforms captured by the price liberalization indicator seem to result in a J-curve-type response. Initial shrinkage of the financial sector is followed by a subsequent expansion of credit. On the other hand, bank sector reform and interest rate liberalization have an immediate effect in driving the interest rate spread down. Moreover, the effect is spread over a one-year lag, with a smaller but significant coefficient.

Conclusion

Our empirical results seem to be consistent with the intuitions offered by McKinnon's (1993) seminal book on the appropriate order of economic liberalization. As with so many other transition phenomena, we observe a J-curve-type response of the volume of credit to reforms. Successful reforms lead to an initial tightening, necessary to overcome the inherited 'soft' budget constraint. This is followed, however, by an expansion of credit.

An important additional detail is that it is not only liberalization, including interest rate liberalization, which matters. One of our results is that the enterprise reforms and corporate governance framework have a positive effect on the finance sector. The latter implies the need to alleviate the agency problems between the providers of finance and enterprises. The link between corporate governance and finance is close.

In line with McKinnon's (1993) argument, macroeconomic destabilization and a government budget deficit have detrimental effects on the financial sector.

And, finally, bank reforms have an unambiguous negative effect on the interest rate spread, increasing the efficiency of the banking sector.

Appendix A   Estimation results: differences between transition economies and others

Table 8A.1 Differences between transition economies and others, dependent variable: ratio of private credit to GDP[a, d, e, i]

	(1)	(2)	(3)	(4)
ln of GDP *per capita*	19.2[c]***	18.9***	18.8***	18.8***
	(1.4)[b]	(1.3)	(1.4)	(1.3)
Transition dummy[f]		−17.5***		−16.7*
		(5.3)		(8.0)
CIS dummy[g]			−16.9***	−2.0
			(4.7)	(9.2)
Constant	−102.0***	−96.4***	−97.7*	−96.2***
	(9.5)	(8.9)	(9.5)	(9.2)
F-statistics	201.6***	105.8***	106.0***	74.4***
R^2	0.56	0.59	0.59	0.59
N	172	172	172	172

	(5)	(6)	(7)	(8)
GDP *per capita*	0.005***	0.005***	0.005***	0.005***
	(0.001)	(0.001)	(0.001)	(0.001)
Square of	-6×10^{-8}***	-6×10^{-8}***	-6×10^{-8}***	-6×10^{-8}***
GDP *per capita*[h]	(1×10^{-8})	(1×10^{-8})	(1×10^{-8})	(1×10^{-8})
Transition dummy		−10.0*		−5.1
		(4.9)		(7.3)
CIS dummy			−17.1***	−12.7†
			(2.7)	(7.4)
Constant	20.4***	22.5***	22.1***	22.7***
	(2.2)	(2.3)	(2.4)	(2.4)
F-statistics	88.6***	58.8***	94.3***	70.7***
R^2	0.58	0.58	0.59	0.59
N	172	172	172	172

Notes:

[a] Estimator: OLS regression.

[b] Robust standard errors (based on the Huber–White estimate of variance) in parentheses.

[c] *** significant at 0.001; ** significant at 0.01; * significant at 0.05; † significant at 0.1.

[d] Data source: World Bank, *World Development Indicators* 2004.

[e] All variables are averages for 1998–2002. Where some annual observations were missing, the averages are computed for available data points.

[f] *Transition dummy*: Twenty seven post-Communist countries in Europe and Central Asia plus Mongolia, China and Vietnam. Please note that for the two remaining Communist economies (Cuba and North Korea) data is missing, and therefore they are not included in estimations.

[g] *CIS dummy*: Twelve former Soviet republics that are members of the CIS. The dummy may be interpreted as a proxy for the time spent under Communism; for the CIS countries, it is approximately seventy years (including the Stalinist period), while for all other transition economies (TE) it is approximately forty years. For the CIS economies, both TE and CIS dummies take value of one, therefore in equations where both are included, the CIS coefficient corresponds to the difference in comparison with other TE.

[h] *GDP per capita*: In constant 1995 US dollars.

[i] *Ratio of private credit to GDP*: Non-equity financial resources provided to the private sector as a percentage of GDP.

Table 8A.2 Differences between transition economies and others, dependent variable: interest rate spread (lending minus deposit)[a, d, e, i]

	(9)	(10)	(11)	(12)
Ln of GDP *per capita*	–2.1[c]***	–2.1***	–1.9***	–1.9***
	(0.3)[b]	(0.3)	(0.3)	(0.3)
Transition dummy[f]		1.2		–2.0†
		(1.5)		(1.1)
CIS dummy[g]			7.4**	9.2***
			(2.4)	(2.5)
Constant	25.6***	25.1***	23.3***	23.6***
	(2.4)	(2.4)	(2.4)	(2.4)
F-statistics	53.6***	27.1***	30.7***	21.8***
R^2	0.20	0.20	0.25	0.26
N	144	144	144	144

	(13)	(14)	(15)	(16)
GDP *per capita*[h]	–0.0002***	–0.0002***	–0.0002***	–0.002***
	(0.0000)	(0.0000)	(0.0000)	(0.000)
Transition dummy		1.0		–2.9*
		(1.6)		(1.2)
CIS dummy			8.4***	10.9***
			(2.3)	(2.4)
Constant	11.1***	10.8***	10.3***	10.8***
	(0.7)	(0.8)	(0.7)	(0.8)
F-statistics	64.7***	33.0***	43.2***	28.4***
R^2	0.14	0.14	0.22	0.23
N	144	144	144	144

Notes:

[a] Estimator: OLS regression.

[b] Robust standard errors (based on the Huber–White estimate of variance) in parentheses.

[c] *** significant at 0.001; ** significant at 0.01; * significant at 0.05; † significant at 0.1.

[d] Data source: *World Bank, World Development Indicators* 2004.

[e] All variables are averages for 1998–2002. Where some annual observations were missing, the averages computed for available data points.

[f] *Transition dummy*: Twenty-seven post-Communist countries in Europe and Central Asia plus Mongolia, China and Vietnam. Please note that for the two remaining Communist economies (Cuba and North Korea) data is missing, therefore they are not included in estimations.

[g] *CIS dummy*: Twelve former Soviet republics that are members of the CIS. The dummy may be interpreted as a proxy for time spent under Communism; for the CIS countries, it is approximately seventy years (including the Stalinist period), while for all other transition economies (TE) it is approximately forty years. For the CIS economies, both TE and CIS dummies take value of one, therefore in equations where both are included, the CIS coefficient corresponds to the difference in comparison with other TE.

[h] *GDP per capita*: In constant 1995 US dollars.

[i] *Interest rate spread*: Interest rate charged by banks on loans to prime customers minus the interest rate paid by commercial or similar banks on deposits.

Table 8A.3 Differences between transition economies and others, dependent variable: ratio of M2 to GDP[a, d, e, i]

	(17)	(18)	(19)	(20)
Ln of GDP per capita	13.7[c]*** (2.0)[b]	13.6*** (2.0)	13.1*** (2.0)	13.2*** (2.0)
Transition dummy[f]		−15.3** (5.7)		−8.9 (8.4)
CIS dummy[g]			−24.5*** (3.6)	−16.5† (8.8)
Constant	−54.5*** (13.9)	−51.0*** (13.4)	−48.4*** (14.0)	−48.3*** (14.0)
F-statistics	46.8***	24.2***	53.1***	35.4***
R^2	0.30	0.32	0.33	0.33
N	158	158	158	158

	(21)	(22)	(23)	(24)
GDP per capita[h]	0.005*** (0.001)	0.005*** (0.001)	0.005*** (0.001)	0.005*** (0.001)
Square of GDP per capita	-9×10^{-8}*** (3×10^{-8})	-9×10^{-8}*** (3×10^{-8})	-8×10^{-8}* (3×10^{-8})	-8×10^{-8}* (3×10^{-8})
Transition dummy		−10.9† (5.6)		−2.5* (8.0)
CIS dummy			−23.7*** (2.9)	−21.5** (8.1)
Constant	30.3*** (3.1)	32.5*** (3.2)	32.7*** (3.3)	33.0*** (3.2)
F-statistics	15.4***	10.8***	49.9***	37.2***
R^2	0.30	0.31	0.33	0.33
N	158	158	158	158

Notes:

[a] Estimator: OLS regression.

[b] Robust standard errors (based on the Huber–White estimate of variance) in parentheses.

[c] *** significant at 0.001; ** significant at 0.01; * significant at 0.05; † significant at 0.1.

[d] Data source: *World Bank, World Development Indicators* 2004.

[e] All variables are averages for 1998–2002. Where some annual observations were missing, the averages computed for available data points.

[f] *Transition dummy*: Twenty seven post-Communist countries in Europe and Central Asia plus Mongolia, China and Vietnam. Please note that for the two remaining Communist economies (Cuba and North Korea), data is missing, therefore they are not included in estimations.

[g] *CIS dummy*: Twelve former Soviet republics that are members of the CIS. The dummy may be interpreted as a proxy for time spent under Communism; for the CIS countries, it is approximately seventy years (including the Stalinist period), while for all other transition economies it is approximately forty years. For the CIS economies (TE), both TE and CIS dummies take value of one, therefore in equations where both are included, the CIS coefficient corresponds to the difference in comparison with other TE.

[h] *GDP per capita*: In constant 1995 US dollars.

[i] *M2–GDP ratio*: money and quasi-money as percentage of GDP.

Appendix B   Estimation results: private credit, interest rate spread and broad money

Table 8B.1   Determinants of private credit[a, b, d, g]

	(25)	(26)
Dependent variable		
1-year lag	0.71 (0.06)[f, h]***	.61 (.05)***
Natural logarithm of GDP	18.3 (4.96)***	19.7 (4.77)***
Inflation rate[c]	−0.001 (0.001)	−0.000 (0.001)
Share of private sector in GDP[e]	0.26 (0.09)**	0.26 (0.09)**
Price liberalization index	−1.45 (1.79)	−1.31 (1.81)*
1-year lag	7.21 (1.56)***	5.10 (1.51)***
Bank reform index	−5.55 (1.58)***	−3.87 (1.49)**
1-year lag	0.42 (1.38)	
Natural logarithm of number of banks	5.64 (1.69)***	
Government balance as % of GDP		0.20 (0.09)*
Constant	−2.57 (5.38)	−6.90 (4.59)
No. of observations	191	198
Second-order autocorrelation: z	−1.17	−1.00
Sargan test for over-identifying restrictions: χ^2	91.14	102.74

Notes:

[a] All variables in first differences. Estimator: Arellano–Bond one-step GMM. Unbalanced panel for twenty-seven transition economies, 1987–2002, using all available data points.

[b] Data sources: EBRD, *Transition Reports* 1995–2005; World Bank, *World Development Indicators* 2004.

[c] *Inflation*: GDP deflator (more observations available than for CPI).

[d] *Private credit*: Non-equity financial resources provided to the sector as percentage of GDP.

[e] *GDP*: In constant 1995 US dollars.

[f] Standard errors in parentheses.

[g] Time controls (annual dummies) included but not reported.

[h] *** significant at 0.001; ** significant at 0.01; * significant at 0.05.

Table 8B.2   Determinants of interest rate spread[a, b, d, f]

	(27)	(28)
Dependent variable		
1-year lag	0.16 (0.05)[e, g]**	0.16 (0.05)**
GDP growth rate	−1.20 (1.10)	
Inflation rate[c]	0.06 (0.02)**	0.07 (0.02)**
Price liberalization index	54.62 (24.79)*	55.56 (24.91)*
1-year lag	−21.52 (21.90)	−26.94 (21.45)
Bank reform index	−48.01 (21.54)*	−47.54 (21.66)*
1-year lag	−36.31 (19.86)†	−33.40 (19.97)†

158

Table 8B.2 (Continued)

	(27)	(28)
Constant	86.77 (75.59)	86.09 (76.02)
No. of observations	206	206
Second-order autocorrelation: z	0.12	0.03
Sargan test for over-identifying restrictions: χ^2	46.75	46.29

Notes:

[a] All variables in first differences. Estimator: Arellano–Bond one-step GMM. Unbalanced panel for twenty-seven transition economies, 1987–2002, using all available data points.

[b] Data sources: EBRD, *Transition Reports* 1995–2005; World Bank, *World Development Indicators* 2004.

[c] *Inflation:* GDP deflator (more observations available than for CPI).

[d] *Interest rate spread:* Interest rate charged by banks on loans to prime customers minus the interest raid paid by commercial or similar banks on deposits.

[e] Standard errors in parentheses.

[f] Time controls (annual dummies) included but not reported.

[g] *** significant at 0.001; ** significant at 0.01; * significant at 0.05; † significant at 0.1.

Table 8B.3 Determinants of broad money[a, b, c, d, f, g]

	(29)	(30)	(31)
Dependent variable			
1-year lag	0.52 (0.06)[e]***	0.63 (0.05)***	0.63 (0.05)***
Natural logarithm of GDP	7.39 (4.68)	0.65 (4.70)	
Natural logarithm of number of banks	2.34 (1.26)†		
Share of state banks in total assets	–0.03 (0.02)		
Price liberalization index	–9.44 (1.49)***	–11.96 (1.59)***	–11.20 (1.58)***
1-year lag	6.32 (1.35)***	8.04 (1.36)***	7.67 (1.35)***
Enterprise reform index	–1.68 (1.36)	0.92 (1.55)	1.03 (1.53)
1-year lag	4.03 (1.11)***	2.14 (1.42)	2.38 (1.42)†
Bank reform index		0.07 (1.42)	0.04 (1.42)
1-year lag		1.76 (1.33)	1.78 (1.36)
Constant	–7.22 (3.61)*	–2.34 (1.20)†	–1.74 (1.08)
No. of observations	187	232	234
Second-order autocorrelation: z	0.25	–1.07	–0.93
Sargan test for over-identifying restrictions: χ^2	74.68	114.95	121.55

Notes:

[a] All variables in first differences. Estimator: Arellano–Bond one-step GMM. Unbalanced panel for twenty-seven transition economies, 1987–2002, using all available data points.

[b] Data sources: EBRD, *Transition Reports* 1995–2005; World Bank, *World Development Indicators*, 2004.

[c] *Inflation:* GDP deflator (more observations available than for CPI).

[d] *Broad money:* Money and quasi-money (M2) as percentage of GDP.

[e] Standard errors in parentheses.

[f] Time controls (annual dummies) included but not reported.

[g] *** significant at 0.001; ** significant at 0.01; * significant at 0.05; † significant at 0.1.

Notes

1. An important theme we do not follow up here is that imperfections in the financial markets have more impact on some specific industries, skill-intensive and R&D-intensive ones in particular. Recent evidence on this is provided by Carlin and Mayer (2003).
2. The creditors' rights index was first applied by La Porta *et al.* (1998).
3. One issue we leave aside is the second-best response to the under-developed financial sectors of internalizing financial markets – in particular, the creation of the internal 'credit markets' of the financial–industrial groups (Peroti and Gelfer 2001), but also finance within multinational structures (FDI): both provide new channels of finance and increase credibility, facilitating access to old ones (Isachenkova and Mickiewicz 2004).
4. See also the paper by Gros and Suhrcke (2000).
5. There is one minor technical point to comment on. For GDP, we tested and reported a logarithmic approximation in addition to the quadratic one used by Gros and Steinherr (2004). The latter turned out to be consistently better in distinguishing between the CIS and non-CIS transition economies. The reason seems to be that the quadratic approximation is more flexible in terms of mapping the distribution of variables (having two parameters instead of one), and may control better for the differences within the non-CIS group. If we consider the difference between new EU member states and some of the SEE economies, many in the latter group are in the lower-middle-income or even low-income group, while the new EU states are in the higher-middle-income group. Thus, while we do not control for reforms and have no additional dummy for SEE, the quadratic approximation of the GDP *per capita* variable is sufficient to differentiate between those two groups, resulting in higher significance.
6. Longer lag structures were attempted, but turned out to be insignificant. More importantly, the magnitude of the first-year negative effect should be treated with caution. It is likely to be inflated in a spurious way, consistently with the phenomenon discussed by Rzońca and Ciżkowicz (2003). See also our discussion in Chapter 10.
7. For all three dependent variables, the impact of the share of foreign banks turned out to be insignificant.

9
Democracy and Reform

This chapter discusses the link between democracy and reform.

We observe first that the gains from reforms may be unevenly distributed. That leads us to conclude that the democratic institutions within which the economic actors mediate may facilitate consensus and remove obstacles to reform. In addition to political democracy, the institutions of a civil society – free media, in particular – may have an important role to play. Low-cost access to information may help to alleviate economic policy capture by special interests.

We then go into more detail. We discuss key reforms, to see which of them are likely to affect both income distribution and special interests. This leads us to form expectations about the relative role of democracy in facilitating particular reforms.

We then test these expectations empirically and present the results, and finally draw some brief conclusions.

Preliminaries: transition as a welfare issue

Our intention here is to discuss the reforms from the point of view of political feasibility. What are the framework conditions that may facilitate reforms, stall them, or result in a policy reversal?

We need to recall a few basic notions. A more detailed discussion may be found in any advanced microeconomic text. Here, we draw from Varian (1992) and Gravelle and Rees (2004).

First, 'allocation' will denote a matrix which describes how much of each good produced in the economy is consumed by each consumer. When we simplify, assuming just one composite good (say, equivalent to real income), the allocations become vectors with the number of components representing the number of consumers. More importantly, to make a graphical illustration easier, we will consider two representative consumers (who are also voters) representing some two major socio-economic groups. From now on, feasible allocations will be denoted by $x^0, x^1, \ldots, x^n$.

After defining allocation, we recall the concept of Pareto-optimality (the Pareto-criterion), the fundamental measure of economic efficiency. An allocation x^* is said to be *Pareto-optimal* if there is no other feasible allocation x^0 which would be preferred by everybody to x^*. In other words, while some economic agents may be better off with a different allocation, it would never be preferred by everybody, so no change away from x^* could be achieved by unanimous voting. Also, in the case where there is an allocation x^*, which is preferred by everybody to x^1, we say that it is *Pareto-preferred*.

The Pareto optimality condition is perfectly rational, but weak. For instance, we may think about a move from the initial allocation x^0 to some allocation x^*, which could lead to a great benefit for a large number of economic agents, with the cost paid by a small number of people. Some of the reforms introduced as part of the transition programme may bear that characteristic. Still, the Pareto-criterion is too weak to distinguish between the two outcomes. Then, the interesting issues are: when can x^* be seen as 'superior' to x^0 in a broader sense (a welfare economics issue) and when may we expect a move from x^0 to x^* (a political economy issue)? The *compensation criterion* aims to answer the first question:

'x^1 is potentially Pareto preferred to x^0, if there is some way to reallocate x^1 so that everyone prefers the new reallocation (x^2) to the original allocation x^0. More formally: x^1 is potentially Pareto preferred to x^0, if there is some allocation x^2, with $\sum_{i=1}^{n} x_i^2 = \sum_{i=1}^{n} x_i^1$ (i.e. x^2 is a reallocation of x^1) such that $x_i^2 > x_i^0$ for all agents i.' (Varian 1992: 405)

The compensation principle is illustrated by Figure 9.1. Take allocation x^0 as a starting point. An economic reform results in a new allocation x^*. However, this is not acceptable for a representative consumer I: in terms of utility she is now worse off than at the beginning of the reforms. Now, curve F' represents a set of allocations that all amount to the same aggregate output as x^*. This curve is called a *utility possibility frontier*[1]. If we can modify the post-reform allocation x^* to compensate the losers, without output loss, we arrive at a point such as x^1, which makes everybody better off as compared with the pre-reform situation.

However, there is one problem with the compensation criterion. Defining the *utility possibility frontier* is not the same thing as assuming that movement *along* the frontier is feasible. The criterion has practical relevance only if we can use some non-distortionary and costless taxation to redistribute – i.e. to move between the points on the frontier. However, 'the first rule of public finance' tells us that 'there is no such thing as a lump-sum tax' (Gravelle and Rees 2004: 303). Thus, to make the framework more realistic, we have

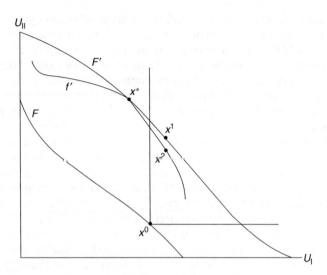

Figure 9.1 Welfare gains from reforms and redistribution

to complement the utility possibility frontier with a '*utility feasibility frontier* showing the utility combinations achievable from the original endowments by varying the level of non-lump-sum transfers' (2004: 304). This is shown as curve f' on Figure 7.1. Here, the reforms followed (accompanied) by compensation (redistribution) result in a move from x^0 to x^* and then to x^2, as the move to x^1 is not feasible due to the deadweight loss resulting from fiscal intervention.

Thus, we may think of transitional reforms as a move from one economic allocation to another. Allocation x^0 corresponds to the old economic regime, and allocation x^1 and the utility feasibility frontier associated with it relates to the post-reform situation. The ideal case of non-controversial reform, with no need for compensation, would correspond to a direct move from x^0 to x^1. While, theoretically, reforms benefiting everybody are possible, in reality it is unlikely that there will be no losers. We will explore why in the next section. The losers, denoted by agent I may not be a large economic group, but a minority. However, if that minority is strong enough to block the reform (as it represents some embedded special interests), a possibility to negotiate compensation (subsequent move from x^* to x^2) becomes a critical issue. Moreover, it is more realistic to see transition as a cluster of reforms, each of them modifying the economic regime with different allocational shifts. In each case, a different group of economic actors is affected and different compensational issues may arise. This leads to the interesting possibility that the allocational effects of some reforms may balance each other, alleviating the need for *ex post* compensation. For instance, it is likely that, for the low-income households, the gains from price liberalization may be lower. However, at least part of that group may be compensated with a particular design of the privatization scheme, where either workers in low-wage occupations (typically, low-capital-intensive branches of industry and services) or the population at large (voucher privatization) are given shares in the privatized companies. A more general example relates to reforms that may result in unemployment being accompanied by the introduction of a social safety net system.

Compensation schemes may be difficult to negotiate and prepare. This argument may lead to the conclusion that, from the political economy point of view, as much as possible should be done immediately during the first move (say from x^0 to x^* on Figure 9.1), leaving the subsequent reallocation to be sorted out later (a move from x^* to x^2). That eliminates the risk that the transition process stalls before the start. The problem with this argument is its reliance on the assumption that voters are myopic. If not then, expecting problems with compensation (the high transaction cost of negotiating the subsequent move from x^* to x^2), they may block the reforms in the first place (see Roland 2000, for a theoretical modelling of this issue). Alternatively, this becomes an argument against democracy. In this latter version, the initial reform decisions should be taken by a group of technocrats and more democratic procedures allowed only after the move from x^0 to x^*.

Is there a contradiction between democracy and the speed of reforms? Not necessarily. The transaction costs of negotiating appropriate compensation may imply that the latter may be a time consuming-task. On the other hand, given the unravelling crisis of the old regime (see Chapter 1), the costs of postponing the reforms may also be high. In this respect, acceptance of fast and far-reaching reforms may crucially depend on the expectation that the appropriate compensating transfers can be negotiated later via democratic institutions. Thus, even if voters accept that the initial reforms will be implemented by knowledgeable technocrats, it may only be because the voters do not expect the technocrats to retain power later. If true, the hypothesis implies that democratic institutions will facilitate the reforms, because they facilitate negotiating and correcting the allocational outcomes after the implementation of the reforms.[2]

We may extend the argument by referring to the Coase theorem (Coase 1960). This says that the efficient allocation of resources is always achieved if it is possible to carry out negotiations at little or no cost. In the course of the negotiations, the relevant parties will take proper account of the effects on all other parties of moving from one allocation of resources to another (from one economic regime to another). The outcome will be efficient, regardless of which party is endowed with the right to block the change (i.e. with property rights).

However, the cost of the negotiations will be small only if the mediating institutions are efficient, the number of well-identified parties is small, full information is available and it is feasible to create a credible contract between the parties. In the context of reforms, we can relate all those characteristics to a developed and well-functioning political system. In the CEE countries, the initial conditions differed in this respect. Some of these countries inherited elements of a civic society which could be developed to represent a variety of interests and ideas. In others, the totalitarian regimes had a far more radical atomizing impact. From this point of view, the fault line may be between (1) Central and South East Europe and the three Baltic states, and (2) the other former republics of the USSR. The latter group came through a far longer period of demolition of civic and democratic institutions, in particular during the long reign of terror under Stalin. In that group, at the onset of transition, there was no generation of an active age with a memory of any kind of alternative political system.

While democratic institutions and political freedom in general may facilitate mediation and therefore make reforms easier, it is not necessarily the case that democracy will always result in efficient outcomes. One important characteristic of the political process, which is associated with lower efficiency, is its susceptibility to *special interests* – i.e. issues that generate substantial individual benefit to a small minority while imposing a small average cost on all other voters. In total, the cost to the majority may exceed the net benefits to the special interest group. However, each member of the majority has no interest in becoming active, while the members of the minority group have such an interest. The special interests problem is typically more acute because of the 'rational political ignorance' effect (Tullock 1967). This relates to the fact that most citizens recognize that their vote is unlikely to determine the outcome of an election. As a result, the citizens have little incentive to seek costly information that will help them cast an intelligent vote. This attitude leaves an opportunity for special interest issues.

Seen from this perspective, it is not only the formal institutions of democracy, but also the availability of low-cost information, which becomes critical. Even if individual voters are not sufficiently motivated to acquire knowledge on all relevant issues, the free, independent and diversified media may play a pivotal role in making the voters more adequately informed, and limiting government capture by special interests. Free and independent media are thus not only the key element of civil liberties, but also a necessary condition for the adequate functioning of the formal institutions of democracy.

For different reforms, the distribution of (relative) losers and winners will vary. The negatively affected minorities may differ considerably with respect to their bargaining power. Compensation schemes may be easy to design in some cases and difficult in others. In the next section, we shall focus on the effects of liberalization, distinguishing between different markets and different sets of winners and losers. Which reforms are more likely to be blocked? In which cases will the role of mediating institutions be most critical?

Liberalization: winners and losers

Internal and external liberalization

We shall organize the analysis of reforms around the four simple models of internal and external liberalization adapted from Gros and Steinherr (1995: 115–17) with some minor modifications. Their analysis is mostly in terms of welfare effects. Building on their work directly, we extend the discussion towards *political economy* issues.

In all the examples below, we shall rely on consumer surplus and producer surplus as measures of welfare. These are approximations based on simplifying assumptions. Nevertheless, they are widely used. Their advantage is that via demand and supply they can be linked to empirical research (assuming that we can overcome the standard identification problems for simultaneous equations in demand and supply systems).

If $x(p)$ is the demand for some good as a function of its price (illustrated in a standard Marshallian way, with price on the vertical axis and quantity on the horizontal axis), then the gain in *consumers' surplus* associated with a price decrease from p_0 to p_1 is equivalent to the area left of the demand curve between p_0 and p_1. However, the consumer surplus is a precise measure of welfare change only when the consumer preferences in the p_0 and p_1 range can be approximated by a quasi-linear utility function, $u(p, m) = u(p) + m$, where m relates to income. This functional form implies that there is no interaction between the effects of price change on utility and the effects of income on utility. In particular, the income effect of price change is zero. In other words, it is useful to bear in mind that consumer surplus becomes a poor analytical tool when we analyze the price changes in a product where demand is sensitive to income (Varian 1992: 164–6).

Similarly, if we have a supply (marginal cost) curve as a function of price (again drawn in a traditional Marshallian way), and the price increases from p_0 to p_1, then the area to the left of the supply curve between p_0 and p_1 can be interpreted as an increase in *producers' surplus*.

Figures 9.2–9.5 (pp. 165–73) describe four cases of price liberalization. Each differs in the characteristics of supply, demand, degree of potential integration with the world market and the nature of initial administrative intervention.

Figure 9.2 illustrates the first, most fundamental case of a representative consumer product market characterized by disequilibrium and shortages. This first model also assumes that the net effect of opening the market to international competition is relatively small and does not affect the main conclusions. We also assume that the domestic supply is price elastic.

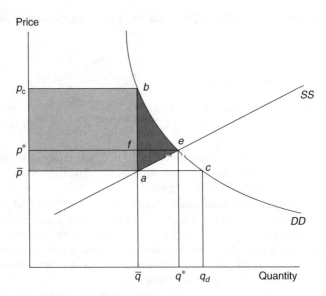

Figure 9.2 Disequilibrium and shortages

Initially, the administrative price is set at $\bar{p}$, and the corresponding supply is $\bar{q}$. There is excess demand ac, given by the section of the price line $\bar{p}$ between the supply curve SS (i.e to the right of the vertical $\bar{q}$ line) and the demand curve DD (point c).

Given the administratively set level of supply $\bar{q}$, removal of price controls alone will result in a jump in market price to p_c, driving demand back from q_d to $\bar{q}$. However, with price controls, goods are not allocated via the price mechanism. In that void, some other means of competition between buyers is needed to re-establish the match between their claims on the product and restricted supply – i.e. decide the final distribution, eliminating the excess demand by adjusting it to $\bar{q}$. The simplest and most common example of such a mechanism is *queuing*. Each consumer pays an additional time cost, which drives up the real consumer price from $\bar{p}$ to p_c. Thus, the real price paid by consumers consists of two components: (1) $\bar{p}$, which is the monetary, nominal price paid for the product plus (2) disequilibrium deadweight cost, which may have both a monetary and a non-monetary component. In the case of queuing, the cost corresponds to the opportunity cost of time lost by consumers. However, it may have some additional components. Time cost may relate not only to queuing, but also to *market search*. The monetary component may reappear in the case of corruption, where scarce products are first acquired by those with privileged access (members of a Communist *nomenklatura*, employees of the retail trade), who realize economic rents by reselling above the official price. In the latter case, the difference between p_c and $\bar{p}$ may come with lower deadweight cost, the latter being replaced by a transfer of income from one group of economic agents to another. However, before concluding that privileged access and resale is economically more efficient than queuing and search, one has also to take into account both the transaction costs, which are likely to be high in the case of resale, and also the negative external effects of corruption. Corruption, while providing some form of allocation mechanism (a popular saying under the command economy was 'corruption is the human face of socialism'), comes with a strong negative external cost: the heritage of the social attitudes developed under Communism is still haunting Central and Eastern Europe.

Full liberalization amounts to the removal of controls over price and production decisions. Ultimately, supply and demand adjust to the market equilibrium point given by *e*. Both consumers and producers gain. Consumers gain from saving on disequilibrium costs (the area p^*fbp_c) and from the net value of additional consumption (*feb*). Producers gain from higher prices (the area $\bar{p}afp^*$) and from the surplus generated from increased production (*aef*). The net welfare gain of both groups of economic agents is given by the area: $\bar{p}aebp_c$. Within it, the area above the equilibrium price line represents the consumer gain; producer gain is shown below the equilibrium price line.

Thus, apparently, everybody gains from price liberalization and reforms should be greeted with overwhelming support. However, this conclusion hinges critically on the *homogeneity* of economic agents, consumers in particular.

First, the opportunity cost of time may differ. Those with a high income gain more from restoring equilibrium, while those with a lower income gain less. Therefore, liberalization has an element of redistribution built in, with an uneven impact on various economic groups. One important example relates to the retired. Their incomes are not work-related and their opportunity cost of time may be relatively low. For that very reason, one of the sad features of the command economy was that within households the oldest people had typically to 'specialize' in queuing. They were also the group unlikely to transform the time gained from eliminating disequilibria into some income-generating activity. This may partly explain why, in spite the protection of the real value of pensions, this group was particulary vocal against the reforms. In a more general perspective, the redistributional aspect of price liberalization implies that democratic institutions may have an important role to play in mediating the compensation mechanisms, including the introduction of a social safety net.

Second, the assessment of liberalization by consumers may be ambiguous, in spite of the welfare gains, if the initial low price ($\bar{p}$) is perceived as equivalent to claims on government. We discussed that issue in Chapter 1, describing the prisoners' dilemma resulting in a reform stalemate during the last period of the command economy. Increasing the price to a market equilibrium level does not decrease real incomes as it replaces non-monetary disequilibrium cost by its (lower!) monetary equivalent. In addition, there are gains from increased supply. The situation differs, however, if there is an expectation that the market could be equalized at the initial price $\bar{p}$. The problem is that with informational asymmetry between the consumers and policy-makers, consumers may not be sure if the new equilibrium price does not contain a hidden element of taxation (resulting in some unwanted redistribution of income), so that price adjustment is used as an opportunity to suppress real incomes. From this point of view, both civil liberties (in particular, the freedom of the media) and political freedom are important. Here, the issue of concern is not redistribution between some income-defined social groups (poor versus rich), but rather between those who may benefit from being close to the power centre (old *nomenklatura*) and those who may not. Because of the nature of the distribution under the old regime, this second classification will only partly overlap with income distribution. For a similar reason, the reforms were more credible when they were introduced by policy-makers not perceived as linked to the old regime.

With Figure 9.3, we extend the analysis to *external liberalization*. We have a tradable good. This time, the initial administrative price ($\bar{p}$) is not below but above the equilibrium level (the world market price). For simplicity, we assume that no imports are allowed initially (a more general intermediate case with tariff barriers and some imports is discussed in most trade and/or public finance texts; see, for instance, Cullis and Jones 1992). When imports are liberalized, the price decreases to p^* and consumption expands. Both effects result in consumers' gain (represented by the area $\bar{p}aep^*$). However, in

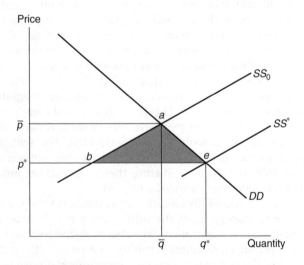

Figure 9.3 External liberalization

this case, the domestic producer loses: the market price is now lower and some domestic production is crowded out by imports; the producers' loss is represented by the area $p^*ba\bar{p}$. Comparing the two areas, we arrive at a net gain *abe*.

Here, the risk of blocking the reforms results from special interest problems. While aggregate consumer gain is substantial, it may be small *per capita*. A typical case, not unique to the transition economies, relates to agricultural products. The irony is that food prices are precisely those which have the strongest impact on the poorest stratum of consumers, for which food represents the most substantial share in their spending. The reintroduction/ preservation of import barriers for food was a typical effect of special interests at the beginning of the 1990s. Ironically, the net impact of liberalization of international exchange in agricultural products may well be positive. While some products may indeed face competition from abroad, for many others new export opportunities may dominate. Indeed, in mid-2004, when the old EU finally widened access for the agricultural production of the new members, it caused a positive average price effect on the domestic prices of food in the latter group, because of export opportunities.[3] However, the problem reaches far beyond agriculture, as will be discussed below.

In general, while (internal) price liberalization brings in partial adjustment, the full effects emerge only when prices move towards the world market level, which in turn is triggered by opening foreign trade and liberalizing exchange rates. Moreover, the effects of the removal of import barriers for consumer products works in the same direction as the removal of export barriers for producers of raw materials and energy, an effect which is discussed in detail by McKinnon (1993).

Again, drawing from Gros and Steinherr (1995), we may now illustrate the liberalization of exports, focusing only on those welfare effects which are relevant from the political economy point of view, with the intention of finding out what special interests may possibly stall the reform process. We again face a product where the effect of external liberalization is important. However, contrary to Figure 9.3, the initial market price is below equilibrium. And, unlike Figure 9.2, the government is implicitly subsidizing consumption by forcing producers to sell on the domestic market instead of exporting (Figure 9.4). Some energy-related products such as oil may be the most important illustration for this example. This is a tradable product, with domestic supply being inelastic in the short run and given by the vertical line $\bar{q}$.

Initially, the domestic price is below the equilibrium price, consumption is subsidized and domestic consumption has priority over exports. Producers are discouraged from exporting; instead they sell cheaply to domestic users of energy, due to some form of export restrictions. To simplify this example (without undermining our general conclusions), we assume that all domestic production is absorbed, leaving no room for exports. The initial level of consumption is thus $\bar{q}$.

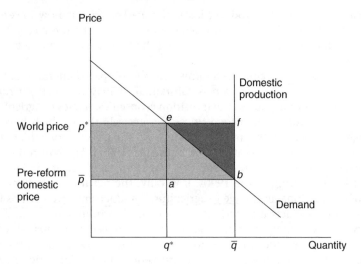

Figure 9.4   Subsidies to consumption

After liberalization, the domestic price adjusts to the world market level p^*. Domestic consumption falls to q^*, as domestic users of energy are forced to restructure and shift to new energy-saving technologies. The welfare outcome of liberalization is thus exactly opposite to the previous one: consumers lose and producers gain. Producers gain from new export opportunities and from higher world market prices amounting to $(\bar{q} - q^*)(p^* - \bar{p})$ and from higher domestic prices amounting to $q^* (p^* - \bar{p})$. On the other hand, the loss to domestic users of energy amounts to $\bar{p}bep^*$. Subtracting the latter from the former we arrive at the *net welfare gain*, which amounts to $efb = 1/2(\bar{q} - q^*)(p^* - \bar{p})$.

The political economy problem results from the fact that the users of energy may represent a strong special interest group. In an economy where cheap energy is a cornerstone of industrial policy, changes may be difficult to implement. The empirical example may come from Russia, a country particularly rich in energy resources, where increasing domestic consumption in the late Communist period systematically drove down exports (see also Chapter 1). At the beginning of the liberalization programme, full adjustment in energy price was blocked by the special interests of energy users. On the other hand, the producers of energy were also compensated with 'soft' tax regimes and a substantial share in the underpriced transfer of assets during the privatization period. Gros and Steinherr (1995) calculate the rough approximation of area *efb* – i.e. the welfare loss from maintaining low domestic prices of energy. Given the initial world market price premium of 150 per cent above the domestic price and the long-run price elasticity of demand of about 0.5, they arrive at a spectacular figure of loss, due to the low domestic price of energy and export controls, equivalent to 5 per cent–10 per cent of FSU GDP in 1990. The situation improved after 1990; nevertheless, the low energy price was the single most important price distortion under the old regime. As pointed out by McKinsey (1999), an additional negative effect was that efficient domestic users were hurt by the prevalence of non-payment among inefficient users. In the steel industry, the providers of energy resources had far more leverage over the large most efficient producers with a direct network connection and vulnerable to the threat of blocked supply. On the other hand, smaller, older-technology, less efficient producers were far less easy to control, and it was difficult to disentangle the provision of energy for them from the provision of heating for local housing.

The important point to note here is again that various components of the liberalization programme are *interdependent*. The change in relative energy prices is insufficient to trigger real adjustment if 'soft' budget channels are present. In fact, the prices of energy resources were to some degree adjusted during the 1990s towards the world market level, yet one could still detect two layers of subsidization, first of domestic producers and to a lesser degree of CIS recipients (Belarus, Kazakhstan, Ukraine). Both energy prices below the world market level and 'soft' budget channels via non-payment for energy imply that producers were forced to subsidize domestic consumption, and that their investment in both production facilities and transport infrastructure (critical for any increase in exports) suffered. The impact on industrial users of energy was that restructuring to increase energy efficiency slowed down. The comparison of the time paths of the use of energy and GDP shows that the former adjusted far less to production in Russia than in those transition economies that were most advanced in reforms.[4]

The difference between the relative domestic price of energy and the world market price was possibly the most important nominal distortion under the command economy. Adjustment towards world market prices made a significant share of industrial production far less profitable. Some of it could even emerge as value-substracting – i.e. where the cost of resources was higher than the value of final production. McKinnon (1993, ch. 12) provides a model which illustrates how price distortions may be maintained by both import and export restrictions. Both have a similar impact in a general equilibrium perspective. Liberalization leads to price adjustment and reveals that much industrial production may be value-subtracting unless it is restructured. Empirical estimates of the extent of value-subtracting activities at the starting point of the reforms are provided by Hughes and Hare (1992). They classify industries into four categories:

- Industries already in long-run competitive equilibrium (a ratio of value-added at domestic prices to that at world prices $\cong 1$)
- Very competitive branches at the global level (a ratio of value-added at domestic prices to that at world prices < 1). Those were branches

which were implicitly discriminated against under the command economy
- Branches protected from foreign competition (a ratio of value-added at domestic prices to that at world prices > 1)
- Value-subtracting branches (a ratio of value-added at domestic prices to that at world prices < 0, because the nominator is negative).

Hughes and Hare's (1992) estimates are reproduced in Table 9.1. Poland looks particularly good; however, that can be easily explained by the early start of the transition process there. In 1992, Poland was already in its third year of reforms, the Czech Republic was into its second year, while the timing for Hungary is more difficult to determine. Nevertheless, the clear outlier is the FSU group, when compared with the three CE countries mentioned above. In the FSU group, 1992 was the first year of reforms, and those were not fully implemented. Thus, comparing Poland with FSU, in a sense, we compare the pre-reform and post-(full) reform outcomes.

The indicators are based on average value-added in branches of industry. They may be misleading, as they do not tell us much about the potential for restructuring. In some industries classified as value-subtracting, the majority of companies may be just below the break-even point, in some others the exit and bankruptcies of many firms may be unavoidable. In addition, in some cases restructuring may be achieved with little investment, by reorientation of production on more value creation, in some other far more financial resources are needed. Comparing results for Poland and the two other Central European economies with those for the former Soviet Union may suggest that fast progress, achieved mostly by reallocation, without significant investment effort was possible. We will come back to this issue in Chapter 10.

We now discuss the final example of the liberalization effects, which focus more directly on the fiscal dimension (see Figure 7.5), with taxpayers as another group of economic agents affected by liberalization. This complements Figure 7.2, as another example where the focus is on internal liberalization,

Table 9.1 Industrial competitiveness, selected transition economies, 1992 (percentages)

	Czech Rep. Output	Czech Rep. Empl.	Hungary Output	Hungary Empl.	Poland Output	Poland Empl.	FSU Output	FSU Empl.
DRC < 1[a]	20.59	36.35	18.18	12.95	17.65	2.67	16.13	13.90
DRC > 2	26.47	22.39	18.18	13.09	5.88	0	38.71	18.36
DRC < 0	23.53	3.20	12.12	3.44	0	0	25.81	50.99

Note:
[a] DRC = domestic resource cost = a ratio of value-added at domestic prices to that at world prices
Sources: Hughes and Hare (1992); ILO (1996).

with external flows after liberalization playing a less significant role. Unlike the previous case, supply is now modelled as elastic.

Initially, domestic price is below the equilibrium price. However, instead of market disequilibrium, this time production is subsidized, and therefore supply is maintained at the market-clearing level. Subsidy is equal to $(p_p - p_c)\bar{q}$, i.e. to area $p_c \, abp_p$. Here, liberalization amounts to the removal of subsidies. As a result, the price increases to p^*, and the quantity produced decreases to q^*. However, both producers and consumers lose, but the taxpayer gains. Consumer loss is equivalent to the area p^*eap_c and producer loss to p^*ebp_p. However, both taken together do not exceed the savings by taxpayer and the resulting net welfare gain is *abe*. In reality, the gain is even higher, as we should add the elimination of the administrative cost of handling the subsidy, influence costs and distortionary cost of tax used to finance it – subsidy does not represent just a pure income transfer based on lump sum tax effortlessly collected.

It is interesting to compare this case (subsidization, Figure 9.5) with that illustrated with Figure 9.2 (market disequilibrium). In the latter case, we have both average producers and average consumers benefiting from liberalization (albeit we pointed out that the gains may not be evenly distributed among consumers). In the former case, those directly interested in the particular market lose, and the gain is acquired by the most dispersed group in the economy – i.e. taxpayers. From the political economy point of view, one should expect a far stronger presence of special interests in case of subsidies than in the case of disequilibria.

In other words, it is more difficult to eliminate the former than the latter.

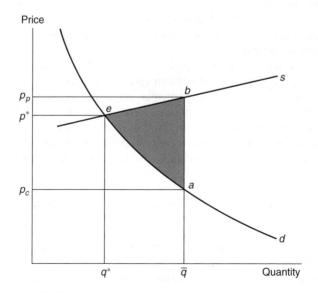

Figure 9.5 Subsidization

Conclusion

We are now able to summarize the political economy conclusions derived from this section.

External liberalization (imports, exports and the exchange rate) is likely to result in the largest distributional effects, and in removing significant economic rents enjoyed by economic actors who are likely to be influential in political terms. However, the redistributional effects are also strong in the case of both (internal) price liberalization and of enterprise reform (removal of subsidies). The latter may be more difficult to implement than the former, due to the fact that the removal of subsidies produces concentrated losses and dispersed larger gains. It may not be only for technical reasons, therefore, that enterprise reform took longer to implement than price liberalization (see Chapter 2). Finally, we did not discuss freedom of entry and small privatization – the remaining key component of the liberalization package. From the formal point of view, this case can be again illustrated by Figure 9.3 a (p. 168). New entrants will shift the supply curve to the right, eliminating the rents enjoyed by 'old' producers, as the price declines. Thus, even if we did not discuss this case in more detail, the conclusions are fairly obvious: again, special interests may still potentially stall the reforms.

From this perspective, there are two main reasons why economic freedom may facilitate reform implementation.

First, democracy and political rights may result in the creation of *mediation institutions*. These may facilitate negotiating compensating transfers between the various parties affected by reforms. Given this possibility, no economic group attempts to stall the reforms. However, an equally or even more important effect relates to the guarantee that the democratic institutions give against the possibility that the costs of reforms are paid by the general public, while the benefits are acquired by the *nomenklatura* – i.e. the main beneficiaries of the old regime.

Second, *civil liberties* are also important. Not only are democratic institutions unlikely to function well without civil liberties, but the latter have an important direct role to play. In particular, acute special interests effects may be most likely where the informational barriers are most significant. This implies that low-cost quality information may be a most efficient method to prevent the reforms being either stalled or captured by special interests. A free media, a key component of civil liberties, is likely to facilitate reforms.

Empirical results on the link between political freedom and reforms

The link between democracy and reforms was tested empirically by Falcetti, Raiser and Sanfey (2002). Using both three-stage least squares (3SLS) estimation of joint growth and reform, a two-equation system and an ordinary least squares estimator, they found robust positive effects of democracy on reforms. We build on their work, extending it in two ways.

First, Falcetti, Raiser and Sanfey's measure of reforms is an average of the EBRD indices of the three key components of reforms: (1) Internal price liberalization, (2) External liberalization of foreign trade and the exchange rate, and (3) Freedom of entry and small-scale privatization. Following the discussion in the previous section, we expect that the significance of democratic and civil society institutions may vary for different reforms. Therefore, in the econometric tests reported below we present tests for all eight basic reform indicators available from the EBRD.

Second, we account for the possibility that the link between political freedom and reforms is non-linear; namely, we hypothesize that the incremental impact on the reforms of achieving a basic threshold of political freedom is higher than the influence of moving between an average and high degree of political freedom.

Variables and empirical models

The standard set of measures of political freedom is available from Freedom House. It includes the ranking of political rights, the ranking of civil liberties and a composite measure which combines both categories in a joint ranking of political freedom status, dividing countries into three categories: 'not free', 'partly free' and 'free'. A detailed description of the criteria used to build each index is available from http://www.freedomhouse.org. We argued in the previous section that political rights have slightly different implications for reforms than civil liberties. The former are directly relevant for democratic mediation mechanisms. The latter may have a critical role in containing the influence of special interests by facilitating access to information, via free media in particular. However, both indices are highly correlated. As noted by Freedom House (New York), civil liberties are a typical prerequisite for political rights. Falcetti, Raiser and Sanfey (2002) report the results for civil liberties, noting that those for the political rights index were highly similar. This was our experience as well; however, in specifications (1)–(8) (Table 9.2, p. 166) we opted for reporting the results for political rights. The latter variable has a flatter distribution and therefore differentiates marginally better between the characteristics of political institutions in the transition economies.[5] In specifications (9)–(16) (Table 9.3, p. 168), we use a composite measure of political freedom reported by Freedom House, which combines both indices. Based on that, we construct two orthogonal contrasts. The first contrast relates to the difference between countries labelled as 'not free' on the one hand and both 'partly free' and 'free' on the other. The second contrast describes the difference between 'partly free' and 'free' categories (see details in the footnote to Table 9.3). The motivation for using both is to check whether the impact of political freedom on reforms is

Table 9.2 Determinants of reform ((1)–(8))[a, b, c, f, g]

	(1) Trade liberalization	(2) Price liberalization	(3) Entry liberalization and small privatization	(4) Enterprise reform	(5) Banking reform	(6) Large-scale privatization	(7) Competition policy	(8) Non-bank finance
Dependent variable, 1-year lag	0.67***	0.45***	0.80***	0.39***	0.51***	0.49***	0.58***	0.55***
	(0.07)[e]	(0.06)	(0.07)	(0.08)	(0.08)	(0.09)	(0.10)	(0.07)
Index of political rights	-0.21***	-0.09**	-0.10**	-0.09***	-0.09***	-0.02	-0.03	-0.01
	(0.00)	(0.03)	(0.04)	(0.02)	(0.03)	(0.03)	(0.03)	(0.02)
Annual real GDP growth rate[d]	0.002	-0.005†	-0.001	0.001	-0.000	-0.003	0.001	-0.001
	(0.004)	(0.003)	(0.003)	(0.002)	(0.002)	(0.003)	(0.002)	(0.002)
Constant	-0.12	0.06	0.03	-0.05	-0.05	-0.00	-0.02	-0.00
	(0.17)	(0.13)	(0.14)	(0.10)	(0.67)	(0.12)	(0.11)	(0.10)
No. of observations	330	330	330	330	330	330	330	330
Second-order autocorrelation: z	-1.09	-0.30	-0.47	-0.49	-1.75†	-1.88†	0.49	-0.69
Sargan test for over-identifying restrictions: χ^2	58.07	75.21	63.06	73.13	197.39	77.15	48.46	71.42

Notes:
[a] All variables in first differences. Estimator: Arellano–Bond one-step GMM. Unbalanced panel for twenty-seven transition economies, 1987–2002, using all available data points.
[b] Data sources: EBRD, *Transition Reports* 1995–2005; Freedom House; World Bank, *World Development Indicators* 2004.
[c] Please note that lower value of the index of political rights corresponds to more political freedom.
[d] *GDP*: In constant 1995 US dollars.
[e] Standard errors in parentheses.
[f] Twelve time controls (annual dummies) included but not reported. They are treated as exogenous and are not first differenced. The number of time dummies is smaller than the number of cross-sections available due to first differencing and use of initial cross-sections as instruments (in levels).
[g] *** significant at 0.001; ** significant at 0.01; * significant at 0.05; † significant at 0.10.

Table 9.3 Determinants of reform ((9)–(16))[c]

	(9) Trade liberalization	(10) Price liberalization	(11) Free entry and small privatization	(12) Enterprise reform	(13) Banking reform	(14) Large-scale privatization	(15) Competition policy	(16) Non-bank finance
Dependent variable, 1-year lag	0.68*** (0.07)	0.48*** (0.05)	0.77*** (0.07)	0.39*** (0.08)	0.50*** (0.08)	0.48*** (0.09)	0.57*** (0.09)	0.55*** (0.07)
'Partly free' and 'free' versus 'not free'[a]	0.22*** (0.05)	0.03 (0.04)	0.08* (0.04)	0.08** (0.03)	0.05† (0.03)	0.01 (0.03)	0.02 (0.03)	0.01 (0.03)
'Free' versus 'partly free'[b]	0.13† (0.08)	-0.06 (0.06)	0.10 (0.003)	0.10* (0.04)	0.07 (0.05)	-0.03 (0.05)	0.01 (0.05)	-0.11** (0.04)
Constant	-0.00 (0.12)	0.05 (0.09)	0.04 (0.10)	-0.00 (0.07)	-0.00 (0.07)	-0.00 (0.08)	-0.00 (0.08)	0.00 (0.07)
No. of observations	349	349	349	349	349	349	349	349
Second-order autocorrelation: z	-1.10	-0.62	-1.03	-0.61	-1.55	-1.85†	0.41	-1.07
Sargan test for over-identifying restrictions: χ^2	50.40	77.95	50.26	73.03	93.12	80.26	50.36	77.05

Notes:

[a] 'Partly free' and 'free' versus 'not free': First orthogonal contrast, which takes the value −2 if the political freedom status (as given by Freedom House) is 'not free', and the value 1 if the status is either 'partly free' or 'free'.

[b] 'Free' versus 'partly free': Second orthogonal contrast, which takes the value −1 if the political freedom status is 'partly free', the value 1 if the status is 'free', and the value 0 if the status is 'not free'.

[c] See also notes to Table 9.2.

non-linear. As already discussed, there may be diminishing returns to democracy if passing some threshold level is most critical.

In addition, we also introduce GDP growth as a control variable to make our specifications comparable with those in Falcetti, Raiser and Sanfey (2002). The expected sign is ambiguous, however. On the one hand, a positive rate of economic growth may facilitate reforms, creating a surplus which may be used to compensate losers. On the other, negative economic growth may increase the pressure for reforms. However, as the variable turned out to be insignificant, we drop it in the second set of specifications ((9)–(16)).

For the same reasons, as described in Chapter 7, our chosen estimator is Arellano and Bond's (1991) GMM dynamic panel estimator, with a lagged value of the dependent variable included in each equation. We thus estimate two sets of equations:

$$Ref_{i,\,t} = \beta_0 + \beta_1 Ref_{i,\,t-1} + \beta_2 PR_{i,\,t} + \beta_3 (\Delta Y/Y)_{i,\,t} + \Sigma T_t + \varepsilon_{i,\,t} \tag{9.1}$$

$$Ref_{i,\,t} = \beta_0 + \beta_1 Ref_{i,\,t-1} + \beta_2 Contrast1_{i,\,t} + \beta_3 Contrast2_{i,\,t} + \Sigma T_t + \varepsilon_{i,\,t} \tag{9.2}$$

where Y denotes real GDP, t is time, i refers to the transition economy, ΣT_i relates to time controls and the remaining variables are defined as described above.

Results

Estimation results are presented in Tables 9.2 and 9.3. Due to construction, negative coefficients on the political rights variable in (1)–(8) correspond to positive coefficients on the two contrasts in (9)–(16), both representing a positive impact of political freedom on the reforms.

The results are consistent with the discussion on pp. 165–73.

In particular, as expected, external liberalization, which creates the most serious challenge (in terms of both wide distributional effects and special interests), stands apart as being most facilitated by the quality of democratic and civil society institutions (specifications (1), (9)). As an additional check on this result, we also estimated an equation with two more variables: a ratio of exports to GDP and external debt servicing expressed as a percentage of exports. A high level of exporting may increase the potential gains from liberalization, generating pressure for it and, similarly, a high debt cost may make the reforms more urgent. Both variables have the expected positive sign, yet the coefficients are insignificant. More importantly, the coefficient on the political rights index remains highly significant (details are available on request).

Next, democracy is important for internal price liberalization, freedom of entry and small-scale privatization, governance and enterprise restructuring and bank reform; for all four reforms, coefficients have the expected signs and are significant.[6] The intuition behind the first two results is as described on pp. 165–74 – both price liberalization and freedom of entry imply *distributional effects*. To understand why 'enterprise restructuring' may be conditional on democracy, one has to take into account that the indicator includes the elimination of the 'soft' budget constraint at the enterprise level, a reform that also has a strong distributional impact. Finally, the link between bank reform and democracy can be interpreted in the same way. As established by PCA in Chapter 2, bank reform and enterprise restructuring are correlated; moreover, the elimination of the 'soft' budget constraint is an important phenomenon which creates a link between the two.

In contrast with the significant results for the five reforms described above, the link with democracy is insignificant for competition policy, NBFls and large-scale privatization. The first two results are very intuitive. The impact of competition policy is limited to a few narrowly defined sectors. Similarly, the stock exchange plays a limited role in the financial systems of the transition countries, and strong redistributional effects are unlikely.

On the other hand, the insignificance of the link between democracy and privatization of large firms may be seen as puzzling. A likely explanation is that while the effects on wealth distribution are important here, the transaction costs of compensating the conflicting claims may not be high. As already discussed in Chapter 4, one of the main political economy issues in privatization is how to compensate the insiders. While very important, the corresponding compensation schemes were relatively easy to design (Blanchard and Aghion 1996; Aghion and Blanchard 1998; Mickiewicz and Baltowski 2003).

Finally, it is interesting to contrast specifications (1)–(8) with specifications (9)–(16), where non-linear effects are accounted for. The general result is that the effect of the difference between regimes which are 'not free' and both 'free' and 'partly free' is far more significant than the difference between 'partly free' and 'free'. There is thus some indication of diminishing returns to democracy. To reach the elementary threshold of political freedom has a more important incremental effect on reforms than a further improvement in the quality of the democratic institutions.

Conclusion

In spite of the apparent technical freedom of action, dictatorships and political oppression are not good for reforms. Democratic institutions may facilitate mediation between economic actors, while dictators risk more than just losing elections if the reforms fail, which may inhibit them from implementing institutional change. Free media and other components of civil liberties may facilitate access to information and limit the extent of state capture by special interests.

The institutional framework of political freedom matters most for reforms for which distributional and special interests effects are large, the effects on income distribution are complex and it is not easy to build compensating effects directly into reforms. As confirmed by empirical results, external liberalization seems to be a prime example of such a situation. On the other hand, while privatization results in spectacular shifts in wealth distribution, it is relatively easy to build the privatization programmes in a way which compensates the losers, insiders in particular. For such reforms, the importance of democratic institutions is smaller.

Finally, it may be that we can see some diminishing returns to democracy, measured as the capacity to reform. The incremental gain from reaching some threshold level of democracy may be higher than from further improvement in the quality of democratic institutions.

Notes

1. One may note that there is no reason to assume that *utility* possibility frontiers must be concave to the origin, unlike the typical *production* possibility frontiers (PPFs). The underlying reason is that changes in utility are not necessary proportional to changes in physical quantities.
2. See also the related discussion in Chapter 1, where we argued that one of the main reasons why the later Communist governments were unable to introduce the far-reaching reforms considered necessary was because of the undemocratic nature of their regimes, which in turn led to concerns about the implications of potential political unrest (a poor substitute for correcting policies via democratic institutions). Romania is a good example of the type of risk faced by Communist despots, when no forms of democratic mediation were able to serve as a safety valve.
3. However, the price levels in the EU are high because of subsidies, and the net effect could be different if the EU were open to imports from outside.
4. This is not illustrated here in detail, but data is easily available. For Russia, the time series for both production and energy are readily available from *Russian Economic Trends*.
5. For pooled data for twenty-seven transition economies (1987–2002), the standard deviation for civil liberties index was 1.52, against 2.03 for political rights.
6. In (9) for trade liberalization, the coefficient for the first contrast ('free' versus 'not free') is positive as expected, but insignificant. It becomes significant when the second contrast is dropped from the specification (not reported).

10
Growth and Transition

In this chapter, we discuss the link between reforms and economic growth. It is organized as follows. The chapter opens with a discussion of the general results from the existing literature on the long-term determinants of economic growth. From there, we move to the discussion of published empirical results on factors affecting long- (medium-) term growth in transition economies. We then turn to the existing evidence based on panel data and short-term effects. Subsequently, we focus our attention on criticism by Rzońca and Ciżkowicz (2003), who show that some reported results may be spurious, and offer our own illustration of this issue, supporting their argument. Finally, we present some additional new estimations and draw some brief conclusions.

Empirical evidence on the determinants of long- (medium-) term growth

By now, the catalogue of the long-term empirical determinants of economic growth is well known. In particular, a thorough meta-study by Sala-i-Martin, Doppelhofer and Miller (2004) gives a list of variables most likely to affect growth. It is based on meta-analysis, which takes into account a full list of sixty-seven variables used to explain long-term growth in reported studies. In particular, two seminal empirical models by Barro (1991) and Levine and Renelt (1992) are considered.

In the light of Sala-i-Martin, Doppelhofer and Miller (2004), modelling growth using a production function approach is justified, as variables, which can be easily interpreted in terms of factor endowment, count. Human capital (especially primary education) is important, and so is human health. The low price of capital goods matters. Rich natural resource endowment has a positive impact, contradicting some earlier insights based on some more restrictive models.

However, growth is driven not only by factor endowment but also by efficient economic organization, characterized by a low level of market distortions and an adequate provision of public goods. The large size of government results in slower growth. Policies resulting in international openness have a positive impact. Interestingly, high transaction costs within the economies may also result from significant ethnolinguistic fractionalization: growth is slower where people cannot communicate with each other using the same language.

Interestingly, culture seems to be important as well: the great Eastern religious traditions (Buddhist, Confucian and Muslim) are associated with more growth, when we control for other factors. On the other hand, the Weberian hypothesis of a Protestant culture being more conducive to growth than a Catholic one is not supported by the data, once we control for the legacy of the Spanish colonies, a tradition which has a negative impact.

Optimistically, countries with a lower GDP *per capita* grow quicker, converging towards the high-income economies, albeit location matters. Clusters of economies (especially in east Asia) grow fast together, others (sub-Saharan Africa (SSA)) remain underdeveloped. In addition, some locational advantages relate to physical geography. In particular, the tropics are not good for growth, and access to the sea spurs GDP growth.

How do the general results compare with those obtained on the transition economies? As already discussed in Chapter 6, the differences between the transition countries in output performance are large. Some transition economies experienced J-curve paths of output, others U-shaped paths, with long recessions. On the one hand, countries such as the Czech Republic, Hungary and Poland emerged from post-Communist crises quickly, on the other, Ukraine and Moldova suffered ten years of recession. Given the relatively similar endowment of those countries in terms of human capital, physical capital and infrastructure, the discussion has concentrated on the comparative significance of macroeconomic policies, liberalization and institutional reforms and initial distortions in explaining differences in output performance.

The empirical literature on economic growth in the transition splits naturally into two parts. First, we have the long-term estimates of economic growth where, following established methodology, GDP growth is averaged over a number of years to eliminate temporary effects. In studies where the endogeneity of explanatory variables is tackled, it is done either by taking the values at the beginning of the period or by use of instrumental variables. Given the enormous policy significance of early transition experience, it is not surprising that a number of studies on the determinants of economic growth in transition were produced in the mid-1990s. If we look at four widely cited studies, those early results showed the following: first, for 1989–95 output changes, Åslund *et al.* (1996) find significant negative effects of macroeconomic instability (inflation) and of war on economic growth. Åslund *et al.* also find that countries which participated in the rouble zone arrangement suffered in terms of economic growth.[1] Second, for the same period, Sachs (1996) shows a clear positive bivariate link between reforms and growth. Next, Heybey and Murrell (1998) base their estimation on growth averages for the first four years of transition and find that in this early period the impact of reforms on growth, while positive, is insignificant and dominated by the negative influence of disruption caused by initial exposure to intra-CMEA trade. Finally, Krueger and Ciolko (1998) extend the model using a number of other variables and a longer time span – i.e. growth averages over 1989–97. The impact of reforms is still positive and significant, and again war hurts economic growth.

Campos (2001) departs from the modelling present in the early studies discussed above, and makes an explicit link to general (non-transition) growth models, in particular, as exemplified by two seminal specifications – Barro (1991) and Levine and Renelt (1992). In line with these general results, Campos finds that both investment and basic education had a positive impact on growth in the transition economies. Interestingly however, the impact of secondary education in the transition economies was ambiguous or even negative, which may be in line with perceptions of the low quality of this sector of education inherited from the old system.

Fidrmuc (2003) presents an analysis which demonstrates how the relative importance of general and transition-specific factors shifted over time. It is unique in its direct account of the fact that the set of factors affecting long- (medium-) term growth may change during the course of transition. Fidrmuc runs a series of regressions with dependent variables taken to be the average growth of five-year periods, starting from 1990–5 (so that the 1990–2000 decade is covered). War has a significant negative impact in the first part of the decade. Similarly, location, as measured by proximity to the EU (Brussels), has some (marginally insignificant) impact at the beginning of decade, which vanishes later. In line with previous studies, the impact of liberalization is strongly significant for most of the period, but becomes insignificant in the most recent one. In contrast, a human capital variable (secondary school enrolment) tends to be insignificant in the first period (similar to Campos 2001), but significant in the later part of the decade.

Based on this, one would be tempted to conclude that the transition-specific set of factors was gradually replaced by a more standard set of explanatory variables, as those economies became more similar to their 'non-transitional' counterparts. However, this is not confirmed by the results on investment, which remains highly insignificant in Fidrmuc's estimations, unlike Campos (2001). However, the former study controls for a larger set of variables. Thus, it seems that the quality of allocation dominated the quantitative effects of investment in transition economies during the whole of the 1990s, which made the quantitative effects of investment insignificant.

Another difference between Fidrmuc (2003) and the non-transition results is that the size of government (as measured by government expenditure) has no significant impact on growth, while a negative effect is standard for the non-transition countries (albeit one may notice that the sign changes from positive in the first two periods to the expected negative in the last five periods). This pattern may be explained by the fact that the collapse of government spending in some transition economies resulted from a lack of tax reform and a crisis in tax collection (see Chapter 7). Thus, small government size in the initial phase of transition may be simply an indicator of fiscal crisis.

Finally, Fidrmuc (2003) finds some evidence of convergence at the beginning of the decade, which ceases in the latter period.

Kronenberg (2004) tests a model explaining average economic growth in the transition countries over 1990–2000. In this long period, basic education again turns out to be a significant factor. On the other hand, in contrast with the general findings on economic growth (Sala-i-Martin, Doppelhofer and Miller 2004), for transition economies natural resource endowment seems to have a negative impact. The explanation of this is that the positive direct effect of natural resources is dominated by their negative effects in stimulating corruption, which in turn has further strong negative external effects affecting the whole economic system. Thus, a natural resource endowment is beneficial only if the system of political, cultural and social norms is strong enough to prevent conflict over economic rents corrupting the business and economic environment. Another disconcerting effect found by Kronenberg (2004) is that during the 1990s, again unlike the general results on economic growth, in the transition countries there was no convergence: the rich were getting richer, and the poor getting poorer, as documented by the positive and consistently significant sign of the initial (1989) GDP *per capita*.

Overall, the results in the literature are consistent. Wars were not good for growth. Liberalization/reforms and macroeconomic stabilization had a positive impact. Towards the end of the first decade of transition, the standard determinants of growth – human capital, in particular – gain in importance, and the significance of transition-specific policies decreases. What is worrying, however, is that the initial differences in income between the transition countries seem to be growing, instead of the expected convergence.

Empirical results from panel data: short-run effects

A second set of results on economic growth in transition comes from a number of empirical studies which focus on short-term effects utilizing panel data techniques. Tables 10.1 and 10.2 summarize the results of seven studies published at the time of writing. Several potentially good working

Table 10.1 Determinant of GDP growth: single-equation models

Authors	Loungani and Sheets (1997)	Selowski and Martin (1997)	Christoffersen and Doyle (2000)	Radulescu and Barlow (2002)	Havrylyshyn and van Rooden (2003)
Estimator	Regression with annual effects; lag dependent included	Pooled regression	Regression with country fixed effect and annual effects	Regression	GLS
Countries and time	EBRD countries 1991–4	EBRD countries 1990–5	EBRD countries 1991–7	EBRD countries 1991–9	EBRD countries 1991–8
Explanatory variables:					
Inflation	Negative Significant		Negative Significant[a]	Negative Significant	Negative Significant
Strong disinflation and exchange rate pegs			Negative Significant		
Dummy for fixed exchange rate regime				Positive Significant	
Fiscal balance	Negative Significant				
Change in index of reform	Positive Significant		Negative Significant		
Index of reform		Negative Significant	Positive Significant	Negative Significant	Negative Significant
Index of reform lagged (−1)		Positive Significant		Positive Significant	Positive Significant
Index of reform lagged (−2)		Positive Significant			Positive Significant
Political freedom					
Export market growth adjusted for Export/GDP			Positive Significant		Ambiguous

Table 10.1 (Continued)

Authors	Loungani and Sheets (1997)	Selowski and Martin (1997)	Christoffersen and Doyle (2000)	Radulescu and Barlow (2002)	Havrylyshyn and van Rooden (2003)
War dummy	Negative Significant	Negative Significant	Negative Significant	Negative, Significant	
Latent variable 1: initial macro distortions, trade dependence on other Communist countries, time spent under Communism					Negative, Significant
As above, interacted with time					Negative, Significant[b]
Latent variable 2: initial GDP *per capita*, urbanization, difference between actual and predicted share of industry in GDP					Negative, Significant
As above, interacted with time					Negative, Significant[b]
Initial level of GDP *per capita*				Negative, significant	

Notes:

[a] Non-linear effects for inflation: only inflation above a threshold level of around 10%–15% has a negative effect on growth.

[b] In specifications where a variable is interacted with time, the same variable with no interaction is also included.

Table 10.2 Determinant of GDP growth: systems of equations

Authors	De Melo et al. (2001)	Falcetti, Raiser and Sanfey (2002)	Merlevede (2003)
Estimator	2SLS four equations: reforms; growth; inflation; freedom	3SLS two equations: reforms, growth; fixed-country effects; quadratic time trend	3SLS two equations: reforms, growth; fixed-country effect and quadratic time trend
Countries and time	'transition time' instead of real time: – FSU 1992–6 – Other EBRD and Mongolia 1990–4, – China 1979–83 – Vietnam 1987–91	'transition time' instead of real time: – FSU and Albania 1991–9 – Bulgaria, Czech Rep., Slovak Rep., FYR 1990–8 – Hungary, Poland 1989–97 (alternatively FSU 1992–)	'transition time' instead of real time: – FSU 1992–2002 – Albania, Bulgaria, Czech Rep., Slovak Rep., 1991–2001 – Hungary, Poland, FYR 1990–2000
Explanatory variables:			
Fiscal balance		Positive Significant	Positive Significant
Index of reform	Negative Significant	Negative Insignificant	Negative Insignificant
Index of reform lagged (–1)	Positive Significant	Positive Significant	Positive Significant
Reform reversal			Negative Significant
Reform reversal interacted with the index of reform			Negative Significant
Political freedom	Positive Significant		
Latent variable 1: initial macro distortions, trade dependence on other Communist countries, time spent under Communism	Negative Significant	Positive Significant	
As above, interacted with time	Negative Insignificant		
Latent variable 2: initial GDP *per capita*, urbanization, difference between actual and predicted share of industry in GDP	Negative Insignificant		Positive Significant
As above, interacted with time			Positive Insignificant

papers are excluded; a summary of most of these is offered by Rousso (2005). The published studies split naturally into two groups. The first five papers ('first-generation' papers) are based on single-equation models (Loungani and Sheets 1997; Selowsky and Martin 1997; Christoffersen and Doyle 2000; Radulescu and Barlow 2002; Havrylyshyn and van Rooden 2003). The next three ('second-generation' papers) tackle the problem of endogeneity of policy variables by using a system of equations modelling. In this latter group, the reforms are instrumented on the set of variables, including indices of political freedom.[2]

The results emerging from all these studies are fairly consistent.

Similarly to the long-run effects, wars had a negative impact on growth. Macroeconomic destabilization had clear-cut negative short-term effects on growth, consistent with the long-term effects. In the 'first-generation' papers, this is approximated by inflation. The 'second-generation' papers rely on fiscal balance, a measure which can be seen as more exogeneous and policy-driven than inflation. Two additional interesting details are offered by Christoffersen and Doyle (2000). First, they found that the effect of inflation is likely to be non-linear. Only inflation above about 13 per cent has a negative effect on growth. Second, in countries where radical disinflation was implemented in the presence of exchange rate pegs, short-term recessionary effects emerged (this effect is discussed in more detail in Chapter 3).

The results on liberalization (reforms) show that the immediate impact is negative. Subsequently, output recovers and the lagged effects are positive, producing a recovery. However, in their contribution, Rzońca and Ciżkowicz (2003) demonstrate that the estimates of reform coefficients may be problematic. The issue deserves careful consideration, and we shall turn to it in the next section.

An interesting addition to the results on the link between reforms and growth is offered by Merlevede (2003), who notes that earlier estimations do not distinguish between the impact of reforms and reform reversals. In a number of countries (the two most prominent examples being Belarus and Uzbekistan), the reforms were reversed in the mid-1990s, and the standard estimation would imply a positive impact on growth of reform reversal (symmetric to the impact of reform implementation). Merlevede (2003) documents that the impact of the reversal was in fact negative.[3]

Finally, an interesting set of results relates to external linkages. Christoffersen and Doyle (2000) demonstrate that countries which were more open initially were affected by developments on their main export markets. These results can be seen as consistent with the 'second-generation' papers which use a latent variable representing the initial conditions. Within this variable, one of the major components is the initial trade dependence on other Communist countries (a measure parallel to that used by Christoffersen and Doyle 2000), which has also an (implicit) negative impact on growth. In particular, the small former Soviet republics were particularly dependent on trade with Russia and suffered from recession in this largest transition economy. In contrast, Russia itself was less dependent on trade with other republics, so that its recession was more affected by policy choice than by external influences. The advantage of Christoffersen and Doyle's (2000) approach is to make this link explicit.

Are the results on the link between reforms and growth spurious?

The starting point of Rzońca and Ciżkowicz's (2003) criticism is that the EBRD indicators used as reform proxies are bounded from above by construction. For that reason, implementation of the reforms is represented by a decreasing rate of change, with the level of indicators converging over time towards the high-income OECD economies' benchmark. A paradoxical implication is that for countries which implemented the reforms quickly, the correlation between change in reforms and economic growth is spuriously negative when all subsequent periods are taken into account (where the residual change in the reform indicator is very small). As the empirical models discussed above include both contemporaneous and lagged reform indicators (which correspond to first differences), the time series characteristics of the reform indicator resulting from its construction imply a spurious effect, where the former term is negative and the latter is positive.

Two points may be noted.

First, the study by Christoffersen and Doyle (2000) differs from all others in the form in which the reform indicators are used in the estimated models. It includes both a first difference of the reform indicator and the reform indicator in levels. While the first may capture the effect discussed by Rzońca and Ciżkowicz (2003) and be spurious, given that it is included the coefficient on the reform level is not affected. It is positive and significant.

Second, if the effect described by Rzońca and Ciżkowicz (2003) is important, it should affect the more recent studies more and those based on earlier periods less, as the time series characteristics of the reform were better as the upper bound is slack, even for the fast reformers. Indeed, a casual look at Figures 2A.2 and 2A.3 (pp. 44–5) demonstrates that before 1998 the upper bound was not reached even by the fastest reformers, which is consistent with figure 2 in Rzońca and Ciżkowicz (2003). This implies that, in this respect, the results from the first three studies reported in Table 10.1 (Loungani and Sheets (1997), Selowski and Martin (1997) and Christoffersen and Doyle (2000)) may be treated with more trust. In the first of these, based on the 1991–4 period, a change in reforms results in higher growth. In the next two, we can detect a J-curve effect, where the lagged positive effect of reforms clearly outweighs the initial negative one.

We intend to investigate the problem in more detail and estimate a series of models, varying the time span of the analysis. We estimate models which are similar to the 'second-generation' growth-in-transition models – i.e. we rely on a system of equations and take account of endogeneity of variables (see Table 10.2, p. 187) – however, with a few differences. First, our panel is larger. The sample is extended from twenty-five to twenty-seven countries, including data on Serbia and Bosnia now available. We also include an early period (starting from 1987) to account for the fact that in some countries (including Hungary, Poland and the former republics of Yugoslavia), limited reforms were introduced before the end of Communism. That leads us to a more important difference, already highlighted in Chapter 7. The 'second-generation' models reorder the time dimension, shifting the time series for particular countries relative to each other, with a starting date defined as the beginning of transition (see Table 10.2). In addition, the estimated equations include quadratic time trends (again, counted in 'transition years'). The potential problem with this approach is that, by construction, the 'transition time trend' is strongly correlated with the reforms.[4] More importantly, also by construction, the time-specific influences common to all transition economies are not controlled for. For these reasons, we do not shift the time dimension in our specifications. All are in real time, with a full set of annual time dummies instead. The advantage of the latter solution is that by not imposing any functional form on the time trend, we can control better for common time-specific shocks.

The second difference is that we do not include any proxies for initial conditions. Instead, in each equation, a full set of fixed-country effects is included. Falcetti, Raiser and Sanfey (2002) and Merlevene (2003) introduce a latent variable representing initial conditions interacted with time in their set of explanatory variables. Because the variable is derived from PCA, analytical interpretation is difficult. More importantly, the measured effects capture only the time-specific effects unaccounted for by the time trend, all the others should already be covered by fixed-country effects. As we opted for the full set of time controls and fixed-country effects, there is no room left for initial condition variables in our specifications.

The third difference is that we introduce inflation into our set of explanatory variable in the growth equations, alongside the reform indicators. However, it is instrumented using the fiscal balance, the index of political rights and the reform index.

Moving from these general remarks to more detailed comments on the specification, we wish to make our set of variables comparable with Radulescu and Barlow (2002), the only paper where the contemporaneous and lagged effects of reform balance each other, so that the effect of reforms on growth is inconclusive (which triggered the response by Rzońca and Ciżkowicz (2003), even if their criticism relates to other papers as well).

Correspondingly, we estimate the following model:

$$(\Delta Y/Y)_{i,t} = \alpha_0 + \alpha_i + \alpha_t + \alpha_1 RI_{i,t} + \alpha_2 RI_{i,t-1} + \alpha_3 (\Delta P/P)_{i,t} + \varepsilon_{i,t} \qquad (10.1)$$

$$(\Delta P/P)_{i,t} = \beta_0 + \beta_i + \beta_t + \beta_1 Fis_{i,t-1} + \beta_2 RI_{i,t-1} + \beta_3 Polit_{i,t} + \eta_{i,t}$$

$$RI_{i,t} = \gamma_0 + \gamma_i + \gamma_t + \gamma_1 (\Delta Y/Y)_{i,t} + \gamma_2 (\Delta Y/Y)_{i,t-1} + \gamma Polit_{i,t} + v_{i,t}$$

Following the existing research tradition, our reform measure is a simple average of the three key liberalization indicators (price liberalization, external liberalization and freedom of entry and small-scale privatization). The results of the estimations are presented in Table 10.3, we report the first equation only. We shall next present the results based on a full model; however, with a different specification, alleviating the problem detected by Rzońca and Ciżkowicz (2003).

Table 10.3's results are consistent with our expectations. For the period of analysis, for which the upper bound of the reform index is not binding (roughly until 1997), we can see that the lagged positive effect dominates over the negative and insignificant contemporaneous effect of reforms. In the latter periods, the importance of the spurious effects detected by Rzońca and Ciżkowicz (2003) prevails.

Additional new results: reforms, stabilization and political rights

To eliminate the effect discussed above, we estimate a model where the reform indicator is included only once in the growth equation:

$$(\Delta Y/Y)_{i,t} = \alpha_0 + \alpha_i + \alpha_t + \alpha_1 RI_{i,t-1} + \alpha_2 (\Delta P/P)_{i,t} + + \alpha_3 (\Delta P/P)_{i,t-1} + \varepsilon_{i,t} \qquad (10.2)$$

$$(\Delta P/P)_{i,t} = \beta_0 + \beta_i + \beta_t + \beta_1 Fis_{i,t-1} + \beta_2 Polit_{i,t} + \eta_{i,t}$$

$$RI_{i,t} = \gamma_0 + \gamma_i + \gamma_t + \gamma_1 (\Delta Y/Y)_{i,t} + \gamma_2 Polit_{i,t} + v_{i,t}$$

Another variant of this model is where we allow for effects of reforms on inflation, that is:

$$(\Delta Y/Y)_{i,t} = \alpha_0 + \alpha_i + \alpha_t + \alpha_1 RI_{i,t-1} + \alpha_2 (\Delta P/P)_{i,t} + + \alpha_3 (\Delta P/P)_{i,t-1} + \varepsilon_{i,t} \qquad (10.3)$$

$$(\Delta P/P)_{i,t} = \beta_0 + \beta_i + \beta_t + \beta_1 Fis_{i,t-1} + \beta_2 RI_{i,t-1} + \eta_{i,t}$$

$$RI_{i,t} = \gamma_0 + \gamma_i + \gamma_t + \gamma_1 (\Delta Y/Y)_{i,t} + \gamma_2 (\Delta Y/Y)_{i,t-1} + \gamma_3 Polit_{i,t} + v_{i,t}$$

Table 10.3 Impact of the time dimension on the estimates of reform coefficients in growth equations^{a-e}

Time period used	1987–94	1987–95	1987–96	1987–97	1987–98	1987–99	1987–2000	1987–2001	1987–2002
RI_t	8.18	−3.21	−15.18	−1.41	−8.97	−22.22†	−35.5*	−48.16**	−61.8**
RI_{t-1}	6.62*	8.4***	12.12**	8.96†	11.48	17.24*	24.11**	31.15**	38.5**
$(\Delta P/P)_t$	0.003	0.000	0.000	−0.000	−0.002†	−0.004**	−0.006***	−0.008***	−0.011***
No. of observations	91	116	142	168	194	220	246	273	300

Notes:

^{a} Estimator: 3SLS. Only coefficients from the first equation of model (1) (see text) are reported.

^{b} Data sources: EBRD, *Transition Reports 1995–2005*; World Bank, *World Development Indicators 2004*

^{c} Inflation: GDP deflator (more data points available than for CPI).

^{d} Time effects (annual dummies) and country fixed effects included in each equation but not reported.

^{e} *** significant at 0.001; ** significant at 0.01; * significant at 0.05; † significant at 0.1.

The results are reported in Tables 10.4–10.6.[5] These are largely consistent with those obtained earlier by other authors:

- First, there is a consistent link between *political freedom* and *reform*.[5] Less freedom implies slower reforms, as is documented by the signs and significance of corresponding coefficients.
- Second, *democracy is also good for macroeconomic stability* (Table 10.4). The results are consistent with De Melo *et al.* (2001, table 8). From the political economy point of view, inflation may be a sign that conflicting claims on government cannot be efficiently coordinated, resulting in the inflationary financing of public expenditure.
- Third, *inflation has an unambiguous effect on economic growth* in transition economies. Both contemporary and lagged effects are negative (with the relative significance varying, depending on the specification).
- And, finally, *reforms have a very significant effect on inflation*. With a one-year lag, liberalization brings a slowdown of inflation. This last result is important, as it suggests that where both inflation and reforms are included in the set of explanatory variables for growth (without instrumenting), we may expect a multicollinearity problem, with the estimates of the reform effects weakened.

Table 10.4 3SLS estimates of model (2)[a–c, f, g]
Reform index = Average of 3 EBRD liberalization indices

Dependent variable	GDP growth ($\Delta Y/Y$)	Reform index (*RI*)	Inflation ($\Delta P/P$)
Reform index, lagged	4.66 (1.05)[e]***		
Inflation[d]	–0.0006 (0.0005)		
Inflation, lagged	–0.0003 (0.001)*		
GDP growth rate		0.12 (0.03)***	
GDP growth rate, lagged			
Index of political rights		–0.04 (0.02)	131.03 (74.38)†
Government balance, lagged			–60.79 (9.48)***
χ^2	342.51***	342.51***	180.72***
No. of observations	294	294	294

Notes:
[a] Estimations based on all available data points for twenty-seven transition economies, 1987–2002.
[b] Data sources: EBRD, *Transition Reports* 1995–2005; Freedom House; World Bank, *World Development Indicators* 2004
[c] Lower value of the index of political rights corresponds to more political freedom.
[d] Inflation: GDP deflator (more data points available than for CPI).
[e] Standard errors in parentheses.
[f] Time effects (annual dummies) and country fixed effects included in each equation but not reported.
[g] *** significant at 0.001; ** significant at 0.01; * significant at 0.05; † significant at 0.1.

Table 10.5 3SLS estimates of model (3)[a-c, f, g]
Reform index = Average of 3 EBRD liberalization indicators

Dependent variable	GDP growth ($\Delta Y/Y$)	Reform index (RI)	Inflation ($\Delta P/P$)
Reform index			
Reform index, lagged	4.34 (1.20)[e]***		–0.94 (0.10)***
Inflation[d]	–1.772 (1.015)†		
Inflation, lagged	–0.376 (0.588)		
GDP growth rate		0.09 (0.02)***	
GDP growth rate, lagged		–0.004 (0.009)	
Index of political rights		–0.054 (0.03)†	
Government balance, lagged			–0.05 (0.01)***
χ^2	440.94***	596.89***	1222.84***
No. of observations	294	294	294

Notes:
[a] Estimations based on all available data points for twenty-seven transition economies, 1987–2002.
[b] Data sources: EBRD, *Transition Reports* 1995–2005; Freedom House; World Bank, *World Development Indicators* 2004
[c] Lower value of the index of political rights corresponds to more political freedom.
[d] Inflation: GDP deflator (more data points available than for CPI).
[e] Standard errors in parentheses.
[f] Time effects (annual dummies) and country fixed effects included in each equation but not reported.
[g] *** significant at 0.001; ** significant at 0.01; * significant at 0.05; † significant at 0.1.

Table 10.6 3SLS estimates of model (3)[a-c, f, g]
Reform index = liberalization (second principal component; see Chapter 2 for details)

Dependent variable	GDP growth ($\Delta Y/Y$)	Reform index (RI)	Inflation ($\Delta P/P$)
Reform index, lagged	3.25 (1.18)[e]**		–0.83 (0.09)***
Inflation[d]	–2.51 (1.16)*		
Inflation, lagged	–0.05 (0.63)		
GDP growth rate		0.10 (0.02)***	
GDP growth rate, lagged		–0.01 (0.01)	
Index of political rights		–0.06 (0.03)†	
Government balance, lagged			–0.05 (0.01)***
χ^2	450.44***	509.75***	1250.90***
Number of observations	294	294	294

Notes:
[a] Estimations based on all available data points for twenty-seven transition economies, 1987–2002.
[b] Data sources: EBRD, *Transition Reports* 1995–2005; Freedom House; World Bank, *World Development Indicators* 2004
[c] Lower value of the index of political rights corresponds to more political freedom.
[d] Inflation: GDP deflator (more data points available than for CPI).
[e] Standard errors in parentheses.
[f] Time effects (annual dummies) and country fixed effects included in each equation but not reported.
[g] *** significant at 0.001; ** significant at 0.01; * significant at 0.05; † significant at 0.1.

Conclusion

Arguably, more attention should be paid to long- (medium-) term estimates than to short-term estimates based on panel data. From all available long-term estimates (including our own estimates of the determinants of recession in Chapter 6), we know that reforms are positively associated with growth. And apart from one study based on the early period, all the reported results are significant.

The problem with panel techniques, as applied in existing research, may be that a longer lag structure is difficult to evaluate, as additional lags are insignificant and the sample size is reduced, resulting in the loss of some important information. What is going on is that the positive impact of reform is spread over a long period of time, and is thus difficult to estimate with a specification which relies on a short-run response. This is an additional, equally important problem, beyond that reported by Rzońca and Ciżkowicz (2003).

Possibly the most interesting result in this chapter is the significance of *macroeconomic stabilization*. Unambiguously, the short-term effects of inflation on economic growth in the transition economies are negative, and the result is established controlling for endogeneity in the spirit of the 'second-generation' transition models. We could not detect any positive, demand-driven response of output to inflationary impulses. This may indicate that demand-based explanations of recessions and output paths in transition may lack empirical support. Instead, with some caveats (as discussed in Chapter 6), the explanations of the 'transitional recessions' based on disorganization (as best represented by Blanchard and Kremer 1997) seem to be standing the test of time well.

Notes

1. The rouble zone experience is discussed in detail by Gros and Steinherr (2004).
2. One may also note that the same approach is also adopted by Fidrmuc (2003) in the context of long- (medium-) term models of growth (see pp. 183–4).
3. In addition, Merlevede (2003) argues that his results support the case for gradualism, as it follows that partial reforms are less costly to reverse than full reforms. However, the overall balance of costs and benefits between gradualism and fast reforms (under aggregate uncertainty) is determined by an option value of early reversal, and the cost of delay of reforms, including those resulting from complementarities between the reform elements (Roland 2000, Section 2.4). There is also one methodological problem with the Merlevede (2003) model on reform reversals. Unlike the basic reform indicators, reversals are not treated as endogeneous. However, we rerun a model similar to Merlevede (2003), treating reversals as endogenous and find that the basic conclusions are not affected: reversals are bad for growth (not reported). Interestingly, political freedom makes reversals less likely and the result is highly significant. We checked all the reversal points listed by Merlevede (2003) and eliminated two: for Bulgaria in 1995 and for Tajikistan

in 1993. In both cases, reversals of some reforms occurred, but those were matched by simultaneous progress in some other reforms. In the first case, a reversal in price liberalization was matched by progress in the freedom of entry and small-scale privatization indicator. In the second case, a reversal in price liberalization was matched by an improvement in competition policy. We also detected some reversals in the additional data we used. Serbia experienced a reversal in price and external liberalization in 1994, and another reversal in price liberalization in 1998. In 2001, the Turkmenistan government inflicted on itself a reversal in large-scale privatization, moving up to third place in the ranking of countries with the largest number of reform reversals, after Belarus and Uzbekistan, unchallenged frontrunners in this category.

4. The argument here is against shifting individual countries along the time dimension, not against defining some threshold level of reforms, seen as equivalent to the beginning of the transition. In fact, the latter is the approach we applied in Chapter 6, where we checked if reaching the threshold level of reforms (liberalization) early affected the length and depth of the post-Communist recession. An early application of the concept of the transition–reforms–liberalization threshold in a different methodological setting can be found in De Melo and Gelb (1997).

5. A diligent reader may notice an insignificant effect reported in Table 10.4: the exact level of significance was 10.3 per cent.

Final Remarks

Our objective in this book was to investigate empirically some of the key issues featuring in the discussion on economic transition in Eastern Europe and Central Asia. One of the main challenges here is that the key dimension of transition – a set of reforms corresponding to liberalization and institutional change – can be measured only in an imperfect way. We have to accept this as a limitation. Nevertheless, we think that conclusions based on empirical testing – even if imperfect – are better than statements which cannot be falsified. In the latter case, economic theories turn into ideologies; and ideologies, as with any other distorted representations of reality, lead to wrong policies.

We found that early implementation of liberalization and stabilization programmes was associated with better output performance, and shorter and less severe recessions. While liberalization resulted in a J-curve-type response of output, the long-term effects were positive.

Why, then, were the paths of reforms, stabilization and output so different within the group of transition economies?

What happened can be partly explained by a historical accident. The reforms in the CE economies were initiated between 1989 and 1991. In 1992, when the first of the fifteen republics of the FSU embarked on their liberalization programmes, recession was all that could be observed as a result of the reforms in the CE economies. The latter were just at the bottom of their corresponding J-curves of output, and wrong conclusions were drawn.

To that, one can add a low level of economic competence (in contrast to a high level of technical skills) and a widespread conviction among policy-makers (possibly over-reacting to Communist uniformity) who believed that in each single case, their own country was so unique that general economic lessons drawn from experiences elsewhere did not apply.

The intellectual endowment therefore did not help, but a more important lesson, this time based on our empirical results, was that political freedom was a factor facilitating economic reforms, liberalization and stabilization programmes. It was also a lack of political freedom that made reform reversals more likely. How difficult the reform process was can be documented by the fact that thirteen out of twenty-seven transition economies faced reform reversals at some point of time between 1989 and 2004.

The strong link between political freedom, civil liberties and economic reforms is not necessarily one which should lead to pessimism.

One may think about Ukraine. Until 2004, it was commonplace to describe this second largest post-Communist country as a 'basket case' of political and economic failure. Yet, in December 2004, the people of Ukraine found enough confidence to topple a corrupt regime in mass, sustained protests.

There is a thin line between optimism and naïvety that one should avoid crossing. However, as has been argued in this book, a free media decrease the cost of access to information and strengthen the position of average voters against special interests. More broadly, democracy facilitates the mediation between different economic actors and helps to reach consensus on those reforms that bring with them a serious redistribution of gains and costs.

Bibliography

Aghion, P. and O. Blanchard (1994) 'On the Speed of Transition in Central Europe', in S. Fisher and J. Rotemberg (eds), *NBER Macroeconomics Annual* (Cambridge, MA: MIT Press), 283–320.

Aghion, P. and O. Blanchard (1998) 'On Privatisation Methods in Eastern Europe and Their Implications', *Economics of Transition*, 6, 87–99.

Ahrend, R. and J. Martins (2003) 'Creative Destruction or Destructive Perpetuation: The Role of the Large State-Owned Enterprises and SMEs in Romania during Transition', *Post-Communist Economies*, 15, 331–56.

Aidis, R. and T. Mickiewicz (2005) 'Growth Expectations of Business Owners: Impact of Human Capital, Firm Characteristics and Environmental Transition', CSESCE Working Paper, 50.

Anderson, T. and C. Hsiao (1981) 'Estimation of Dynamic Models with Error Components', *Journal of the American Statistical Association*, 76, 598–606.

Applebaum, A. (2003) *Gulag: A History* (New York: Doubleday).

Arellano, M. and S. Bond (1991) 'Some Tests of Specification for Panel Data: Monte Carlo Evidence and an Application to Employment Equations', *Review of Economic Studies*, 58, 277–97.

Åslund, A. (2001) 'The Myth of Output Collapse after Communism', Carnegie Endowment for International Peace Working Paper, 18.

Åslund, A. (2002) *Building Capitalism* (Cambridge: Cambridge University Press).

Åslund, A., P. Boone, S. Johnson, S. Fisher and B. Ickes (1996) 'How to Stabilise: Lessons from Post-Communist Countries', *Brookings Papers on Economic Activity*, 1, 217–313.

Balcerowicz, L. (1992) *800 Dni* (Warsaw: BGW).

Balcerowicz, L. (1995) *Socialism, Capitalism, Transformation* (Budapest: Central European University Press).

Balcerowicz, L., C. Gray and I. Hashi (eds) (1998) *Enterprise Exit Processes in Transition Economies* (Budapest: CEU).

Barr, N. (ed.) (1994) *Labour Market and Social Policy in Central and Eastern Europe* (Oxford: Oxford University Press).

Barr, N. (2001) 'Reforming Welfare States in Post-Communist Countries', in L. Orlowski (ed.), *Transition and Growth in Post-Communist Countries: The Ten-Year Experience* (Northampton, MA: Edward Elgar), 169–217.

Barro, R. (1991) 'Economic Growth in a Cross Section of Countries', *Quarterly Journal of Economics*, 106 (2), 407–43.

Barro, R. (1997) *Determinants of Economic Growth: A Cross-Country Empirical Study* (Cambridge, MA: MIT Press).

Basel Committee on Banking Supervision (2004) *International Convergence of Capital Measurement and Capital Standards. A Revised Framework* (Basel: Bank for International Settlements).

Bauc, J., M. Dąbrowski and P. Senator (1994) *Źródła Inflacji w Polsce w Latach 1989– 1993* (Warsaw: CASE).

Begg, D. (1998) 'Pegging Out: Lessons from the Czech Exchange Rate Crisis', *Journal of Comparative Economics*, 26, 669–90.

Bell, J. and J. Rostowski (1995) 'A Note on the Confirmation of Podkaminer's Hypothesis in Post-liberalisation Poland', *Europe–Asia Studies*, 47, 527–30.

Berg, A. (1994) 'Does Macroeconomic Reform Cause Structural Adjustment? Lessons from Poland', *Journal of Comparative Economics*, 18, 376–409.

Berglof, E. and P. Bolton (2002) 'The Great Divide and Beyond: Financial Architecture in Transition', *Journal of Economic Perspectives*, 16 (1), 77–100.

Blanchard, O. (1997) *The Economics of Post-Communist Transition* (Oxford: Clarendon Press).

Blanchard, O. and P. Aghion (1996) 'On Insider Privatisation', *European Economic Review*, 40, 759–66.

Blanchard, O. and M. Kremer (1997) 'Disorganisation', *Quarterly Journal of Economics*, 112, 1091–126.

Blanchard, O., R. Dornbush, P. Krugman, R. Layard and L. Summers (1991) *Reform in Eastern Europe* (Cambridge, MA: MIT Press).

Blanchflower, D., A. Oswald and A. Stutzer, (2001) 'Latent Entrepreneurship across Nations', *European Economic Review*, 45, 680–91.

Boeri, T. (1997) 'Labour Market Reforms in Transition Economies', *Oxford Review of Economic Policy*, 13 (2), 126–40.

Bofinger, P., H. Flassbeck and L. Hoffman (1997) 'Money-Based versus Exchange Rate-based Stabilisation', *Economic Systems*, 21 (1), 1–33.

Bond, S. (2002) 'Dynamic Panel Data Models: A Guide to Micro Data Methods and Practice,' *Portuguese Economic Journal*, 1, 141–62.

Boycko, M., A. Shleifer and R. Vishny (1995) *Privatising Russia* (Cambridge, MA: MIT Press).

Boycko, M., A. Shleifer and R. Vishny (1996) 'A Theory of Privatisation', *Economic Journal*, 106, 309–19.

Brada, J. (1989) 'Technological Progress and Factor Utilisation in Eastern European Economic Growth', *Economica*, 56 (224), 433–48.

Buiter, W. and C. Grafe (2002) 'Anchor, Float or Abandon Ship: Exchange Rate Regimes for the Accession Countries', *EIB Papers*, 7, 51–71.

Calvo, G. and F. Coricelli (1992) 'Stagflationary Effects of Stabilisation Programmes in Reforming Socialist Countries: Enterprise-side and Household-side Factors', *World Bank Economic Review*, 6, 71–90.

Calvo, G. and F. Coricelli (1993) 'Output Collapse in Eastern Europe: The Role of Credit', *IMF Staff Papers*, 40 (1), 32–52.

Campos, N. (2001) 'Will the Future Be Better Tomorrow? The Growth Prospects of Transition Economies Revisited', *Journal of Comparative Economics*, 29, 663–76.

Campos, N. and F. Coricelli (2002) 'Growth in Transition; What We Know, What We Don't and What We Should', *Journal of Economic Literature*, 60, 793–836.

Carlin, W. and C. Mayer (2003) 'Finance, Investment and Growth', *Journal of Financial Economics*, 69, 191–226.

Christoffersen, P. and P. Doyle (2000) 'From Inflation to Growth: Eight Years of Transition', *Economics of Transition*, 8, 421–51.

Chudzik, R. (2000) 'Banks and the Privatisation of Enterprises in Poland', in E. Rosenbaum, F. Bönker and H. Wagner (eds), *Privatisation, Corporate Governance and the Emergence of Markets* (Basingstoke: Macmillan), 155–70.

Cirera, X. and J. Hölscher (2001) 'Exchange Rate Regimes and Monetary Policies in Transition to Monetary Union: The Case for Capital Controls', ACE-Phare Project P98–1065-R Paper, University of Sussex and University of Brighton, mimeo.

Coase, R. (1960) 'The Problem of Social Cost', *Journal of Law and Economics*, 3, 1–44.

Coffee, J. (1996) 'Institutional Investors in Transitional Economies', in R. Frydman, C. Gray and A. Rapaczynski (eds), *Corporate Governance in Central Europe and Russia*, 1 (Budapest: CEU Press), 111–86.

Colombo, E. and J. Driffill (2003) 'Financial Markets and Transition', in E. Colombo and J. Driffill, *The Role of Financial Markets in the Transition Process* (Heidelberg: Physica-Verlag), 1–12.

Corker, R., C. Beaumont, R. van Elkan and D. Iakova (2000) 'Exchange Rate Regimes in Selected Advanced Transition Economies – Coping with Transition, Capital Inflows and EU Accession', IMF Policy Discussion Paper, 3.

Cullis, J. and P. Jones (1992) *Public Finance and Public Choice* (London: McGraw-Hill).

De Melo, M., C. Denizer, A. Gelb and S. Tenev (1997) 'Circumstance and Choice: The Role of Initial Conditions and Policies in Transition Economies', World Bank Policy Research Working Paper, 1866.

De Melo, M., C. Denizer, A. Gelb and S. Tenev (2001) 'Circumstance and Choice: The Role of Initial Conditions and Policies in Transition Economies', *World Bank Economic Review*, 15, 1–31.

De Melo M. and A. Gelb (1997) 'Transition to Date: A Comparative Overview', in S. Zecchini (ed.), *Lessons from Economic Transition* (Dordrecht: Kluwer), 59–78.

Desai, P. and T. Idson (2000) *Work Without Wages: Russia's Nonpayment Crisis* (Cambridge, MA: MIT Press).

Djankov, S., C. McLiesh and A. Shleifer (2005) 'Private Credit in 129 Countries', NBER Working Paper, 11078.

Djankov, S. and P. Murrell (2002) 'Enterprise Restructuring in Transition: A Quantitative Survey, *Journal of Economic Literature*, 60, 739–792.

Drewnowski, J. (ed.) (1982) *Crisis in the East European Economy* (Beckenham: Croom Helm).

Driffill J. and T. Mickiewicz, (2003) 'The Order of Financial Liberalisation: Lessons from the Polish Experience', in E. Colombo and J. Driffill, *The Role of Financial Markets in the Transition Process* (Heidelberg: Physica-Verlag), 13–42.

Earle, J. and S. Estrin (1996) 'Employee Ownership in Transition', in R. Frydman, C. Gray and A. Rapaczynski (eds), *Corporate Governance in Central Europe and Russia*, 2 (Budapest: CEU Press), 1–61.

Earle, J. and K. Sabirianova (2000) 'Equilibrium Wage Arrears: A Theoretical and Empirical Analysis of Institutional Lock-in', IZA Working Paper, 321.

EBRD (1994–2005) *Transition Reports* (London: European Bank for Reconstruction and Development).

Estrin, S. (1994) 'The Inheritance', in N. Barr (ed.), *Labour Market and Social Policy in Central and Eastern Europe* (Washington, DC: World Bank), 53–76.

Estrin, S. and R. Stone (1996) 'A Taxonomy of Mass Privatisation', *Transition*, 7(11–12), 8–9.

European Commission (2003) *Employment in Europe: Recent Trends and Prospects*, Brussels: Directorate-General for Employment and Social Affairs.

Falcetti, E., M. Raiser and P. Sanfey (2002) 'Defying the Odds: Initial Conditions, Reforms and Growth in the First Decade of Transition', *Journal of Comparative Economics*, 30, 229–50.

Fidrmuc, J. (2003) 'Economic Reform, Democracy and Growth during Post-Communist Transition', *European Journal of Political Economy*, 19, 583–604.

Filatotchev, I. (2003) 'Privatisation and Corporate Governance in Transition Economies: Theory and Concepts', in D. Parker and D. Saal (eds), *International Handbook on Privatisation* (Cheltenham: Edward Elgar), 323–46.

Filatotchev, I., M. Wright and M. Bleaney (1999) 'Privatisation, Insider Control and Managerial Entrenchment in Russia', *Economics of Transition*, 7, 481–504.

Fischer, S. (1988) 'Devaluation and Inflation', in R. Dornbush, F. Leslie and C. Helmers (eds), *The Open Economy* (Washington, DC and Oxford: World Bank and Oxford University Press), 108–27.

Fischer, S. (2001) 'Exchange Rate Regimes: Is the Bipolar View Correct?', *Journal of Economic Perspectives*, 15, 3–24.

Fischer, S. and R. Sahay (2000) 'The Transition Economies after Ten Years', IMF Working Paper, WP/00/30.

Fries, S., D. Neven and P. Seabright (2004) *Competition, Ownership and Bank Performance in Transition*, EBRD, unpublished paper.

Fries, S. and A. Taci (2002) 'Banking Reform and Development in Transition Economies', EBRD Working Paper, 71.

Frydman, R., A. Rapaczynski and J. Earle (1993) *The Privatisation Process in Central Europe*, 2 vols (Budapest: CEU Press).

Funck, B. and L. Pizzati (eds) (2002) *Labor, Employment and Social Policies in the EU Enlargement Process* (Washington, DC: World Bank).

Gacs, V. and P. Huber (2003a) 'Quantity Adjustment in Candidate Countries Regional Labour Markets', in *Adjustment Capability of Regional Labour Markets*, Workpackage no. 2., ACCESSLAB 5th Framework Project (Vienna: WIFO).

Gacs, V. and P. Huber (2003b) 'Regional Labour Market Problems in the Candidate Countries: A Descriptive Analysis', in *Adjustment Capability of Regional Labour Markets*, Workpackage no. 2., ACCESSLAB 5th Framework Project (Vienna: WIFO).

Golinowska, S. (2001) 'Welfare State Reforms in Post-Communist Countries: A Comment on Barr', in L. Orlowski (ed.), *Transition and Growth in Post-Communist Countries: The Ten Years' Experience* (Northampton, MA: Edward Elgar), 219–35.

Gomulka, S. (1992) 'Polish Economic Reform: Principles, Policies and Outcomes', *Cambridge Journal of Economics*, 16, 355–72.

Gomulka, S. (1995) 'The IMF-Supported Programs of Poland and Russia, 1990–1994: Principles, Errors and Results', *Journal of Comparative Economics*, 20, 316–46.

Góra M. and C. Schmidt (1998) 'Long-Term Unemployment, Unemployment Benefits and Social Assistance: The Polish Experience', *Empirical Economics*, 23 (1–2), 55–85.

Gravelle, H. and R. Rees (2004) *Microeconomics* (Harlow: Pearson).

Gregory, P. and R. Stuart (1995) *Comparative Economic Systems* (Boston, MA: Houghton Mifflin).

Gros, A. and D. Steinherr (1995) *Winds of Change* (London: Longman).

Gros, A. and D. Steinherr (2004) *Economic Transition in Central and Eastern Europe* (Cambridge: Cambridge University Press).

Gros, A. and M. Suhrcke (2000) 'Ten Years After: What is Special about Transition Economies', EBRD Working Paper, 56.

Hart, O. (2001) 'Financial Contracting', *Journal of Economic Literature*, 39, 1079–100.

Havrda, M. (2003) 'The Czech Republic: The Case of Delayed Transformation', in M. Federowicz and R. Aguilera (eds), *Corporate Governance in a Changing Economic and Political Environment* (Basingstoke: Palgrave Macmillan), 121–43.

Havrylyshyn, O. and R. van Rooden (2003) 'Institutions Matter in Transition, but do Policies?', *Comparative Economic Studies*, 45, 2–24.

Heybey, B. and P. Murrell (1998) 'The Relationship between Economic Growth and Speed of Liberalization During Transition', *Policy Reform*, 3, 121–37.

Hughes G. and P. Hare (1992) 'Industrial Policy and Restructuring in Eastern Europe', *Oxford Review of Economic Policy*, 8, 82–104.

ILO (1996) *World Employment 1996/97. National Policies in a Global Context* (Geneva: International Labour Office).

IOSCO (2003) *Objectives and Principles of Securities Regulation* (Madrid: International Organisation of Securities Commissions).

Isachenkova, N. and T. Mickiewicz (2004) 'Ownership Characteristics and Access to Finance: Evidence from a Survey of Large Privatised Companies in Hungary and Poland', William Davidson Institute Working Paper, 666.

Jackman R. and M. Rutkowski (1994) 'Labour Markets: Unemployment', in N. Barr (ed.), *Labour Markets and Social Policy in Central and Eastern Europe* (Oxford: Oxford University Press).

Jensen M. and W. Meckling (1976) 'Theory of the Firm: Managerial Behaviour, Agency Costs and Ownership Structure', *Journal of Financial Economics*, 3, 305–60.

Judson, R. and A. Owen (1999) 'Estimating Dynamic Panel Data Models: A Guide for Macroeconomists', *Economics Letters*, 65, 9–15.

Kamela-Sowinska, A. (2003) 'Szansa ale niepewna', *Rzeczpospolita*, 10–11 May, B3.

Kiviet, J. (1995) 'On Bias, Inconsistency and Efficiency of Various Estimators in Dynamic Panel Data Models', *Journal of Econometrics*, 68, 53–78.

Kolodko, G. (1979) 'Fazy wzrostu gospodarczego w Polsce', *Gospodarka Planowa*, 3, 137–43.

Kolodko, G. (1987) *Polska w swiecie inflacji* (Warsaw: Ksiazka i Wiedza).

Kornai, J. (1979) 'Resource-Constrained versus Demand Constrained Systems', *Econometrica*, 47, 801–19.

Kornai, J. (1980) ' "Hard" and "Soft" Budget Constraints', *Acta Oeconomica*, 25, 231–45.

Kornai, J. (1986) *Contradictions and Dilemmas: Studies on the Socialist Economy and Society* (Cambridge, MA: MIT Press).

Kornai, J. (1992) *The Socialist System: The Political Economy of Communism* (Oxford: Clarendon Press).

Kornai, J. (1995) 'Transformational Recession: The Example of Hungary', in C. Sanders (ed.), *Eastern Europe in Crisis and the Way Out* (Basingstoke: Macmillan), 29–77.

Kornai, J., E. Maskin and G. Roland (2003) 'Understanding the Soft Budget Constraint', *Journal of Economic Literature*, 61, 1095–136.

Kronenberg, T. (2004) 'The Course of Natural Resources in the Transition Economies', *Economics of Transition*, 12, 399–426.

Krueger, G. and M. Ciolko (1998) 'A Note on Initial Conditions and Liberalisation during Transition', *Journal of Comparative Economics*, 26, 718–34.

Kurowski, S. (1991) *Polityka Gospodarcza PRL* (Warsaw: Editions Spotkania).

Kutan, A. and J. Brada (2000) 'The Evolution of Monetary Policy in Transition Economies', *Federal Reserve of St. Louis Review*, March, 31–40.

Kutan, A. and T. Yigit (2005) 'Real and Nominal Stochastic Convergence: Are the New EU Members Ready to Join the Euro Zone?', *Journal of Comparative Economics*, in press.

Lange, O. (1936) 'On the Economic Theory of Socialism: Part One', *Review of Economic Studies*, 4, 53–71.

La Porta. R., F. Lopez-de-Silvanes, A. Shleifer and R. Vishny (1998) 'Law and Finance', *Journal of Political Economy*, 106, 1113–55.

Lavigne, M. (1999) *The Economics of Transition* (Basingstoke: Macmillan).

Lehmann, H. (1998) 'Active Labor Market Policies in Central Europe: First Lessons', in R. Riphahn, D. Snower and K. Zimmermann (eds), *Employment Policy in the Transition: Lessons from German Integration*, Berlin: Springer.

Leontief W. and F. Duchin (1983) *Military Spending* (Oxford: Oxford University Press).

Levine, R. and D. Renelt (1992) 'A Sensitivity Analysis of Cross-Country Regressions', *American Economic Review*, 82 (4), 942–63.

Loungani, P. and N. Sheets (1997) 'Central Bank Independence, Inflation and Growth in Transition Economies', *Journal of Money, Credit, and Banking*, 29, 381–99.

Mau, V. (1996), *The Political History of Economic Reform in Russia, 1985–1994* (London: Centre for Research into Communist Economics).

McKinnon, R. (1992) 'Taxation, Money and Credit in a Liberalizing Socialist Economy', in C. Clague and G. Rausser (eds), *The Emergence of Market Economies in Eastern Europe* (Cambridge, MA: Blackwell) 109–28.

McKinnon, R. (1993) *The Order of Economic Liberalisation* (Baltimore, MD: Johns Hopkins University Press).

McKinsey (1999) 'Report on Russian Economic Performance', McKinsey Global Institute, http://www/mckinsey.com

Megginson, W., R. Nash and M. van Randenborgh (1984) 'The Financial and Operating Performance of Newly Privatised Firms: An International Empirical Analysis', *Journal of Finance*, 69, 403–52.

Megginson, W. and J. Netter (2001) 'From State to Market: A Survey of Empirical Studies on Privatisation', *Journal of Economic Literature*, 39, 321–89.

Megginson, W. and J. Netter (2003) 'History and Methods of Privatisation', in D. Parker and D. Saal (eds), *International Handbook on Privatisation* (Cheltenham: Edward Elgar), 25–40.

Mejstrik, M. (2003) 'Privatisation and Corporate Governance in the Czech Republic', in D. Parker and D. Saal (eds), *International Handbook on Privatisation* (Cheltenham: Edward Elgar), 372–401.

Merlevede, B. (2003) 'Reform Reversals and Output Growth in Transition Economies', *Economics of Transition*, 11, 649–69.

Mickiewicz, T. (1988) 'Gra o reforme', *Res Publica*, 2 (12), 112–14.

Mickiewicz, T. (2003) 'Convergence in Employment Structures. Transition Countries versus the EU: Reforms, Income Levels or Specialisation Patterns?', in K. Piech (ed.), *Economic Policy and Growth of Central and East European Countries* (London: SSEES UCL), 59–82.

Mickiewicz, T. and M. Baltowski (2003) 'All Roads Lead to Outside Ownership: Polish Piecemeal Privatisation', in D. Parker and D. Saal (eds), *International Handbook on Privatisation* (Cheltenham: Edward Elgar), 402–26.

Mickiewicz, T. and J. Bell (2000) *Unemployment in Transition: Restructuring and Labour Markets in Central Europe* (Amsterdam: Harwood Academic).

Mickiewicz, T., C. Gerry and K. Bishop (2005) 'Privatisation, Corporate Control and Employment Growth: Evidence from a Panel of Large Polish Firms, 1996–2002', *Economic Systems*, 29, 98–119.

Milanovic, B. (1998) *Income, Inequality and Poverty during the Transition from Planned to Market Economy* (Washington, DC: World Bank).

Milgrom, P. and J. Roberts (1992) *Economics, Organisation and Management* (Upper Saddle River, NJ: Prentice Hall).

Mihalyi, P. (2000) 'Corporate Governance during and after Privatisation: The Lessons from Hungary', in E. Rosenbaum, F. Bönker and H. Wagner (eds), *Privatisation, Corporate Governance and the Emergence of Markets* (Basingstoke: Macmillan), 139–54.

Mises, L. von (1966 [1949]) *Human Action: A Treatise on Economics* (Chicago: Contemporary Books/Yale University Press).

Modigliani, F. and M. Miller (1958) 'The Cost of Capital, Corporation Finance and the Theory of Investment', *American Economic Review*, 48, 261–97.

Newell, A. and F. Pastore (2000) 'Regional Unemployment and Industrial Restructuring in Poland', Discussion Paper, 194, University of Sussex, Department of Economics.

Nuti, M. and R. Portes (1993) 'Central Europe: The Way Forward', in R. Portes (ed.), *Economic Transformation in Central Europe* (London: CEPR), 1–20.

OECD (1992) *Economic Surveys: Poland* (Paris: Organisation for Economic Cooperation and Development).

Peroti, E. and Gelfer, S. (2001) 'Red Barons or Robber Barons? Governance and Investment in Russian Financial–Industrial Groups', *European Economic Review*, 45, 1601–17.

Pinto, B., M. Belka and S. Krajewski (1993) 'Transforming State Enterprises in Poland: Evidence on Adjustment by Manufacturing Firms', *Brookings Papers on Economic Activity*, 1, 213–70.

Pirtillä, J. (2001) 'Fiscal Policy and Structural Reforms In Transition Economies', *Economics of Transition*, 9, 29–52.

Podkaminer, L. (1987a) *Szacunki struktury i rozmiarów nierównowagi na rynkach konsumpcyjnych Polski w latach 1965–1986* (Warsaw: PWN).

Podkaminer, L. (1987b) 'On Polish Disequilibrium Once Again', *Soviet Studies*, 39, 509–12.

Porket, J. (1984) 'The Shortage, Use and Reserves of Labour in the Soviet Union', *Osteuropa Wirtschaft*, 29 (1), 8–24.

Portes, R. (ed.) (1993) *Economic Transformation in Central Europe* (London: CEPR).

Portes, R. (1994) 'Transformation Traps', *Economic Journal*, 104, 1178–89.

Poznanski, K. (1996) *Poland's Protracted Transition: Institutional Change and Economic Growth 1970–1994* (Cambridge: Cambridge University Press).

Radosevic, S. (1999) 'Transformation of Science and Technology Systems into Systems of Innovation in Central and Eastern Europe: The Emerging Patterns and Determinants', *Structural Change and Economic Dynamics*, 10, 277–320.

Radulescu, R. and D. Barlow (2002) 'The Relationship between Policies and Growth in Transition Countries', *Economics of Transition*, 10 (3), 719–45.

Rebelo, S and C. Vegh (1995) 'Real Effects of Exchange-rate-based Stabilisation: An Analysis of Competing Theories', in B. Bernanke and J. Rotemberg (eds), *NBER Macroeconomics Annual* (Cambridge, MA: MIT Press), 125–74.

Rein, M., B. Friedman and A. Wörgötter (eds) (1997) *Enterprise and Social Benefits after Communism* (Cambridge: Cambridge University Press and CEPR).

Riboud, M., C. Sanchez-Paramo and C. Silva-Jauregui (2002) 'Does Eurosclerosis Matter? Insititutional Reform and Labour Market Performance in Central and East European Countries', in B. Funck and L. Fizzati (eds), *Labor, Employment and Social Policies in the EU Enlargement Process*, Washington, DC: World Bank, 243–311.

Riedel, J. and B. Comer (1997) 'Transition to a Market Economy in Vietnam', in S. Parker and J. Sachs (eds), *Economies in Transition: Comparing Asia and Europe* (Cambridge, MA: MIT Press), 189–216.

Roland, G. (2000) *Transition and Economics: Politics, Markets and Firms* (Cambridge, MA: MIT Press).

Rousso, A. (2005) 'Progress in Transition and the Link to Growth', *Beyond Transition: The Newsletter About Reforming Economies*, 15 (1), 22–3.

Rozelle, S. and J. Swinnen (2004) 'Success and Failure of Reform: Insights from the Transition of Agriculture', *Journal of Economic Literature*, 52, 404–56.

Rutkowski, M. (1990) 'Labour Hoarding and Future Unemployment in Eastern Europe: The Case of Polish Industry', Discussion Paper, 6, LSE Centre for Economic Performance.

Rutkowski, M. (1995) 'Workers in Transition', Policy Research Working Paper, 1556, Washington, DC: World Bank.

Rutkowski, M. and M. Przybyla (2002) 'Poland: Regional Dimensions of Unemployment', in B. Funck and L. Fizzati (eds), *Labor, Employment and Social Policies in the EU Enlargement Process* (Washington, DC: World Bank), 157–75.

Rzońca, A. and P. Ciżkowicz (2003) 'A Comment on the Relationship between Policies and Growth in Transition Countries', *Economics of Transition*, 11 (4), 743–8.

Sachs, J. (1993) *Poland's Jump to the Market Economy* (Cambridge, MA: MIT Press).

Sachs, J. (1996) 'The Transition at Mid Decade', *American Economic Review, Papers and Proceedings*, 86, 128–33.

Sala-i-Martin, X., G. Doppelhofer and R. Miller (2004) 'Determinants of Long Term Growth: A Bayesian Averaging of Classical Estimates (BACE) Approach', *American Economic Review*, 94, 813–35.

Schaffer, M. and G. Turley (2001) 'Effective versus Statutory Taxation: Measuring Effective Tax Administration in Transition Economies', EBRD Working Paper, 62.

Schroeder, G. (1986) *The System versus Progress* (London: Centre for Research into Communist Economies).

Selowsky, M. and R. Martin (1997) 'Policy Performance and Output Growth in the Transition Economies', *American Economic Review, Papers and Proceedings*, 87, 349–53.

Shleifer A. and R. Vishny (1994) 'Politicians and Firms', *Quarterly Journal of Economics*, 109, 995–1025

Shleifer A. and R. Vishny (1997) 'A Survey of Corporate Governance', *Journal of Finance*, 52, 737–83.

Sirc, L. (1981) 'The Decline in Growth Rates East and West', *Revue d'Etudes Comparatives Est-Ouest*, 12, 63–77; translated into English and published in L. Sirc, *Why the Communist Economies Failed* (London: Centre for Research into Communist Economies, 1994).

Smith, A. (1996) *Russian Foreign Trade in the Transition* (London: Royal Institute of International Affairs).

Stiglitz, J. (1992) 'The Design of Financial Systems for the Newly Emerging Democracies of Eastern Europe', in C. Clague and G. Rausser (eds), *The Emergence of Market Economies in Eastern Europe* (Cambridge, MA: Blackwell), 161–86.

Stiglitz, J. and A. Weiss (1981) 'Credit Rationing in Markets with Imperfect Information', *American Economic Review*, 71, 393–410.

Sztanderska, U. and B. Piotrowski (1999) *Background Study on Labour Market and Employment in Poland* (Warsaw: European Training Foundation).

Takla, L. (1999) 'Privatisation in the Czech Republic', in P. Hare, J. Batt and S. Estrin (eds), *Reconstituting the Market* (Amsterdam: Harwood), 135–54.

Tanzi, V. and G. Tsibouris (2000) 'Fiscal Reform Over Ten Years of Transition', IMF Working Paper, 113.

Temkin, G. (1989) 'Economic Calculation under Socialism', *Communist Economies*, 1 (1), 31–60.

Temkin, G. (1996) 'Information and Motivation: Reflections on the Socialist Economic System', *Communist and Post Communist Studies*, 29 (1), 25–44.

Tolba, M. and O. El-Kholy (eds) (1992) *The World Environment 1972–1992: Two Decades of Challenge* (London: Chapman & Hall on behalf of UNEP).

Tosovsky, J. (1996) 'Disinflation in the Czech Republic: Looking both Backward and Forward', in *Achieving Price Stability* (Jackson Hole, KS: Federal Reserve Bank of Kansas City), 147–60.

Tullock, G. (1967) *Toward the Mathematics of Politics* (Ann Arbor, MI: University of Michigan Press).

Varian, H. (1992) *Microeconomic Analysis* (New York: W.W. Norton).

Voszka, E. (2003) 'Ownership and Corporate Governance in the Hungarian Large Enterprise Sector', in E. Rosenbaum, F. Bönker and H. Wagner (eds), *Privatisation, Corporate Governance and the Emergence of Markets* (Basingstoke: Macmillan), 171–94.

Ward, B. (1958) 'The Firm in Illyria: Market Syndicalism', *American Economic Review*, 48(4), 566–89.

Wiles, P. (1982) 'Introduction: Zero Growth and the International Nature of the Polish Disease', in J. Drewnowski (ed.), *Crisis in the East European Economy* (Beckenham: Croom Helm), 7–17.

Winiecki, J. (1987) *Economic Prospects – East and West* (London: Centre for Research into Communist Economies).

Winiecki, J. (2002) *Transition Economies and Foreign Trade* (London: Routledge).

Winiecki, E. and J. Winiecki (1992) *The Structural Legacy of the Soviet-Type Economy* (London: CRCE).

Zemplinerova, A. and M. Machacek (2003) 'Privatisation in the Czech Republic: Strengths and Weaknesses', in Y. Kalyuzhnova and W. Andreff (eds), *Privatisation and Structural Change in Transition Economies* (Basingstoke: Palgrave Macmillan), 202–24.

Index

208